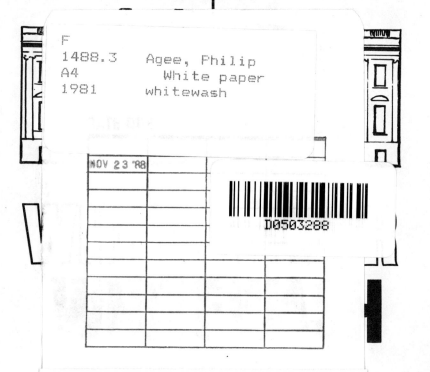

of the CIA and El Salvador

Edited by
WARNER POELCHAU

ii

Published by
DEEP COVER BOOKS
P. O. Box 677
New York, NY 10013

June 1981

TABLE OF CONTENTS

ACKNOWLEDGEMENTS

Excerpts from *On Company Business*, Copyright © 1980 by Isla Negra-Blanca Films and Alan Francovich.

Article by Juan de Onis (*New York Times*, February 6, 1981), Copyright © 1981 by The New York Times Company. Reprinted by permission.

Excerpts from *Inside the Company: CIA Diary*, Copyright © 1975, Stonehill Communications, Inc.

Excerpts from "The CIA and The White Paper on El Salvador," by Ralph McGehee, *The Nation*, April 11, 1981, Copyright © 1981, The Nation Associates, The Nation Magazine.

Interview with Ambassador White reprinted from *U.S. News & World Report*, January 26, 1981, Copyright © 1981, U.S. News & World Report, Inc.

PART 1

EDITOR'S FOREWORD

Before taking office the Reagan foreign policy team and the President-elect himself made it abundantly clear that the new American administration would take a much harder line on dealings with the socialist countries, in particular with the Soviet Union. Once in the White House, the new President wasted no time in letting the world know that he equated armed struggles for national liberation with international terrorism and as extensions of Soviet power. In this context the new Secretary of State, Alexander Haig, surprised many by suggesting that "some things are more important than peace."

In February 1981 the London *Times* observed that "the new Administration had cast its eye around the world to find a suitable place where it could make an early and firm stand against communism." El Salvador was the country where Reagan and Haig would demonstrate to the world — to friends and foes alike — that America was going to "draw the line." The President and the Secretary of State assumed a tone of belligerence not heard from Washington in many years — certainly not since the ignominious evacuation from Vietnam.

For many observers the warlike threats over El Salvador seemed equally aimed at the people of the United States in a conscious effort to prepare the psychological climate for public acceptance of renewed foreign interventionism and eradication of the "Vietnam syndrome." In the Federal Republic of Germany and other countries of Western Europe, many people were reminded of the political climate during the 1962 Cuban missile crisis.

The key for the Reagan-Haig Salvadoran crisis was alleged foreign intervention in the bloody civil war on behalf of the left-wing insurgents who, during 1980, showed increasing strength and good possibilities for repeating the Sandinista victory in Nicaragua the year before. Using documents said to have been captured from the guerrillas by Salvadoran military and security forces as "proof," the Reagan administration justified a massive increase in military aid to the Salvadoran military junta headed by the Christian Democrat, Napoleon Duarte. The Duarte government, as presented through U.S. government eyes, was caught between the inhuman violence of extreme right and extreme left, while trying as hard as it could to install fundamental reforms in banking, commerce and land tenure. These reforms, it believed, would rob the guerrillas of the issues on which they had steadily gained in strength over ten years of armed struggle. Opponents of the junta belittled the reforms as cosmetic and limited, while citing continuing repression of innocent civilians as evidence that the junta's security forces and the right-wing terrorist organizations were one and the same.

The opposition analysis was generally accepted by Western Europe's Social Democrats. The West German, Swedish and Dutch Social Democrats, for example, had very good relations with the Salvadoran rebels, largely because the leader of the Revolutionary Democratic Front (FRD), Guillermo Ungo, is a Social Democrat who has worked for some years with the parties of the Socialist International. For leaders like Willy Brandt and former Swedish Prime Minister Olaf Palme, the Salvadoran revolutionaries were not "international terrorists" but freedom fighters and democrats in their majority.

So the Reagan administration — including the Vice President, former CIA Director George Bush — needed some way to convince allied governments and the Social Democrats of an international communist plot against freedom in El Salvador. Like Phoenix rising from ashes, the State Department produced "documentary proof" that El Salvador had been "progressively transformed into another case of indirect armed aggression against a small Third World country by Communist powers acting through Cuba."

The Reagan government first surfaced the "captured documents" through the *New York Times*, just as Haig was about to dispatch high-level teams of diplomats to Europe and Latin America to convince leaders of the rightness of the American position. Juan de Onis, an old *Times* Latin American hand, was given a peek at two of the documents which he reported in a sensational story, repeated in the press the world over, on February 6, 1981. One of the documents given to de Onis showed a massive commitment by Soviet bloc countries to provide arms and other military equipment to the Salvadoran guerrillas, with Cuba serving as a logistics base for transshipment to El Salvador. De Onis reported that "U.S. intelligence agencies" consider the documents "authentic."

This "official leak" to the press was followed by the well-prepared diplomatic offensive. Targets were not only European and Latin American governments, but also the social democratic parties. The aim was to convince them to withdraw or withhold political and financial support for the FRD, the political front associated with the guerrilla movement. An initial willingness to compromise with the Americans was evident in some quarters. In West Germany, for example, a government spokesman and the Deputy Chairman of the Social Democratic Party (SPD), in separate press conferences, spoke for the first time of "respectable democrats" on *both* sides of the Salvadoran civil war.

Central to the February diplomatic campaign was "the mass of captured documents" that supposedly proved the massive flow of arms through Cuba and Nicaragua to the Farabundo Marti National Liberation Front (FMLN) — the umbrella grouping of four different guerrilla forces whose common political front is the FRD.

When Philip Agee read the de Onis article he told me that the whole story sounded suspicious. He described to me a number of operations from his twelve-year CIA experience in which he participated in falsifying documents for ends very similar to those being made with the "captured" Salvadoran documents. Having seen the sudden new position of the Bonn government — which after minor differences is still America's junior partner in important questions — after the initial surfacing of the documents through de Onis, Agee's examples from the 1960's made me suspicious too. These doubts were supported by the U.S. government itself, as it seemed in no hurry to produce the originals or copies of them, for general scrutiny.

As the diplomatic mission headed by Lawrence Eagleburger, the Assistant Secretary of State for European Affairs, arrived in Bonn to begin the rounds of European capitals — using the "captured documents" as evidence of Soviet intervention — Agee decided to have a press conference. On February 20 he discussed with journalists in Bonn his CIA experience in falsifying documents in Latin America along with other indications of current CIA activities in El Salvador.

He prepared for the journalists a massive amount of documentation, including excerpts from his first book, *Inside the Company: CIA Diary*, and from the documentary film about the CIA, *On Company Business*. He also distributed at the press conference copies of formerly secret CIA documents captured when the U.S. Embassy in Teheran was taken over by student militants in 1979 — and which I brought back from several trips there. The falsified passports and other documentation clearly showed that the CIA is still in the falsification business.

Agee's attempt to stimulate skepticism toward the "captured documents" failed to have the impact that he had hoped. The Western media, particularly in the United States, seemed uninterested in questioning the authenticity of the "captured documents" or their use in justifying the diplomatic and propaganda offensive against the Salvadoran liberation movement. He told me he was convinced that the international offensive and the internal U.S. campaign against the FMLN-FRD could be the preparation for a Dominican Republic-style invasion if the guerrillas started a new, more successful push following their January stalemate. He remembered that in 1965, while he was working for the CIA in Uruguay, the then-Senior Roving Ambassador of the U.S., Averell Harriman, led a diplomatic mission to Latin American capitals — just as Vernon Walters, the former CIA Deputy Director, was now heading the special diplomatic mission to Latin America on El Salvador. Harriman made his trip to explain and to seek support for the invasion.

Harriman's "proof" that another Cuba had been in the making in 1965 was a list of "58 trained communists" who had infiltrated the ranks of the Constitutionalists — the side that the invasion defeated. Agee believed that the "captured documents" could well be a similar pretext for an escalation of U.S. intervention in El Salvador.

Although Agee's February 20 press conference was reported in African and Latin American journals and in some liberal publications in Western Europe, the reaction in the United States was meager — and in one case astounding. Ten days after the press conference the *Washington Post* ran a long op-ed article by one R. Emmett Tyrrell Jr. (not a *Post* staff writer and unidentified in the article) in a clear, and even ludicrous, diversionary tactic.

Tyrrell wrote that Agee ("this cryptic figure") had "emerged from one of his vaporous foreign haunts to hold a well-timed press conference in Bonn" in which Agee "divulged that certain documents now being used by our own State Department to sully the good name of El Salvador's rebels are, in very truth, forgeries." Tyrrell added: "For 90 minutes Agee held reporters in the grip of his hand. . . ."

Going on to attack Agee's politics and his support of Cuba's revolution, Tyrrell denied that El Salvador might become "another Vietnam" and that the "captured documents" were forgeries — implying that Agee had said at his press conference that they were fabricated, whereas in fact Agee had urged skepticism until the documents could be examined.

Tyrrell then attacked the Salvadoran liberation movement as "this attempt to establish yet another Marxist colony in our back yard" and ended with a suggestion that shows how far the *Washington Post* has come from its journalism of Watergate days. Tyrrell "guessed" that Agee's work against the CIA for ten years was a CIA plot designed to "win the confidence of the Soviets" and thereby to become a double agent. Tyrrell, without a hint of satire, warned the Soviets to be on their guard: "Once a CIA agent, always a CIA agent."

Since Agee has lived with his family openly in Hamburg for three years, and I have known him much of this time, I was astonished by this article when I considered it along with the failure of other American mainstream media to question the "captured documents." Their cozy partnership with the U.S. government was all too apparent, and I agreed with Agee that something should be done.

Agee had a tape of his press conference, and I decided to transcribe it and publish it with documentation he had distributed. The first six Parts of this book consist of the edited transcript of the February 20 press conference with selected examples of documents. One item in Part 4, about the CIA's falsification of documents to provoke the slaughter of a million or more Indonesians in 1965-1966, is based on an article by another former CIA officer, Ralph McGehee, who also raised doubts about the "captured" Salvadoran documents.

At the same time as I decided to publish Agee's material, the Department of State put out some of the "captured documents" in its *White Paper on Communist Interference in El Salvador*. We decided to get a copy, which wasn't easy, and to analyze it — looking for indications that any of the documents might have been falsified. Neither Agee nor I were experts on El Salvador, so we did intensive research in Hamburg press archives to compare names, dates and other factual content of the documents with public information and accounts of events. We also spoke to knowledgeable people, including Salvadoran revolutionaries. We examined the Spanish originals with the English translations of the White Paper, and these with the interpretations and conclusions reached by the State Department.

Our findings astonished us. The White Paper contained gross errors in translations, conclusions with no basis in the documents, and outright inventions. In the end, Agee concluded, and I agreed, that the most important of the "captured documents" show strong signs of being fabrications, probably inserted with documents really captured, and then conveniently discovered. Our critique of the White Paper is in Part 7 of this book, and the entire White Paper itself is in Appendix A.

No one simply examining machine copies of documents can scientifically prove a case of falsification — neither can he prove whether a document is genuine. However, the contradictions with known facts in several documents, along with glaring inconsistencies, make for extreme skepticism regarding the most important ones contained in the White Paper. But equally notable is the invention, fabrication, embellishment and exaggeration found in the State Department analyses when compared with what the documents actually say.

I had a unique problem in preparing this book because since 1980 Philip Agee has been restricted in his ability to communicate by a U.S. court order that requires him to present all his writings and formal speeches to the CIA for censorship. However, he is allowed to make "extemporaneous comments without prior preparation, and oral expressions of information, personal views, opinions and judgments on matters of public concern" — so long as he doesn't reveal classified American government information.

So I decided to accomplish this book in a complicated way. After editing Parts 1 through 6 and integrating the documentation from Agee's February 20 press conference, I had many hours of informal interviews with him on the White Paper. The result is perhaps the world's first spoken book, which, I hope, will clarify American policy in El Salvador, contribute to opposition to escalation and regionalization of the conflict, and create skepticism toward this and future White Papers.

There still remains a question: Do the Salvadoran guerrillas obtain arms from outside El Salvador? The answer can only be, of course! The West Berlin newspaper, *Die Tages Zeitung*, has raised one-and-a-half million marks in a public campaign emphasizing that the money will be used for arms for the guerrillas. Soon this campaign alone will pass two million marks (equivalent to $1,000,000). And, as everyone knows, the Salvadoran guerrillas have raised many millions of dollars through kidnappings and other action with which they can buy arms on the international market.

But there is another factor. Even if the Soviet Union were really delivering arms to the Salvadoran guerrillas — who are fighting injustice, illiteracy, exploitation, torture and murder — my reaction would be: Wonderful! Their cause is just and the more support they get, from whatever source, the better. The United States, after all, sent arms to the Soviet Union not so long ago to help resist aggression by Hitler. But today, the United States, far from the Soviet Union (even if you believe the White Paper), is the main outside power introducing arms into El Salvador. And day after day we read how those arms are being used to massacre innocent civilians and to sustain a reign of terror that is unusually cruel, even for a civil war.

The international crisis over El Salvador clearly threatens other countries. The new American interventionism is aimed also at the Sandinistas in Nicaragua, Cuba, Grenada, Angola, Mozambique, the Persian Gulf and all liberation movements. It must be exposed for what it is in El Salvador and stopped right there.

The reader should consider this book as one more sign of support for the FMLN-FDR from the "Free World." I believe we have effectively reduced the White Paper to fantasy and pretext, to one more example of the classical Big Lie.

Warner Poelchau
Hamburg, 1981

PART 2

INTRODUCTION

Good morning, and welcome . . .

I hope there are seats available for all of you; I had not expected such a large turnout. You have in front of you copies of many documents that I assembled for this discussion.

I invited you to come and discuss the CIA's falsification of documents as a matter of standard method, and how this relates to El Salvador, because I have been reading in the newspapers lately, as have you all, about documents supposedly captured from the Salvadoran liberation movement showing Ethiopian, Vietnamese, Soviet and Cuban intervention. The pile of documents you have includes some previously secret CIA documents together with examples of how the CIA has falsified documents in the past. Since the diplomatic offensive based on the supposedly captured Salvadoran documents is going ahead so fast these days, I thought it was important to do this quickly. As we all know, the documentation is being used to justify an American effort to cut away international support from the Revolutionary Democratic Front and to swing it in favor of the military junta.

On top of the pile you see the prologue of the film script *On Company Business*, a three-hour historical documentary on the CIA directed by Alan Francovich of Berkeley, California. It was 5 years in the making and it won the International Critics' Award at the Berlin Film Festival last year. It has already been seen on national television in the United States, Finland and Sweden and will be shown on television and in theaters all over the world. I worked on this film as a consultant, and it contains interviews with many former CIA officers and agents who describe past operations. I gave you this prologue as a reminder for other extracts from the film script, and because of the paragraph from the *Doolittle Report*, which shows the philosophy adopted by the U.S. Government in 1951 with respect to using the CIA as an instrument for subversion.

> We are facing an implacable enemy. There are no rules in such a game. We must learn to subvert, sabotage and destroy our enemies by more clever, more sophisticated, more effective means than those used against the United States.
> — The Doolittle Report on the CIA, 1951

I will go as quickly as I can through the documents, which I have arranged in the different categories that I wish to discuss. First is the press reporting now coming out on supposed support from Ethiopia and Vietnam and other countries for the Liberation Front in El Salvador. Then there are examples of documents captured in the United States Embassy in Teheran, some of which are falsified. Next I have about ten cases of my own experience in which I and others in the CIA fabricated documents, for which this recent reporting on El Salvador could almost be a carbon copy. I also have documentation from newspapers in Latin America from the time I was work-ing there, which I copied from microfilm in the British Museum in London while doing research on my first book. This shows the tremendous impact of falsified documents once they have surfaced — one way or another.

I am also going to speak about the American Institute for Free Labor Development because that is the U.S. agency responsible for technical assist-ance to the Salvadoran junta's agrarian reform. It is one of the key programs being implemented by the military officers who seized power toward the end of 1979. The AIFLD, as it is known, has been a front for the CIA since it was founded in 1961. I have various documents about the CIA's work through this front, and they bring together the connection between the espionage agency and a program like agrarian reform, which right now is very relevant to El Salvador because what is in the making there is another Vietnam. The use of this front by the CIA is an application of old methods of rural pacification that were tried and failed in Vietnam and that include the infamous Phoenix program wherein tens of thousands of Vietnamese were assassinated.

Finally, I am going to speak of various programs which the CIA has had with local security services in Latin America, as they undoubtedly have with Salvadoran services today, and how these connect with paramilitary murder squads such as those at work in El Salvador, Guatemala and Hon-duras. You can be certain that ten to fifteen CIA officers are working from an office in the American Embassy in San Salvador right now, and passing information and other support to the Salvadoran security forces is one of their top priorities.

So that, in a nutshell, is what I want to talk about. I will try to make it as painless as possible with all these documents I've given you.

First, I would like to comment on this *New York Times* article writ-ten by Juan de Onis from Washington (reproduced in the *International Herald Tribune*).

Russia, Cuba Agreed to Supply Captured U.S. Arms to Salvadoran Rebels, Papers Say

By Juan de Onis, *New York Times Service*

WASHINGTON — Secret documents captured from El Salvador's Marxist-led guerrillas that are considered authentic by U.S. intelligence agencies indicate that the Soviet Union and Cuba agreed last year to deliver tons of weapons to the guerrillas from stockpiles of U.S. arms taken over by Vietnam and Ethiopia. Copies of the doc-uments obtained by The New York Times include a report on a trip by a Salvadoran guerrilla, believed to be Shafik Handal, secretary-general of the Salvadoran Commu-nist Party, to the Soviet Union, Vietnam, Ethiopia and Eastern European capitals where top-ranking party officials agreed to provide arms, uniforms and other military equipment for up to 10,000 guerrillas.

Arms Flow

During the last two months, in which the guerrillas of the Farabundo Marti Liberation Front unleashed an unsuccessful but large-scale offensive, many of the arms captured by El Salvador's armed forces have been U.S.-made rifles, mortars and ma-chine guns. There have also been Chinese-made weapons, as well as a variety of small arms available through commercial channels.

U.S. officials said they did not have information that showed the arms and supplies described in the document had reached El Salvador. But State Department and Pentagon sources have said that there has been a flow of arms to the Salvadoran guerrillas in recent months that is believed to be coming, in part, from Cuba.

Secretary of State Alexander M. Haig Jr. said in his first press conference last week that the Soviet Union had been involved in "unprecedented risk-taking" in support of revolutionary movements in Latin America and Africa, using what Mr. Haig called "the Cuban proxy."

The documents captured in El Salvador by government security forces last month describe the extent of collaboration between the Soviet Union and its allies in support of the Salvadoran guerrillas that has been approved at the highest levels of Communist leadership in East Europe and in Vietnam.

In one document, apparently written in Havana, the Salvadoran guerrilla reports on a visit to Hanoi June 9-15, 1980, in which he was received by Le Duan, secretary-general of the Vietnamese Communist Party, Xuan Thuy, vice president of the National Assembly, and Lt. Gen. Tran Van Quang, vice minister of defense.

The report said the Vietnamese agreed to supply 60 tons of arms and ammunition, mainly from weapons abandoned by U.S. and South Vietnamese forces. The list included 1,620 M-16 automatic rifles, 162 M-30 and 36 M-60 machine guns, 48 mortars, 12 anti-tank rocket launchers, 1.5-million rounds of ammunition and 11,000 mortar rounds.

In Ethiopia, the report says the Salvadoran guerrilla met July 3-6 with Lt. Col. Mengistu Haile Mariam, president of the revolutionary council. The report said he was promised 150 submachine guns, 1,500 M-1 rifles, 1,000 M-14 rifles, and more than 600,000 rounds of ammunition.

The Ethiopian armed forces were supplied by the United States before the overthrow of Emperor Haile Selassie by revolutionary officers opened the way to Soviet military influence. The Ethiopian armed forces are now supplied almost entirely with Soviet and East European weapons.

The Salvadoran guerrilla leader reported that he visited Bulgaria, where he was received by Dimitur Stanishev, a secretary of the Communist Party Central Committee, who offered 300 submachine guns with 200,000 rounds.

In Czechoslovakia, he reported that he had met Vasil Bilak, second secretary of the Communist Party's Central Committee, who offered some Czech arms and said they would be transported in East German ships to Cuba.

In Hungary, the report said the Salvadoran emissary was received by Janos Kadar, secretary-general of the Socialist Workers' Party. The Hungarians offered radio equipment, medical kits and 10,000 pairs of boots and uniforms.

Financial Aid

In East Germany, the report said the emissary was received by Erich Honecker, the party chief and president, and Hermann Axen, party secretary for international relations. The report said they promised $1 million in financial aid through a "committee of solidarity," but no arms.

In Moscow, where the report said the guerrilla emissary made two visits, first on June 2 before going to Vietnam, and another in July, the main topics were how to transport the arms to El Salvador.

Meetings were held with Karen Brutents, deputy chief of the Soviet Central Committee's department of international relations, and his deputy, Mikhail Kudashkin.

The report said the officials had agreed to give military training to 30 young Salvadoran Communists who were studying in the Soviet Union.

But the Salvadoran's report complained that he left Moscow without a firm decision on how the arms were to be shipped, whether by ship or air transport, and he complained that he had been unable to see Boris Ponomarev, the chief of the party's international relations department.

On July 29, after reaching Havana, the emissary said he had been notified by the Soviet Embassy that the Soviet Communist Party's Central Committee wanted him to return for further talks in September or October.

"The comrade expressed his concern that the lack of decision by the Soviets could affect not only the aid which they can give, but also that which has been offered by other parties of the European Socialist camp," the report said.

Another document, also written from Havana, refers to meetings that took place between the Salvadoran guerrilla leader and Gustavo Carvajal Moreno, president of Mexico's ruling Revolutionary Institutional Party, who was in Cuba during a visit there by President Jose Lopez Portillo last year.

This document said the Salvadoran guerrilla was guest at a dinner given by Mr. Lopez Portillo for Fidel Castro. As a result of talks with Mr. Carvajal, the Salvadoran reported that Mexico had agreed to allow the political front of the guerrillas to set up an office in Mexico City.

The report said Mr. Carvajal had offered to coordinate a front of Latin American political parties that would work against U.S. military intervention in El Salvador if the guerrillas overthrew the military-backed government of President Jose Napoleon Duarte.

But the report said Mr. Carvajal had said that neither the Mexican government nor the governing party could provide military assistance.

As I read the article, it struck me as almost a carbon copy of falsified CIA "proof" that I remembered. So I was suspicious of this document — or about this article — and I spoke to Juan de Onis, the *New York Times* reporter who received the documents from the government and wrote this article. I spoke to him three times this week.

De Onis is refusing to give out copies of the documents on which he based his article, and the U.S. government will not give copies of the documents for analysis by other people. I spoke to Congressman Ronald Dellums' office — he is the member of the House of Representatives from Berkeley, California — two days ago and asked if they had copies of the documents, because I was extremely interested in looking at them and analyzing them. It turned out that his office has been trying to get copies for over a week, and the government refuses.

De Onis told me that the way he got the documents was not through an unauthorized leak. Giving him the documents was an official act so that the information would appear in the *New York Times*. He said they were typed and not difficult to read. But the curious thing about the documents is that the way the de Onis story is written, you think there are a lot of documents involved. He mentions "secret documents" twice, and you think of an archive having been captured. And then he gives us an example — the one with all the military support listed — and then another example — the supposed political agreement between the President of the Mexican ruling party and the El Salvador revolutionaries.

During my conversations with de Onis he eventually admitted that he had only seen two documents, and he said that these documents were from among others captured in December by the El Salvador security forces from the guerrillas. But in his article he said they were captured last month, January, so I called him back asking him when they were captured. I asked if he knew where they were captured or from whom or what the circumstances were, the date or place or battle, or whether they were in someone's knapsack — and he had none of those details. Apparently he hadn't asked. He said: "The people who gave me the documents know."

I wondered why de Onis didn't ask for those details to have a better idea of their authenticity, because I remembered an operation that was very important in Lima, Peru. There were some legitimate documents captured, and the CIA then inserted false documents with the legitimate ones. For all we know, not having seen these Salvador documents, and the government refusing to give them, they may be false, and they may have been fabricated by the CIA precisely to provide so-called proof of support by Communist countries for the revolutionary movement in El Salvador.

I think this is extremely important to talk about. Because in the American press at least, I have not seen a word of skepticism about the legitimacy of these documents and that is what I want to raise today. I can't say, of course, not having seen the documents, whether they are false or whether they are real. At the very least, you would think that the United States government would have published a White Paper on the matter and put out copies of the originals. Who knows if there are any more than two, or there could be 150, and the two that are most important were fabricated by the CIA, inserted with the others, and then surfaced.

What is also curious about this is that the Salvadoran government is not exploiting the documents themselves. They supposedly captured the documents. But then they gave them to the United States government, and the United States is carrying the whole ball diplomatically with this offensive all over the world and, from what I have been able to discover, the Salvador government is doing nothing and has not even exploited the documents which they themselves captured.

What makes it most doubtful to me is that the United States government has not given these documents out. Juan de Onis said they were going to give them out — that he understood that they were going to give them out yesterday, and then they were going to give them out today, and now it seems like Monday. He said that the situation in Washington over these documents is extremely fluid and confused.

I might ask the question if anyone here knows whether the Eagleburger mission is actually showing copies of these documents. I have heard that they are not. They are trying to convince the governments of Western Europe to do certain things with respect to the Front or the government in El Salvador, but I have heard that they are not giving out copies of the documents themselves. The more they hold on to them and play them so closely to the chest, the more suspicious I get. I hope that as a result of this press conference and your efforts, people will get the documents and analyze them. Even after analysis it is not always easy to tell whether they are false or not, but one can try.

General Vernon Walters, the former CIA Deputy Director, has been sent on a mission for the same purpose as Eagleburger, to convince the Mexican and other Latin American governments to take some action. They probably want the Mexicans to withdraw support from the Revolutionary Democratic Front because they are one of the Front's principal backers in Latin America.

General Walters, for those who don't remember, was used by Nixon to begin the coverup of the Watergate break-in in 1972. When Walters was

Deputy Director of the CIA, the Nixon administration asked him to intervene with the FBI to stop an investigation in Mexico City about the money found on the burglars when they were arrested in the Watergate office building. And Walters contacted the FBI, saying that he had been told that if the FBI continued its investigation it might run afoul of CIA operations in Mexico — which was totally false.

PART 3

RECENT FALSE DOCUMENTS FROM THE U. S. EMBASSY IN IRAN

Now the Iranian documents. I bring these just in case anybody has the naive idea that the CIA may have stopped falsifying documents in recent years. Because my cases — the ones I participated in and know about from having worked in the CIA — are all from the 1960's. But these documents from Iran are from 1979. They were among those captured at the Embassy.

The first one is a secret cable from the Teheran Embassy to the State Department in Washington in which the Charge, Bruce Laingen, concurs in the assignments of two new CIA officers, and he mentions a little further down that there are now four of them there. Written in his handwriting at the top is: "Show to Tom A." That is Tom Ahern, who was the CIA Chief of Station, and one of the hostages captured. "SRF" in this document means CIA. When I was in the CIA, the State Department referred to us as CAS (Competent American Source). "SRF" is a new designation for the CIA, perhaps meaning Special Research Facility or some such euphemism.

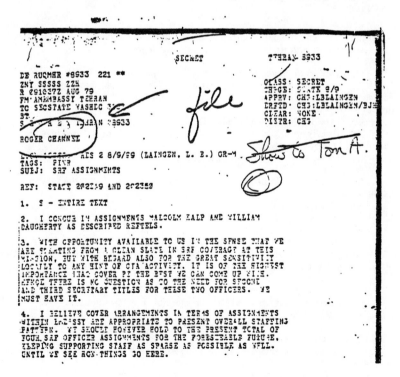

```
 8.  WE ARE MAKING EFFORT TO LIMIT KNOWLEDGE WITHIN EMB
 OF ALL SEP ASSIGNMENTS; THAT EFFORT APPLIES PARTICULARLY
 TO LAUGHERTY. PURSUANT TO NEW PROGRAM OF WHICH HE IS A
 PRODUCT AND ABOUT WHICH I HAVE BEEN INFORMED.

 9.  I SUPPOSE I NEED NOT MIND THE DEPARTMENT THAT THE CIA
 AND APPARENTLY INSOLUBLE PROBLEM OF A DESIGNATION FOR SRF.
 OFFICERS WILL INEVITABLY COMPLICATE AND TO SOME DEGREE
 YEALIN OUR COVER EFFORTS LOCALLY, NO MATTER HOW MUCH WE
 WORK AT IT.  LAINGEN
 BT
 #6923

 NNNN                          SECRET                 TEHRAN 6923
```

The next document is the confession by Ahern published in the Teheran press in July 1980. It appeared in *Azadegan*, one of Teheran's daily newspapers. The translation was by a service called The Flame. Notice that Ahern discusses the use of cryptonyms within the CIA's internal communications and identifies Iranian collaborators to the militants.

The confession is obviously an extract from a longer transcript. Efforts to obtain the full transcript were unsuccessful. Amir Entezam, identified by Ahern as SDPROBE (internal CIA cryptonym), was Iran's Deputy Prime Minister in the first revolutionary government headed by Mehdi Bazargan.

Azadegan: Moslem students following Imam's line's interview with one of spies in connection with Amir Entezam, Qashqai, and Madani

Q: Explain more about your activities and operations. . . ?
A: Every officer of the CIA was responsible for establishing contacts with a number of sources and obtaining the required information. This was mainly done by direct meetings with the sources.
Q: How did you arrange the meetings?
A: Usually meetings used to be set up before hand, i.e. in meetings the date and place of the next meeting was set. . .
Q;   Did any of you have a code name?
A: Yes.
Q: And your code name was Penguin (the closest we get to the Persian translation: Ed.)
A: Yes. That is right.
Q: And your sources had a code name too?
A: Yes. This is also true.
Q: For which sources was Penguin responsible?
A: His sources were "Rotor", "Probe", "Tramp" and the other one was "Genius 13" (again as above, e.g. they could also be "Rather", "Pert" and "Tramp": Ed.)
Q: Were you responsible for four sources?
A: That is right.
Q: Therefore you personally were responsible for four sources?
A: That is right.
Q: Explain to us one thing. The names of all these start with "S" and "D". What is the meaning of this "S" and "D"?
A: These two letters indicate that the source person or the activity is in connection with Iran.
Q: But it does not necessarily mean that they are Iranians?
A: No, not necessarily.
Q: Were the four sources in contact with you Iranians. . . ?
A: Yes.

Q: Were all four Iranians?
A: I must think to be sure. Yes, I am sure.
Q: Do other countries have two indicating letters?
A: Yes, they have.
Q: Well then, all were Iranians?
A: That is right.
Q: What missions did you assign to each of these sources. Name them with the code name.
A: In connection with "S.D. Probe" in the first phase I was interested in reports of the sessions of the Experts Assembly. In connection with "S.D. Tramp", because he knew different persons (our) demands were broader. From information about the biography of individuals in relations between the government and leaders of the revolution, to information about Kurdestan and also brief reports about the leadership and the morale in the armed forces. These are points which I can remember now. . . .
Q: What about other sources?
A: "S.D. Rotor" used to give reports about one of the racial minorities. . . Rotor used to give reports about the security situation of one of the tribes of the tribal areas and about their relations with the local officials and central government.
Q: Well then, did "S.D. Rotor" know that he was facing CIA agents? Did you pay anything to him? If not, what were his motives for contacting the CIA?
A: I believe that he knew that I am the representative of the CIA. I did not pay him anything. About the reason of his readiness to contact us, I do not remember that we had any discussion about it. There is no specific reference in the dossier about what his precise expectations from his contact with me or other agents before me were.
Q: In your view what was his motive in contacting the CIA?
A: I think he was interested in a secret contact with the U.S. government and this was in the form of a contact with the CIA. I do not know. I am guessing, because we never discussed this. However the leaders of tribes like more than others to be insured by such contacts.
Q: Well. About this newspaper, did "Rotor 4" know what was the purpose of this newspaper which you wanted to launch, and what are the U.S. interests in the newspaper?
A: No. Are you still . . . (could not be read) talking with Rotor? This was not put to him. He knew about my and Washington's interest in the work which he intended to do. But because of his successive delays, and that in effect they did the work, I intentionally delayed the discussion about these instances so that it appears to my mind that in effect it should be a paper that can be talked about.
Q: With whom did he intend to publish this newspaper?
A: With whom?
A: I know that he had put this to Admiral Madani. But I do not know if it was decided that he would become a partner or colleague and if Madani would have a role or not. I remember that Rotor made a reference to Admiral Madani in this regard. At least they had not discussed it together.
Q: Was Madani an obstacle for you in this path?
A: He, what?
Q: Obstacle, a problem.
A: Not as far as I know. On the contrary, as I understood from "Rotor" Madani was at least encouraging him to set up this newspaper. Now, whether he was prepared to get actively involved or not, I was never sure, but I never got the impression that Madani would be an obstacle to this plan.
Q: Let's get to the names.
A: The names of the source and who they have been in contact with?
Q: Who is "S.D. Probe"?
A: "S.D. Probe" is Entezam.
Q: Who is "S.D. Rotor"?
A: Khosrow Qashqai.
Q: And who is . . . . .

At the time of the takeover of the American Embassy in Teheran, the militants captured false identity documents prepared for Ahern. These were released to the press and included a Belgian passport containing Ahern's photograph with the name Paul Timmermans as the bearer of the passport.

The next document is the CIA's instructions to Ahern on how to use the false documentation. You won't find Ahern's name here, but if you check the reports that came out right after the takeover in 1979, you will see that the Iranians published the photograph in the Belgian passport — and it was a photograph of Ahern.

These pages which instruct him how to use this false passport also tell him how to use the little cachet devices so that he could print in the passport false dates of arrival and departure at the Teheran airport. The false passport also shows trips in 1977 and 1978 to Madrid, New Delhi, Helsinki, Lisbon and Athens "to enhance its validity." Note also the false International Vaccination Certificate that goes with the false passport.

PAGE 1

COVER CONSIDERATIONS

ACCORDING TO PERSONAL DATA IN YOUR PASSPORT, YOU ARE
SINGLE, WERE BORN IN ANTWERP, BELGIUM 08JUL34, HAVE BLUE
EYES, HAVE NO DISTINGUSHING CHARACTERISTICS, AND ARE APPROXI-
MATELY 1.88 METERS TALL. YOUR COVER OCCUPATION IS THAT OF
A COMMERCIAL BUSINESS REPRESENTATIVE.

IT IS NOT UNCOMMON TO FIND A BELGIAN WHOSE NATIVE
LANGUAGE IS FLEMISH LIVING IN A NOMINALLY FRENCH-SPEAKING
SECTION OF BELGIUM, SUCH AS JETTE: YOU CAN SAY THAT YOU
WERE BORN IN ANTWERP, BEGAN WORK WITH A COMPANY WITH A
REGIONAL OFFICE IN ANTWERP, THEN WAS TRANSFERRED TO THE
MAIN OFFICES IN BRUSSELS. DESPITE THE FACT IT IS ONLY
ABOUT 90 MINUTES DRIVING TIME BETWEEN BRUSSELS AND ANTWERP,
YOU DECIDED TO LIVE IN ONE OF THE SUBURBS OF BRUSSELS, JETTE.
THIS WOULD EXPLAIN THE ISSUANCE LOCALE OF YOUR DOCUMENTATION.
WORKING FROM YOUR BRUSSELS BASE, YOU HAVE TRAVELLED IN EUROPE
ON BUSINESS IN THE PAST (AS REFLECTED IN YOUR PASSPORT) AND
ARE NOW ASSIGNED TO THE MIDDLE EAST SECTION OF YOUR COMPANY.
YOUR NON-BACKSTOPPED ADDRESS IN JETTE IS 174 AVENUE DE JETTE,
JETTE, BELGIUM.

NITS-8792

S E C R E T

PAGE 2

INSTRUCTIONS FOR ACTIVATING PASSPORT

YOUR BELGIAN PASSPORT #N745653 WAS OSTENSIBLY ISSUED IN
JETTE, BELGIUM (A SUBURB OF BRUSSELS) ON 16 MARCH 1977, WAS
REVALIDATED IN JETTE ON 15 MARCH 1978, AND IS SET TO EXPIRE
ON 14 MARCH 1982.

TO ENHANCE ITS VALIDITY, THE FOLLOWING BACK TRAVEL WAS
ADDED: A TRIP TO MADRID, SPAIN IN APRIL 1977; A TRIP TO LISBON,
PORTUGAL IN AUGUST 1977; A TRIP TO DELHI, INDIA IN JANUARY
1978; A TRIP TO MADRID, SPAIN IN MARCH 1978; A TRIP TO HEL-
SINKI, FINLAND IN JUNE 1978; AND A TRIP TO ATHENS, GREECE
IN NOVEMBER 1978.

UNDER CURRENT (AUGUST 1979) REGULATIONS, A BELGIAN DOES
NOT NEED A VISA TO ENTER IRAN; INSTEAD, HE WOULD BE LIMITED
TO A STAY OF NINETY (90) DAYS. TO ACTIVATE THIS PASSPORT
YOU WILL HAVE TO ENTER OSTENSIBLE ENTRY AND EXIT CACHET IM-
PRESSIONS INTO THE PASSPORT. FIRST YOU MUST ASCERTAIN WHICH
CALENDAR SYSTEM WAS IN USE FOR YOUR OSTENSIBLE ENTRY AND/OR
EXIT DATES. WOLOCK HAS SEEN THREE VERSIONS: 1) USING THE
PERSIAN CALENDAR; 2) USING THE MOSLEM CALENDAR BUT WITH THE
LAST TWO DIGITS OF THE YEAR ONLY; AND 3) USING THE MOSLEM
CALENDAR AND USING THE FULL FOUR DIGITS OF THE YEAR.

NITS-8792

S E C R E T

Facsimile   S E C R E T

PAGE 3

IF THE PERSIAN CALENDAR IS IN USE, USE THE ENTRY/EXIT CACHET
MOUNTED ON WOODEN BLOCKS IN CONJUNCTION WITH THE "PERSIAN
CALENDAR" DATE CHIPS. SELECT A CORRECT DATE AND SET THE
CHIPS INTO THE CUT-OUT PORTION OF THE CACHET(S). USING THE
#280 INK PAD FOR AND ENTRIES OR THE #295 INK PAD FOR ANY
EXITS, INK THE CACHET(S) WITH THE DATE CHIPS SET IN, THEN
MAKE AN IMPRESSION INTO THE PASSPORT.

FOR THE MOSLEM CALENDAR SYSTEMS, YOU WILL FIRST IMPRESS
THE DATE USING THE BANDED DATERS, THEN USE THE ENTRY/EXIT CACHET
MOUNTED ON THE CLEAR PLASTIC. FIRST, SELECT THE CORRECT
BANDED DATED (EITHER TWO-DIGIT YEAR OR FOUR-DIGIT YEAR) AND
THE CORRECT INK PAD (#280 FOR ENTRIES, #295 FOR EXITS), THEN
ENTER THE DATE INTO THE PASSPORT. THEN, INK THE CORRECT CACHET
(EITHER ENTRY OR EXIT) IN THE CORRECT PAD, AND ENTER THIS IMPRESSION

SO THAT THE DATE APPEARS MORE OR LESS CENTERED IN THE IMPRESSION.
PEER THROUGH THE PLASTIC TO ASSURE THE DATE IS CORRECTLY PLACED.
PLEASE SEE PAGE 4 FOR MOCK-UPS AND EXEMPLARS.

SHOULD YOU NOTICE ANY CHANGES, EITHER IN THE CACHET STYLES
OR INK COLORS, SEND COLOR EXPOSURES TO EZNOVA, WITH SCALE AND
COLOR PATCH INCLUDED IN EACH PHOTO: EZNOVA WILL THEN REPRODUCE
THE NEEDED MATERIAL AND FORWARD IT/THEM TO YOU.

S E C R E T   NITS-8792

PAGE 3A

YOUR CACHET IMPRESSIONS SHOULD BE LEGIBLE--~~NOT GOT SO~~
~~SMEAR TEST~~. PRACTICE ON THE ENCLOSED PAPER UNTIL YOU FEEL
ABLE TO ADD THE CACHETS INTO THE PASSPORT.

N.B.: SINCE MEHRABAD ENTRY AND EXIT CACHETS EACH HAVE A
DIFFERENT INSPECTOR NUMBER AND IS WOULD BE MOST UNLIKELY THAT
A TRAVELER WOULD HAVE THE SAME CACHET NUMBERS FOR CONSECUTIVE
TRIPS, THE ATTACHED CACHETS SHOULD ONLY BE USED ONCE IN THE
PASSPORT. CACHETS NEEDED FOR ADDITONAL IRANIAN ENTRY/EXITS
SHOULD BE REQUESTED FROM EZNOVA OR THE DOCUMENT SHOULD BE
FORWARDED THERE FOR UPDATING.

SECRET

NITS-0701

S E C R E T

PAGE 4

— 22 —
VISAS — VISA — SICHIVERMERKE — VISAS

— 23 —
VISAS — VISA — SICHIVERMERKE — VISAS

EXEMPLAR
ENTRY CACHET WITH PERSIAN YEAR

EXEMPLAR
EXIT CACHET WITH MOSLEM YEAR AND
USING ONLY LAST TWO DIGITS

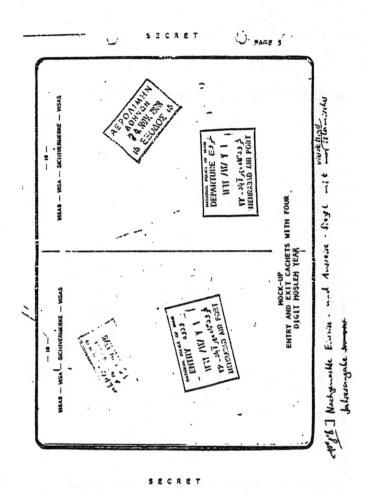

NITS-8792

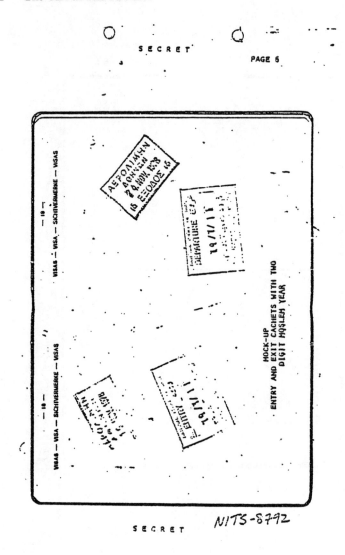

MOCK-UP
ENTRY AND EXIT CACHETS WITH TWO
DIGIT MOSLEM YEAR

SECRET

INSTRUCTIONS FOR THE INTERNATIONAL CERTIFICATE OF VACCINATION

CACHETS FOR OSTENSIBLE SMALLPOX, YELLOW FEVER, AND CHOLERA VACCINATIONS HAVE ALREADY BEEN ENTERED INTO THE SHOT RECORD. PLEASE SIGN IN ALIAS UNDERNEATH YOUR NAME FOR EACH SHOT.

THE SMALLPOX VACCINATION IS VALID FOR THREE YEARS: IT WILL BE RENEWED IN JULY 1982. PLEASE CONTACT EZNOVA OR WOLOCK IF YOU WILL NEED THE SHOT RECORD BEYOND THIS DATE.

THE YELLOW FEVER VACCINATION IS GOOD FOR TEN YEARS: NOTHING FURTHER HAS TO BE DONE FOR THIS VACCINATION.

THE CHOLERA VACCINATION IS VALID FOR ONLY SIX MONTHS. NEW CACHET ENTRIES WILL HAVE TO BE MADE, BEGINNING IN JANUARY 1980. CONSULTING THE MOCK-UP (OVERLEAF) USE THE "DR R. COOSEMANS" AND "OSSOM-FI" CACHETS AND REFLEX BLUE INK PAD. USING ANY BALL POINT OR WET INK PEN, ENTER A SUITABLE DATE USING A DAY-MONTH-YEAR ORDE (WITH THE MONTH IN ROMAN NUMERALS) AND SIGN ABOVE THE DOCTOR'S NAME CACHET. UPDATE THE CHOLERA VACCINATION AS NEEDED EVERY SIX MONTHS, USING THE SAME CACHETS AND INK PAD. REMEMBER, YOU WILL OSTENSIBLY GET THESE SHOTS IN BELGIUM, AND YOUR PASSPORT SHOULD NOT SHOW YOU IN IRAN WHEN YOU UPDATE YOUR CHOLERA SHOT.

SECRET

53 %

NITS-8792

SECRET   PAGE 8

INTERNATIONAL CERTIFICATE OF VACCINATION OR REVACCINATION
AGAINST CHOLERA

CERTIFICAT INTERNATIONAL DE VACCINATION OU DE REVACCINATION
CONTRE LE CHOLÉRA·

This is to certify that / PAUL TIMMERMANS   date of birth /8·7·1934 sex / M
Je soussigné(e) certifie que /   né(2) le   sexe/
whose signature follows / Paul Timmerman
dont la signature suit   /

has on the date indicated been vaccinated or revaccinated against cholera.
a été vacciné(e) ou revacciné(e) contre le choléra à la date indiquée.

SECRET   NITS - 8792

The documents that follow are photocopies of false documentation
sent out to a second man in the CIA station in Teheran whose name is
George O'Keefe. The first page is the envelope in which the false documents
were sent, and you see that it was partially burned — probably while going
into the incinerator at the time of the takeover. This envelope comes from
the CIA office in Frankfurt as you can see from "OTS" Frankfurt, which
might stand for "Office of Technical Services."

The second page is the CIA dispatch which covers the sending of the
false documents to the Teheran station. It describes them. One is a Federal
Republic of Germany passport, number so-and-so, issued in Hanover; another is a West German driver's license; another is a West German international
driver's license. These documents are in the name of Josef Schneider. The

man's real name is George O'Keefe — but the name on the documents is Schneider.

Sorry — it's confusing. The first document following the Dispatch form is a West German driver's license in O'Keefe's true name. This would not have been included in the envelope containing the false documents, but was probably found by the militants and placed with the falsified documents to show that the photos on the false documents are O'Keefe. Note that O'Keefe's 1976 address is Aurikelstieg 1, Hamburg. A check at this address revealed that O'Keefe lived there until about June 1978 and that the contract for his apartment was in the name of the U.S. Consulate General in Hamburg — simply confirming that the CIA has an office in that Consulate. The other documents (following the driver's license in true name) are false documents in the name of Josef Schneider for which O'Keefe used his true year of birth but reversed the day/month combination.

So here you have a second case of falsified documents of very recent origin having to do with a West German passport. I show them to confirm that the CIA is still falsifying documents. With the Eagleburger mission having come to West Germany, and having gone to Belgium, to try to convince these governments to follow American policy, you have to wonder, when the CIA, by falsifying their passports, has jeopardized the lives of every Belgian and every West German living in Iran or travelling there. But the CIA couldn't take care of these documents. They let them fall into the hands of the militants. They were published — and every Belgian and West German in Iran became suspect of being there as an undercover man for the CIA. It is presumptuous, I think, to come and ask for help when you have jeopardized the nationals of a country that way.

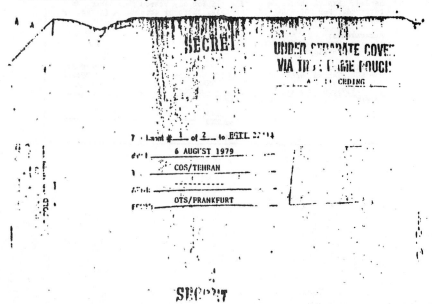

DISPATCH	SECRET	

Chief of Station, Tehran

C/NE; C/EZVIVID; COS, Germany; C/WOGAME; D/WOLOCK/GAD

Chief, EZNOVA

TECHS LPGAMIN - Transmittal of Alias Documentation for JAUMOTTE

REF: DIRECTOR 461951

WARNING NOTICE - SENSITIVE INTELLIGENCE SOURCES & METHODS INVOLVED

1. Forwarded USC/TNP and preceding this dispatch are the following backstopped FRG documents for JAUMOTTE in alias number 203472:

    A. FRG passport number D1797931 issued in Hannover on 21 March 1973 and revalidated on 13 July 1979. Document is valid until 21 March 1983. Prior travel per ref request has been entered.

    B. FRG internal driver's license number 9941/79 issued in Hannover on 16 July 1979 and valid indefinitely.

    C. FRG International Driving Permit issued Hannover on 24 July 1979 and valid for one year.

2. A non-backstopped Hannover address is shown on the driver's license.

3. Forwarded as attachment number two, herewith is cachet kit containing inks, cachets, date chips and instructions. Please monitor Tehran entry and exit cachets and advise EZNOVA if ink color and/or dating system changes. (Germans may remain up to 3 months without visa, so JAUMOTTE must be stamped out within 3 months of his ostensible entry.)

4. These documents should be returned to EZNOVA when no longer needed. EZNOVA should be notified if for any reason they cannot be returned. Per DOI-F 240-10, any loss, theft or compromise (actual or presumed) should be reported to EZNOVA.

Attachments:
#1 - One Envelope, USC/TNP & Preceding
#2 - One Envelope, H/W
                                  Alan J. NAGLUND

Distribution:
  2 - COS, Tehran, w/att a/s   2 - COS, Germany, w/o att
  2 - C/NE, w/o att   2 - C/WOGAME, w/o att
  2 - C/EZVIVID, w/o att   2 - D/WOLOCK/GAD, w/o att

RVW6AUG99, DRV D9c.2.

EGTT-22411	6 AUGUST 1979

SECRET

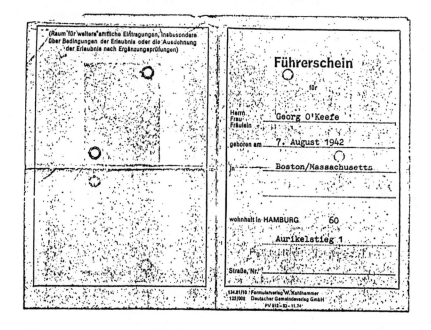

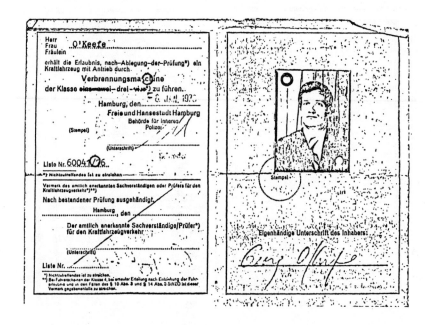

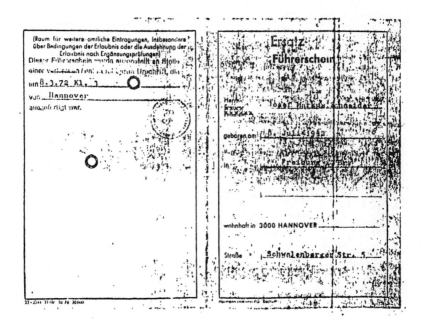

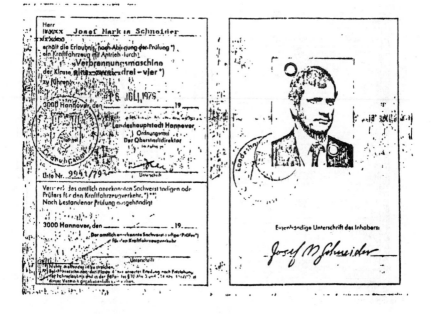

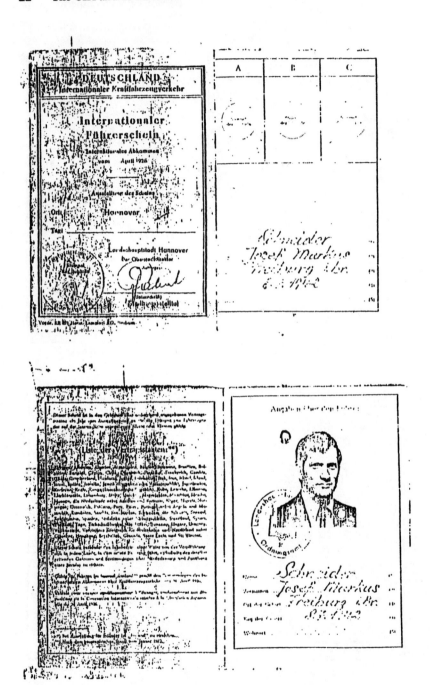

The next document is a copy of the official note from the Embassy to the Iranian Foreign Ministry announcing O'Keefe's arrival in June 1979 and asking that a diplomatic carnet be issued for him. (The almost illegible line in the Embassy note reads: "as Second Secretary of this Embassy. Mr. O'Keefe is married.")

No. P-143

The Embassy of the United States of America presents its compliments to the Islamic Republic's Ministry of Foreign Affairs and has the honor to inform the Ministry that Mr. George E. O'Keefe arrived Tehran on June 23, 1979 and assumed his duties . . . . Mr. O'. . . . .

Mr. O'Keefe's name should be added to the Diplomatic list taking precedence among officers of the Embassy immediately following Mr. Michael J. Metrinko, Second Secretary.

The Embassy has the honor to request the Ministry to register and authorize the issuance of a diplomatic identity card for Mr. O'Keefe, holder of Diplomatic Passport No. X140736.

The Embassy avails itself of this opportunity to renew to the Ministry the assurances of its highest consideration.

2 closures: Passport and photographs.

Embassy of the United States of America
Tehran, July 2, 1979

With O'Keefe there is confusion from the fact that he has his true name, George O'Keefe — the false name, Josef Schneider — and still a third name which is his secret name inside the CIA, because every CIA operations officer has a pseudonym for use inside the Agency. In this case the CIA pseudonym for O'Keefe is Jaumotte. If you look at that CIA Dispatch, you see under "Subject": "Transmittal of Alias Documentation for Jaumotte." Jaumotte is the code name he used inside the CIA, and the importance of pointing this out is found in the following document.

This is a CIA cable from headquarters in Langley, Virginia, to the New York field office of the CIA with information copies to the CIA station in Teheran and to the field office in Los Angeles. It advises that Jaumotte, that is, O'Keefe, is to arrive in New York on October 31, 1979 to meet the Iranian agent whose internal cryptonym is SDPLAYER/1.

```
                                                    30 OCT 79  8J 30z

S E C R E T 292327Z OCT 79 STAFF
CITE DIRECTOR 541895.
TO:  PRIORITY FR/NEW YORK INFO TEERAN, FR/LOS ANGELES.
VNINTEL AJAJA TORRES SDPLAYER
REF:  DIRECTOR 542716
     1.  JAUMOTTE WILL ARRIVE NEW YORK MORNING 31 OCTOBER FOR
INTRODUCTION SDPLAYER/1.
     2.  PLEASE ADVISE CONTACT INSTRUCTIONS.
     3.  FILE 201-953302.  RYW 29OCT99 DRV D9C.1 ALL SECRET.
S E C R E T
BT
'1394
```

```
                 SD = Ivan
                 ON = France
                 Gv = Britil
                 CA = Germ.
```

The next cable shows that the Iranian was not able to attend the
meeting with O'Keefe because of a family problem.

```
                                                    1 Nov 79  04 43z

S E C R E T 312321Z OCT 79 STAFF
CITE FR/NEW YORK 57904
TO:  IMMEDIATE DIRECTOR INFO TEERAN, FR/LOS ANGELES.
VNINTEL AJAJA TORRES SDPLAYER
REF DIRECTOR 541995
     1.  REF INTRODUCTION OF JAUMOTTE TO SDPLAYER/1 (P/1) DID
NOT TAKE PLACE DUE TO MEDICAL EMERGENCY ON PART OF P/1'S SISTER-
IN-LAW'S DAUGHTER.  P/1 AVAILABLE 1 NOV 79 UP TILL 1330 HOURS
RPT 1330 HOURS.  PER DISCUSSION WITH BASE, JAUMOTTE PREPARED
RETURN NEW YORK 1 NOV 79.  SUGGEST JAUMOTTE PLAN ARRIVE NEW YORK
AT 1000 HOURS.
     2.  FILE: 201-963308.  RYW 31OCT99 DRV D9C1
S E C R E T
BT
#7803
```

The next document is the cabled report on training given to this Iranian spy by O'Keefe and another CIA officer, probably from the Office of Training, whose internal CIA pseudonym is Quaranta. You will notice from the report on these 10 hours of training that they concentrated on clandestine communications and the use of car pickups for their meetings.

(Copy---Ed. Note)

3 Nov 79

1. RE PARA FIVE REF B, SDPLAYER/1 (P/1) GIVEN TOTAL OF TEN HOURS OF TRADECRAFT TRAINING IN NEW YORK BY QUARANTA. INITIAL TWO HOUR BLOCK OF INSTRUCTION COVERED OPERATIONAL SECURITY (PERSONAL, PHYSICAL, WORK ENVIRONMENT) WITH PARTICULAR EMPHASIS ON TELEPHONE SECURITY AND METHODS OF AGENT COMMUNICATION. P/1 WAS GIVEN BRIEF INTRODUCTION ON THEORY OF LIVE DROPS, DEAD DROPS, BRUSH PASSES, CAR TOSSES, SW AND CAR PICKUPS. IT WAS NOTED TO S/1 THAT A SEPARATE BLOCK OF INSTRUCTION WOULD BE DEVOTED TO CAR PICKUPS AND CAR MEETINGS.

2. THREE HOUR BLOCK OF INSTRUCTION WAS DEVOTED TO OBSERVATION, ELICITATION AND REPORTS WRITING. TWO HOUR BLOCK WAS DEVOTED TO COMMUNICATION SYSTEMS (REGULAR, WARNING AND RESERVE) AND SAFETY/WARNING SIGNALS. AN HOUR AND ONE HALF BLOCK ON SURVEILLANCE (VEHICULAR, FOOT AND FIXED) AND COUNTERSURVEILLANCE. FINAL HOUR AND A HALF WAS DEVOTED TO CAR PICKUPS (FIXED POINT, FLOATING CONTACT, HEAD-ON APPROACH AND FOLLOW ME METHOD). GRAPHIC ILLUSTRATIONS WERE USED FOR AGENT COMMO AND TRADCRAFT SUBJECTS. AFTER BRIEFING PORTION OF CAR PICKUPS COMPLETED, RENTAL VEHICLE WAS USED FOR LIVE EXERCISE.

3. IN ALL ASPECTS OF TRAINING, P/1 EXHIBITED ABILITY TO GRASP QUICKLY AND RETAIN TEACHING POINTS. HE ALSO WAS NOT BASHFUL ABOUT ASKING FOR ADDITIONAL EXPLANATION OR CLARIFICATION. P/1 HAS GOOD MEMORY AND FULLY UNDERSTANDS AND ACCEPTS REASONING BEHIND CLANDESTINITY OF RELATIONSHIP. P/1 SHOWED KEEN INTEREST IN TRADECRAFT SUBJECTS AND WAS MOST RECEPTIVE TO OVERALL SCOPE OF TRAINING.

```
                                           3 Nov 79    7  7

S E C R E T  621953-1 NO7 73 STAFF

CITE IB/NEW YORK 37577

TO:  DIRECTOR INFO TEHRAN.

VN INFTL AJAJA FORMS SDSIAXGR

REF A FL/NEW YORK 37543
    B FL/NEW YORK 57505

    1.  RE PARA FIVE REF B. EXPLAINED (3/1) GIVEN TOTAL
OF TEN HOURS OF TRADECRAFT TRAINING IN NEW YORK 9V QUARANT.
INITIAL TWO HOUR BLOCK OF INSTRUCTION COVERED OPERATIONAL SECURITY
(PERSONAL, PHYSICAL, COMMUNICATIONS) WITH PARTICULAR EMPHASIS
ON TELEPHONE SECURITY AND MEANING OF SIGNS COMMUNICATION.
P/1 WAS GIVEN BRIEF INTRODUCTION ON THEORY OF LIVE DROPS, DEAD
DROPS, BRUSH PASSES, CAR PASSES. HE AND CAR PICKUPS. IT WAS
NOTED SO 3/1 THAT A SEPARATE BLOCK OF INSTRUCTION WOULD BE
DEVOTED TO CAR PICKUPS AND CAR MEETINGS.

    2.  THIRD HOUR BLOCK OF INSTRUCTION WAS DEVOTED TO
SURVEILLANCE, DETECTION AND REPORTS THEREOF. NEXT FOUR BLOCK
WAS DEVOTED TO COMMUNICATIO SYSTEMS (REGULAR WARNING AND
RESCRAPET AND SAFETY WARNING SIGNALS, AND HOUR ONE-ON- HALF
BLOCK ON SURVEILLANCE (VEHICULAR, FOOT AND FIXED) AND
COUNTERSURVEILLANCE. FINAL HOUR AND A HALF WAS DEVOTED TO
CAR PICKUPS (FIXED POINT, RELOADING CONTACT, STAND-ON APPROACH
LAND FOLLOW ME METHOD). GRAPHIC ILLUSTRATIONS WERE USED FOR
AGENT COMMO AND TRADECRAFT SUBJECTS. AFTER BRIEFING PORTION OF
CAR PICKUPS COMPLETED, RENTAL VEHICLE WAS USED FOR LIVE
EXERCISE.

    3.  IN ALL ASPECTS OF TRAINING, P/1 EXHIBITED ABILITY
TO GRASP QUICKLY AND RETAIN TEACHING POINTS.  HE ALSO WAS NOT
BASHFUL ABOUT ASKING FOR ADDITIONAL EXPLANATION OR CLARIFICATION.
P/1 HAS GOOD MEMORY AND FULLY UNDERSTANDS AND ACCEPTS REASONING
BEHIND CLANDESTINITY OF RELATIONSHIP.  P/1 SEEMED REAL INTEREST
IN TRADECRAFT SUBJECTS AND WAS MOST RECEPTIVE TO OVERALL SCOPE
OF TRAINING.

    FILE 201-823348.  GPT: GINOVICO DET DICI
      B B
  #75
```

Then we have another CIA cable from the New York office revealing that the Iranian was to return to Teheran in early November with the first Teheran meeting between him and O'Keefe set for November 17, with O'Keefe waiting in his parked car on Niku Street. Notice also in this document that the Iranian has a bank account in Houston, Texas, and that his CIA salary payments were to be deposited to this account.

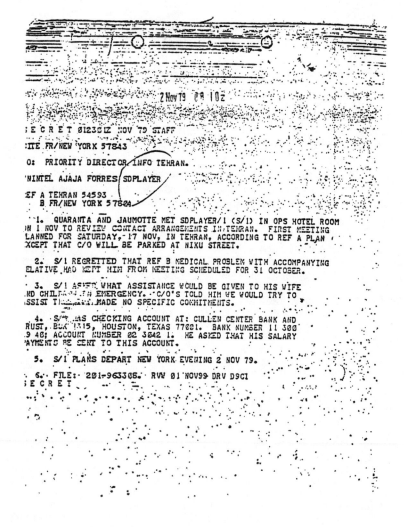

As a final remark on these false documents provided by O'Keefe, I would point out that from among the names of all the hostages in Tehran, O'Keefe never appeared because, as you can see from these documents, he had returned to New York from Teheran and was there when the Embassy was taken over.

PART 4

CASES OF FALSE DOCUMENTATION AND FALSE PRESS STORIES PREPARED BY THE C I A

Now I want to give you examples of the CIA's falsification of documents and information for the purpose of connecting the Soviets or Cubans or some other socialist country with indigenous left and socialist movements. You should consider these examples as representative of hundreds of others undoubtedly concocted by the CIA over the years. Don't put these down as "old" cases because, as you will see, they had an impact in their day comparable to the impact that Washington hopes will come from the current documents about El Salvador.

A.   The Raid on the Cuban Embassy in Lima, Peru, 1960
The first case is from 1960 and is about the break in diplomatic relations between Peru and Cuba. The CIA's role is described in these extracts from my first book: *Inside the Company: CIA Diary.*

Quito — 30 December 1960
There seems now to be little doubt that the InterAmerican Conference will be postponed. Peru insists it won't attend because of Ecuador's intention of raising the Protocol issue; Venezuela and the Dominican Republic are still in a crisis over Trujillo's attempt to assassinate Betancourt; and U.S.-Cuban relations are getting still worse. We all know the invasion is coming but certainly not until Kennedy takes over.

Peru's break in relations with Cuba today hasn't helped prospects for the Conference. The break is partly a show of appreciation to the U.S. for the October ruling by the Guarantors on the Protocol, but it's also the result of a Lima station operation in November. The operation was a commando raid by Cuban exiles against the Cuban Embassy in Lima which included the capture of documents. The Lima station inserted among the authentic documents several that had been forged by TSD including a supposed list of persons in Peru who received payments from the Cuban Embassy totalling about 15,000 dollars monthly.

Another of the forged documents referred to a nonexistent campaign of the Cuban Embassy in Lima to promote the Ecuadorean position on the Rio Protocol. Because not many Peruvians believed the documents to be genuine, the Lima station had great difficulty in getting them publicized. However, a few days ago a Conservative deputy in the Peruvian Congress presented them for the record and yesterday they finally surfaced in the Lima press. Although the Cubans have protested that the documents are apocryphal, a recent defector from the Cuban Embassy in Lima — present during the raid and now working for the Agency — has "confirmed" that the TSD documents are genuine. The Conservative Peruvian government then used the documents as the pretext for breaking relations with Cuba.

B.   The Flores Case, Quito, Ecuador, 1963
The next extracts from *Inside the Company* describe an important case in which I myself concocted a false document. This operation had a huge impact and contributed to a military coup in Ecuador.

Quito — 14 April 1963
Each day, it seems, a new wave of rumors spreads around the country signaling the

imminent outbreak of guerrilla warfare and terrorism. Partly the rumors reflect our continuing propaganda campaign to focus attention on communism in order to provoke a serious crackdown by the government.

Quito — 19 April 1963
Another important trip to wonder about — this time it's Antonio Flores Benitez, one of Echeverria's lieutenants, who left today for Cuba. What we can't figure out is why Echeverria would send Flores to Cuba when Araujo is there and Roura is in China.

Quito — 24 May 1963
John Bacon, the Station Reports Officer, and I suggested to Dean that we prepare an incriminating document to be used against Antonio Flores Benitez — to be planted on Flores when he arrives at the airport. There's a chance, of course, that he'll come overland from Colombia or that he'll arrive in Guayaquil, but Dean likes the plan and asked us to go ahead. The document will appear to be Flores's and Echeverria's own report to the Cubans on the status of their organization and on their plans for armed action. We are describing what we know about the organization, filling in with imagination where necessary, on the basis of the information from the ECWHEAT telephone tap and reports from Cardenas and Vargas, our two best penetrations of the Echeverria group. We are emphasizing (for propaganda afterwards) Flores's penetration agents in the Ministry of Defense, Army communications, the presidential bodyguard and the presidential archives. We are also planning to mention relations with Araujo's group and Gonzalo Sono Mogro, who seems to be training a separate organization in explosives and weapons.

Quito — 26 May 1963
It has been a busy weekend. Bacon and I finished the "Flores Report" yesterday and he took it out to Mike Burbano to put in final form, correct Spanish and proper commie jargon. He knows this usage best because he's the cutout for Cardenas and Vargas. No question but that we've got a really sensational and damaging document.

Bacon included in the report a general analysis of the Ecuadorean political scene with appropriate contempt for the Saad PCE leadership for its "reformist" tendencies. He infers that the Echeverria group has already received funds from Cuba and that this report is the justification for new funds. The date for commencing an all-out terrorism campaign will be late July (since we already have a report that the CTE plans to announce a general strike for that date). Bombing targets and guerrilla attacks will be set for the homes of police and military officers as well as key installations such as the water-works and the telephone and electric companies.

Burbano passed it back and I typed it this morning — it filled five sheets of flimsy blue copy paper. Then Dean came to the office and we agreed that Juan Sevilla, the Minister of the Treasury, would be better for getting it planted than Jaime del Hierro, the Minister of Government. I went to see Sevilla; he agreed immediately and said he'll use Carlos Rendon, the same secretary and customs inspector who nailed Roura. When I got back to the Embassy Dean was acting like a little boy. He had gone over to the "Favorita" to buy a tube of toothpaste and had spent three hours squeezing out the paste and cleaning the tube. Then he crumpled the papers, ground them a little with his shoe, folded them to fit into the tube and pronounced the report genuine beyond doubt. I took the tube, now with the report neatly stuffed inside, back over to Sevilla and tomorrow he will give it to Rendon who will plant it if possible. Rendon won't move from the airport until Flores arrives, and if he comes via Colombia or Guayaquil, we'll figure out some other way to get the document out. One way or another this one should really provoke a reaction.

Quito — 2 June 1963
Flores is hooked and we've got another big case! Juan Sevilla and I were playing golf together this morning when a caddy came running out to call him to the telephone. We rushed into the clubhouse and sure enough it was Carlos Rendon, his personal

secretary, calling to say that Flores had arrived and that the plant had worked perfectly. Sevilla rushed straight to the airport and I went home to wait. Late in the afternoon he telephoned and when I went to his house he explained that Rendon had seen Flores arrive and had put the toothpaste tube up his sleeve. He let it fall out carefully while he was reviewing Flores's luggage, "found it" and began to examine it, finally opening it and "discovering" the concealed report.

Arriving with Flores was another well-known communist, Hugo Noboa, who was discovered to be carrying 1,400 dollars in cash in a secret pocket. This money, propaganda material, and phonograph records of revolutionary songs were confiscated along with the Flores report, and both Flores and Noboa were taken under arrest to the political security offices for questioning.

Now to get the publicity going.

Quito — 3 June 1963

We're going to have to fight for this one. Only a small notice appeared in the press today on the Flores and Noboa arrests, and the only reference to the "Flores Report" was an allegation that microfilm had been found in his suitcase. Flores, according to this notice, is protesting that if any microfilm was found it was planted either in San Juan, Puerto Rico, where he was transit, or here in Quito.

I checked with Juan Sevilla and he told me that he thinks Arosemena is going to try to quash the whole case including the false document. This is why, according to Sevilla, Flores is still in custody of the political security office instead of the police investigations department under Major Pacifico de los Reyes. He added that the key figure is Jaime del Hierro, the Minister of Government and added that if I know del Hierro, I should confirm the importance of Flores and the document. (Neither Sevilla nor del Hierro knows that I am in a working relationship with the other.)

For most of the afternoon I've tried to get either del Hierro or Manuel Cordova, the Sub-Secretary of Government, by telephone. It's not like them to avoid me like this, and Dean is about to blow up because the report hasn't been surfaced.

Quito — 4 June 1963

There's no doubt now that Arosemena has tried to cover up the case and protect Flores, but we're prying it loose almost by the hour. Sevilla threatened to resign if the case were suppressed and the rumors of a new Cabinet crisis were so strong yesterday and today that the Secretary-General of the Administration made a public denial of the crisis.

Del Hierro finally called me back today, and when we met at Cordova's house he gave me the "Flores Report" asking that I check it for authenticity because it is so grave. I couldn't simply give it a moment's look and pronounce it genuine so I took it back to the station. When I told Dean of this he went into a fury, stamped up and down and said I'd better get that report surfaced or else. He's really disgusted with del Hierro, whom he thinks is trying to delay making it public in order to protect the Liberal Party from embarrassment; the document, after all, is pretty damaging to the government, even though it is primarily aimed at exposing the Echeverria group.

A positive sign is that Flores has been passed from the political security office to the police, which places him directly under del Hierro. In his declaration Flores only said that he had been in Europe on a forty-five-day trip as a journalist (he writes for the leftist weekly *La Manana*) with no mention of travel to Cuba.

Quito — 5 June 1963

Dean's fit of temper shows no signs of diminishing. This morning he demanded Jaime del Hierro's private telephone number at the ministry, which I gave him. He called del Hierro and told him angrily that of course the document is authentic and that every Ecuadorean should read it. Dean was careful to record this call on his dictaphone just in case del Hierro complains to the Ambassador.

Then I proposed to Dean that I give a copy of the document to Jorge Rivadeneira Araujo, the brother of Rodrigo Rivadeneira — the transcriber of the Flores telephone tap. Jorge has long participated in the clandestine printing operation, along with his brothers, and is a writer for *El Comercio*, Quito's leading daily. We don't usually place propaganda through Jorge, but Dean agreed since it is the fastest way to put pressure on del Hierro to release the original document. Later I took a copy to Rodrigo which he is passing to Jorge who will show it to his editors at the newspaper. This may destroy my relationship with del Hierro and Cordova but Dean doesn't care – he doesn't think Arosemena and the Liberals can last much longer anyway.

Quito – 6 June 1963

Our ploy against del Hierro worked like a charm. This morning about ten o'clock Cordova called me from the Embassy receptionist's desk and when I went down he took me out back to del Hierro who was waiting in his car. He said he urgently needed back the Flores document because the press had somehow got a copy and he would have to release the original later today. I rushed up for the document, returned it to del Hierro and told Dean who whooped for joy. Then I called Rodrigo Rivadeneira to alert his brother Jorge that the Ministry of Government would release the document later today. It may not be printed in today's evening newspapers but already the whole town is buzzing about it. . . .

Both Mario Cardenas and Luis Vargas report that Echeverria has been crushed psychologically by this blow. He fears that with the Roura arrest and now Flores he'll surely be reprimanded by the Saad leadership, possibly even expelled from the PCE. He has now gone into hiding and the agents are trying to find out where.

Quito – 7 June 1963

Finally it's in print and the sensation is immense. Everything's included: description of Saad and the PCE Guayaquil leadership as "old bureaucrats full of bourgeois vices, faithful to the Moscow line and acting as a brake on revolution." Also: "We (the Echeverria group) are faithful to the experiences of the Cuban revolution and the necessity to prepare for armed insurrection." Araujo is described as having a good number of trained and armed teams and the Rivadeneira group is cited as possibly useful for "our" purposes. All the different critical government offices where Flores has his contacts are mentioned – including the Presidential Palace – and the date for commencing operations (urban terrorism and rural guerrillas) is given as late July to coincide with "our" urging of the CTE to call a general strike for that time.

As if this document weren't enough in itself, by sheer coincidence the CTE yesterday announced a general strike for late July. Our agents had reported that this announcement would come some time and we had included it in the Flores document. This announcement was carried in the press today, alongside the Flores document, as proof that the latter is genuine. . . .

Quito – 5 July 1963

The chain of recent cases, particularly the Roura and Flores cases, has produced one of the results we wanted. At a special meeting of the PCE Central Committee the whole Pichincha Provincial Committee under Echeverria was dismissed, with Roura expelled from the party and Echeverria suspended. Already Jaime Galarza, one of Echeverria's lieutenants, has published an article suggesting that Pedro Saad, PCE Secretary-General, was behind the revelations in the Flores document and Roura's arrest, because such information could only come from highly placed party members.

The momentum of the last three months' campaign is having other effects. Most of our political-action agents, particularly the rightists in the ECACTOR project, are reporting improving disposition to a military rather than a Congressional move against Arosemena, what with the alarm and gravity of the current situation. At the Ambassador's reception yesterday, moreover, the politicians talked considerably of their surprise that communist preparations have progressed so far. Moreover, everyone seemed to be apprehensive over the spectre of Velasco's return and the probability that he'll win again next year. Some members of Congress are anxious to begin proceedings against Arosemena, but many realize the odds favor Arosemena and his patronage over a weak and divided Congress.

Quito — 11 July 1963

Arosemena's out and a four-man military junta is in.

It began last night at a banquet Arosemena gave for the President of the Grace Lines — W. R. Grace and Co. has large investments in Ecuador — to which high-ranking Ecuadorean military men were invited because the Grace Lines President is a retired U.S. Navy admiral. During the toasts Arosemena made favorable commentary about U.S. business operating in Latin America but he insulted our Ambassador by derisive reference to U.S. diplomatic representatives. In his drunkenness Arosemena also demonstrated incredible vulgarity and finally left the banquet and his guests.

This morning the chiefs of the military services decided at a meeting at the Ministry of Defense to replace Arosemena with a junta and about noon the Presidential Palace was surrounded by tanks and troops. I went down to the Hotel Majestic just in front of the Palace where Jorge Andino, a support agent and owner of the hotel, arranged a room where I could watch the action. I also monitored the military intelligence radio and reported by telephone and walkie-talkie back to the station where frequent progress reports on the *coup* were being fired off to headquarters and to Panama (for the military commands there who receive all Agency intelligence reporting in Latin America).

Several hours of tension passed as Arosemena, known to be armed, refused to receive a delegation from the new junta. He remained in the presidential living quarters while the junta members arrived and went to work in the presidential offices. Eventually Arosemena was disarmed by an aide and taken to the airport where he was placed on a military aircraft for Panama — the same place that Velasco was sent to less than two years ago. . . .

The junta is composed of the officers who commanded the Army, Air Force and Navy plus a colonel who was Secretary of the National Defense Council. The Navy captain is the junta chief but Colonel Marcos Gandara of the Defense Council is said unanimously to be the brains and main influence. No question that these men are anticommunist and will finally take the kind of action we want to disrupt the extreme left before they get their serious armed operations underway.

The "Flores" falsified document was only one of a number of similar cases that occurred during the period from January to June of 1963. What we were doing was preparing the ground for a military coup, and in fact the coup did occur the month after the Flores document surfaced. The President was thrown out, a military junta was established, and we began to work with the new military government. They immediately cracked down on the Communist Party and all left-wing groups. Hundreds of people were arrested — which was exactly what we wanted. I mention this Flores document but it is not the only one of that period. I can't go into all of it — my first book was 640 pages long — but this one was sensational.

C.   The Forged Waksman Letter, Montevideo, Uruguay, 1965

The next extracts from *Inside the Company* are about a falsified letter. I was transferred in early 1964 from Ecuador to Uruguay, and in this case I am down in Montevideo in the CIA office in the U.S. Embassy. There was going to be a continent-wide meeting in Montevideo bringing together people from all over Latin America for the Seminar on Latin-American Social and Economic Integration — and it was sure to have an anti-American flavor.

A CIA station obtained a letter from the conference organizer in Montevideo named Daniel Waksman to an organization which he was inviting to come to the seminar. The Technical Services Division in Washington reproduced the stationery with the exact letterhead and reproduced the signature at different places on different sheets of paper so that we could then type in our own letter and make it appear that it had been signed by Waksman.

An officer in the Montevideo station wrote a letter which he addressed to the Cultural Attache of the Soviet Embassy in Montevideo. The letter, with Waksman's signature, thanked the Soviets for all the support, assistance and guidance they had given in preparing and bringing off this big conference. Then, through journalists who were on our payroll, we got the letter published in the principal afternoon newspaper in Uruguay, *El Plata*. On December 13, 1965, enormous headlines appeared in the newspaper: "Documents for the break with Russia." Because we also had a campaign under way to force a break in relations between Uruguay and the Soviet Union.

The year before, Uruguay was forced to break relations with Cuba largely as a result of CIA operations. So now we were trying to force them to break relations with the Soviets — and I've got a number of other examples about that. But in the case of this letter, when it was published it caused a sensation. Naturally we established a link that didn't exist by the falsification of the letter — or, at least, a link we had no proof of. But the damage was already done because denials afterwards are never as effective as the first, well-prepared accusation.

Montevideo — 10 December 1965
Big news! Alberto Heber, the Blanco NCG Councillor who will take over as NCG President in March, today proposed that Uruguay break diplomatic relations with the Soviet Union because of Soviet interference in Uruguayan labor troubles. We don't have direct access to Heber but can check with Colonel Rodriguez. I have no means of seeing the Soviet chauffeur until next week to discover their reaction, but Conolly is concentrating on the AVENGEFUL tapes. Headquarters is delighted and confirms that we should support the break in any way we can. Already Lee Smith, the new covert-action operations officer, who recently replaced Alex Zeffer, is preparing a black letter linking the Soviet cultural attache with leftist student activities. Lee is using the stationery with the letterhead of the Seminar on Latin American Social and Economic Integration that the TSD prepared for us last month.

Montevideo — 11 December 1965
The black letter connecting the Soviet cultural attache with the Seminar on Social and Economic Integration will be put out in *El Plata*, the afternoon daily belonging to the Blanco faction led by the NCG President. The letter is a statement of appreciation for technical advice, and refers to instructions relating to the Seminar and brought by a colleague who recently returned to Montevideo. Thanks are also given for "other assistance." Although the letter is vague, Soviet financing and control of the Seminar is easily inferred. The forged signature is that of Daniel Waksman, the Seminar Secretary for Foreign Relations.

Montevideo — 13 December 1965
Somewhat anti-climactic but useful, our black-letter operation against the FEUU and the Soviet cultural attache caused a sensation when it was published by *El Plata* this afternoon. Banner headlines announce "Documents for the Break with Russia" and similar treatment will be given in tomorrow morning's papers. Denials from Daniel Waksman, the FEUU leader to whom the letter is attributed, were immediate,

but they will be given scant coverage except in the extreme-leftist press. AVBUZZ-1 has arranged for Alberto Roca, publisher of the station-financed student newspaper *Combate*, to take responsibility for the black letter in order to relieve *El Plata* of liability.

Through AVBUZZ-1 we'll place new propaganda, in the form of editorial comment, using the unions' "capitulation" to avoid the break with the Soviets as proof of Soviet influence over the unions (although in fact the government conceded quite a lot more than the unions).

D.   The Falsified Documents Connecting the Uruguayan Trade Unions with the Soviet Embassy, Montevideo, 1965-1966

The next extracts from *Inside the Company* describe an operation in Uruguay wherein we falsified documents in order to "prove" that the Soviet Embassy was directing a continuous series of strikes by the Uruguayan labor movement in 1965. We falsified these documents to justify a break in diplomatic relations.

This was a 19-page report which purported to prove that the Soviet Union, that is, the Soviet Embassy, was organizing and giving all the orders for a long and very disruptive series of strikes occurring in Uruguay. The strikes in fact were occurring because of economic conditions — inflation, etc. We wanted to use our falsified documents with the President and with the Minister of the Interior, with whom I was working, to show a Soviet hand behind the strikes. As it turned out, the strikes subsided before a break in diplomatic relations, but the government used these and others we falsified over the coming months to justify expulsions. From December 1965 to December 1966, six Soviets, three North Koreans, two East Germans and one Czechoslovakian were expelled — all because of our false documents. As a matter of fact, I also have here press material taken from Uruguayan publications at the time describing this whole question of our documentation and the expulsions of the Soviets and others from Uruguay.

Montevideo — 11 December 1965
We have worked all day preparing a report for NCG Councillor Alberto Heber that will justify both a break in diplomatic relations with the Soviets and the outlawing of the PCU. We began the project last night when John Cassidy, who replaced O'Grady as Deputy Chief of Station, got an urgent call from one of his contacts in the Uruguayan military intelligence service. They had been asked by Heber earlier yesterday for a report on the Soviets, but since they had nothing, they called on the station for assistance.

This morning all the station officers met to discuss the problems of trying to write the Heber report. After we decided to write it on a crash basis, Conolly chose the names of four Russians to be in charge of their labor operations, and then went through his files to find concrete information to give weight to this fantasy report. Similarly Riefe selected certain key CNT and government union leaders as the Uruguayan counterparts of the Soviets, together with appropriate true background information that could be sprinkled into the report, such as trips by PCU leaders to Prague and Moscow in recent months. Cassidy, Conolly, Riefe and I then wrote the final version which Cassidy and I translated into Spanish. Tonight Cassidy took it out to AVBUZZ-1 for correction and improvement of the Spanish, and tomorrow he'll turn it over to the military intelligence service (cryptonym AVBALSA). For a one-day job the twenty-page report is not bad. Certainly it includes enough information that can be confirmed to make the entire report appear plausible.

We prepared this report with media operations in mind, apart from justifying the break with the Soviets and outlawing the PCU. Heber has already said publicly that he has strong evidence to support the break, though without the details which he hasn't yet got, but if the break is not made we can publish the report anyway and attribute it to Heber — he is unlikely to deny it. In that case it will cause a sensation and prepare the way for the later decisions we want, and also provide material for putting to the media by other stations, such as Buenos Aires and Rio de Janeiro. According to Heber, the Blanco NCG Councillors will meet tomorrow (Sunday) to decide on the break, and formal NCG action will follow on Monday or Tuesday. The Minister of Defense, meanwhile, has suggested outlawing the PCU and closing propaganda outlets such as *El Popular*.

Montevideo — 12 December 1965

This morning before Cassidy turned over the Heber report to military intelligence, Horton decided first to show it to Colonel Ventura Rodriguez, the Chief of Police, as the top military officer in public security. We took it over to Rodriguez's office, where we sat around the conference table with Rodriguez and Colonel Roberto Ramirez, Chief of the Guardia Metropolitana, who was listening to a soccer game on his little transistor radio.

As Rodriguez read the report, I began to hear a strange low sound which, as it gradually became louder, I recognized as the moan of a human voice. I thought it might be a street vendor trying to sell something, until Rodriguez told Ramirez to turn up the radio. The moaning grew in intensity, turning into screams, while several more times Rodriguez told Ramirez to turn up the soccer game. By then I knew we were listening to someone being tortured in the rooms next to the AVENGEFUL listening post above Rodriguez's office. Rodriguez at last finished reading the report, told us he thought it would be effective and Horton and I headed back for the Embassy.

Back at the Embassy the Ambassador told Horton that the NCG President had just this morning asked him if he had any information that might be used to justify breaking relations with the Soviets. Horton showed him the Heber report and the Ambassador suggested he should give it to Washington Beltran, the NCG President. The Ambassador took the original out to Beltran's house while a copy went to the military intelligence service, with the warning that if it were passed to Heber he should be advised that Beltran already has a copy.

Giving the report to the Ambassador for Beltran has certain advantages but Heber may be reluctant to use it now. Too bad, because Heber is the councillor who convinced the others to reinstate the state of siege, the one who suggested the break, and will moreover be the NCG President in less than three months' time.

Montevideo — 13 December 1965

The impasse is broken and the break with the Soviets is off for the time being. Last night the government and bank unions reached agreement that the firings of previous months would be canceled and that sanctions against strikers will be spread out over many months as painlessly as possible. The agreement was followed last night by the release of all the bank workers who had been arrested late last week. Early this morning similar agreements were reached with central administration unions. Communist and other militant leaders of the CNT had no choice, as the government unions accepted these solutions, but to cancel the general strike scheduled for tomorrow.

With the general strike broken and agreements with unions being made, the government has dropped the threat of breaking relations with the Soviets. The report prepared for Heber will not be brought out by the government for the time being — we can do so later. The state of siege will continue until firm agreements with all the government unions are reached. The leftist daily *Epoca* is still closed for inflammatory propaganda, and almost 30 are still under arrest.

Montevideo — 20 January 1966

Vargas, the Director of Immigration, is very excited about promoting action against communist bloc diplomatic and commercial missions in Montevideo. He showed me the Heber report of last month, without telling me how he got it – probably from Heber himself, and asked if I would use it and any other information we have in order to justify the expulsion of key Soviets instead of a break in diplomatic relations. He and Storace (and presumably Heber) now want us to prepare a report naming whichever Soviets we want as those responsible for meddling in Uruguayan labor and student organizations. At the appropriate moment the report will be used for declaring those Soviets *persona non grata*. Conolly, Riefe, Cassidy and I have already started on this new report. We will have to work fast to take advantage of the resentment caused by the Rashidov speech and the Tri-Continental and of Heber's clear intention to use expulsions and the threat of expulsions as a tool against the unions. Vargas is also going to begin action against the non-diplomatic personnel of communist missions, especially those who are here as officials of the commercial missions, which would include Soviets, Czechs, East Germans and the North Koreans. He's going to start with the North Koreans. He has discovered several ways in which he is going to prepare expulsions of Soviet bloc diplomatic and commercial officers. These expulsions will be mainly on technicalities he has found in the 1947 immigration law that forbids entry to persons who advocate the violent overthrow of the government, on irregularities in the issue of visas, and on interpretations of the status of Soviet bloc commercial officers. Little by little he hopes to cut down the official communist representation here by expelling the Koreans, East Germans and certain Czechs and Soviets – none of whom have diplomatic status – and by the *persona non grata* procedure where diplomatic officials are concerned.

Montevideo — 2 February 1966
Expulsion of the North Koreans was approved yesterday by Storace and will be ordered by Vargas in a matter of hours. . . .

Montevideo — 4 February 1966
The NCG President has raised suddenly the specter of a move against the Soviet mission again. Today he told newsmen at Government House that the Minister of the Interior, Storace, is preparing a new report on infiltration by communist diplomats in Uruguayan labor and student organizations. He also said that from what his own sources tell him, and from what Storace told him orally, there can be no doubt of illegal intervention by communist diplomats. He added that Storace's report will be presented to the NCG next week and will lead to an announcement of great moment.

The "Storace report" is the one we wrote for Storace and Vargas two weeks ago to justify the expulsion of eight Soviet and two Czech diplomats. This report is already in Storace's hands and if all goes well we should have some sensational expulsions next week. The Soviets were selected very carefully in order to produce the desired effects. Both Khalturin, the KGB chief, and Borisov, the Consul and a KGB officer, were left off the expulsion list, so that we can continue to monitor the liaison between Khalturin and Borisova. We included on the list, however, Khalturin's most effective and hard-working subordinates, including the cultural attache whom we made trouble for in the spurious Waksman letter last year, so that Khalturin will have to take on an even greater work load. Reports from Salgueros and from the AVBLIMP observation post reveal that Khalturin is working extremely long hours and appears to be under severe strain. By forcing still more work on him we might trigger some kind of breakdown. We also included the Embassy *zavhoz* (administrative officer) because his departure will cause irritating problems in the Soviet mission's housekeeping function. I added the two Czechs in order to demonstrate KGB use of satellite diplomats for their own operations and in order to get rid of the most active Czech intelligence officers.

Montevideo — 11 February 1966
The North Koreans are out but the Soviet expulsion is postponed. Vargas couldn't get the Koreans to go to his office to be advised, so he sent police to bring them in by force. The three officials and their families left today. Expulsion of the Soviets is postponed for the time being because Washington Beltran, the outgoing NCG President,

wants Alberto Heber, who comes in as NCG President on 1 March, to make the expulsion. Storace's presentation of our report to the NCG is also postponed but Vargas assured me that action will be taken sooner or later. At the moment he is going to proceed with progressive harassment and expulsion – if politically acceptable – of the East German trade mission, the Czech commercial office and the Soviet commercial office. Because officials of these offices haven't got diplomatic status, Vargas can assert control without interference from the Foreign Ministry. He is also proceeding on the new decree granting the Ministry of the Interior and the Immigration Department equal voice with the Foreign Ministry for approval of all visas, diplomatic included, for communist country nationals.

Washington, D.C. – 7 October 1966

This morning at the Uruguay desk there was a celebration. The government at last expelled some Soviets – four left yesterday – and now the Montevideo press is speculating on whether the NCG will cancel a recent invitation to Gromyko to visit Uruguay. The expulsions are the result of Luis Vargas's persistence – when I said farewell he told me that when the government unions started agitating again before the elections, the Soviets would suffer. (Before leaving Montevideo I wrote a memorandum recommending that Vargas be given a tourist trip to the U.S. as a reward if he finally got any thrown out, and it'll be small compensation since I never paid him a salary.)

The expulsion order was based on the same false report we prepared for Storace last January, with minor updating, and it accuses the Soviets of meddling in Uruguayan labor, cultural and student affairs. Only four Soviets are being expelled right now because the cultural attache and one other on the original list are on home leave in Moscow and their visa renewals can be stopped by Vargas. The other two not included in the expulsion are commercial officers and they will be expelled, according to Vargas, as soon as these four with diplomatic status leave.

The Montevideo station and others will be using the expulsions for a new media campaign against the Soviets. Our report for Storace ties the most recent wave of strikes to the PCU Congress in August and to the Soviet participation therein, together with the usual allegations of Soviet-directed subversion through the KGB, GRU and local communist parties. Proof of the authenticity of the subversion plan outlined in the report, according to Storace, are the eleven different strikes occurring in Uruguay at this moment. The Soviets were given forty-eight hours to leave Uruguay. Recently, too, the decree expelling the two remaining East Germans, Vogler and Kuhne, was approved. They were given thirty days to clear out. The gambit on Soviet expulsions may have worked against the unions last year but not this time.

Washington, D.C. – 1 December 1966

In last Sunday's elections in Uruguay the Blanco-Colorado constitutional-reform pact was adopted, and the Colorados won the presidency – it'll be General Gestido who resigned from the NCG last April to campaign for reform. . . . Yesterday Heber decided to take a two-month vacation – his term as NCG President has only three months left – and Luis Vargas resigned as Director of Immigration.

It is unlikely that any additional action against the Soviets, East Germans or others will be taken, but the record for expulsions during the eleven months since we started working with Storace and Vargas is impressive: six Soviets, three North Koreans, two East Germans, and one Czech.

E.   The CIA's Argentine Newsreel

The next extract is from the script of the film *On Company Business*. Joseph Burkholder Smith, a former CIA officer, describes how the CIA was running a newsreel service in Argentina in which false information was inserted. Smith was in the CIA from 1951 until 1973, and he wrote a memoir: *Portrait of a Cold Warrior*, G. P. Putnam's Sons, New York, 1976.

Joseph Burkholder Smith: "Well, what we did in that instance was to take stories, news stories, and world events, Russian activities or U.S. activities regarding Cuba, and Cuban activities in Latin America, and we would twist the story. So that it would have a context, perhaps, or sometimes an explicit statement of *information which was really not true*, but supported the position that we had. This was how the news was presented. We worked in a commentary that presented the slant we wanted."

F. The False Report of Rapes by Cuban Soldiers in Angola, 1975-1976

Next is an extract from a filmed interview with John Stockwell, also from *On Company Business*. Stockwell was the Headquarters Chief of the CIA's intervention in Angola in 1975 and 1976 to support the Holden Roberto and the Savimbi forces against the MPLA. Stockwell resigned from the CIA in 1976 and wrote *In Search of Enemies* (W. W. Norton, New York, 1978), a book exposing the Angolan intervention in great detail. In the film interview he tells the story of the CIA's Lusaka Station fabricating a story against Cuban soldiers in Angola.

John Stockwell: "This imaginative station chief in Lusaka put out a story in which he reported a fictitious scene in which Cuban soldiers had raped some 15-year-old Ovimbundu maidens, and this was the perfect touch. Sheer nonsense! Very much contradictory of what the Cubans were doing and the way they were conducting themselves in Angola. And then he kept that going for three months. He had these same Cuban soldiers captured in a battle. He had them put on trial before a tribunal of the same women who had been raped. And then, eventually, executed. With photographs, mind you, of the trial and photographs of the execution, of these young women who had been raped killing the Cubans who had raped them."

G. Falsification of Documents in the White House

Lest one might think that the CIA has a monopoly on falsifying documents, we should not forget the work of E. Howard Hunt when he was employed at the White House during the Nixon administration. In his book, *Under Cover — The Memoirs of an American Secret Agent* (Berkley Publishing Corporation, New York, 1974), Hunt describes how he fabricated documents that he made appear to be telegrams from the State Department in Washington to the U.S. Embassy in Saigon. The documents implicated the Kennedy administration in the assassination of the Vietnamese President, Ngo Dinh Diem, in 1963. His purpose was to discredit Senator Edward Kennedy, who was thought at that time to be the principal danger to Nixon's re-election. Hunt eventually surfaced the false information through an American network television documentary on the Vietnam war.

H. The Venezuelan Arms Cache, 1963-1964

There is another interesting case — and I think you will find it just as interesting as I do. Some of you might remember a cache of guerrilla arms that was discovered on the coast of Venezuela in 1963 and supposedly traced to Cuba. I never knew for sure, but I always strongly suspected that the CIA had planted this arms cache because we, in Ecuador, were discussing doing the same thing. The idea was to get Czech arms, or Belgian arms, and plant them in the country, then have them discovered and traced back to Cuba. This actually happened in Venezuela in the fall of 1963. Venezuela then brought it before the Organization of American States, and in 1964 the OAS voted that all of its members should break diplomatic and commercial relations with Cuba. Until this arms case, the U.S. government, and especially the CIA, had not been totally effective in isolating Cuba. In the end, after the arms cache case ran its course, the only Latin American country that did not break relations with Cuba was Mexico. We had considerable success against Cuba in the early 1960's, and I mention the arms cache because, although it is not about false documents, it involves falsification of events.

I am not the only one who believed that the CIA planted the arms cache. The following is another extract from *On Company Business* in which Joseph Smith, formerly the CIA's Venezuelan desk officer, describes his similar belief. The same extract goes on to show Dean Rusk, then Secretary of State, expressing satisfaction before news cameras that the Venezuelan resolution against Cuba had been adopted by the OAS.

Joseph Burkholder Smith: "While I was in Argentina the most interesting thing we had to do regarding Castro was to drum up support on the part of the Argentine government for the Venezuelan charge that Castro was supplying guerrillas in Venezuela with arms. The arms cache was found in November, 1963. I had served, before going to Argentina, as Venezuela desk officer, and I was apprised that one of the things that was developed as proof of, was a series of statements by one man who had been captured, back in the time when I was a desk officer. And somehow these arms which are supposed to be delivered two years later, are supposed to be tied in with an urban guerrilla plot that he confessed to. And knowing what our directives were, and what we had to do to try to convince the Argentines of this, I have some suspicion about the reality of this arms stash as a Cuban operation. I think it might all have been planted by us."

Dean Rusk, U.S. Secretary of State, 1964: "What do I say to our brothers in Venezuela? We are with you in full solidarity and will act with you to ensure the safety of your democracy."

Smith: "Venezuela did get its resolution condemning Castro passed by the OAS and Castro was ostracized economically and politically in the rest of the hemisphere. And this, of course, was that major objective of Kennedy's policy toward Cuba."

Rusk: "The hemisphere is now solid with respect to Cuba. Nineteen of the twenty nations have broken diplomatic relations. The foreign ministers of the hemisphere have now applied all of the, what might be called the peaceful remedies under the Rio treaty. Castro's course is not the path of the future."

That is all I brought today in terms of false documents and false cases. Nevertheless these show that the CIA has produced false documents as a matter of standard methodology for the past 25 years, and the Iranian documents clearly show that they are still doing it. I, for one, would be very skeptical of current documents relating to El Salvador, and the supposed assistance from Vietnam, Ethiopia, the Soviet Union and Cuba, until they are proven to be legitimate.

Because of the CIA's history, I think the onus of proof is on the government. You will see in the *New York Times* article by de Onis that the main document is believed to be a report by the General Secretary of the Salvadoran Communist Party, whose name is Handal, on a trip to all those different countries.

Handal, even though he is a Salvadoran guerrilla leader and living in clandestinity, immediately issued a statement of denial. Can you imagine a General Secretary of a political party, having gone on a mission as they say he has, committing all of that to paper down to how many thousand rounds of ammunition, how many rifles and so on, and taking it back to El Salvador where he is in danger of being captured at any moment, or leaving it where it could be captured by the Salvadoran security forces? That, to me, is incredible. In my 12 years in the CIA I never have known a case like that. As a matter of fact, it was the very lack of that kind of documentation which led us to falsify "proof."

I.   The CIA Role in the Indonesian Mass Slaughter of 1965-1966
(Editor's Note: The following story on the CIA's role in provoking the slaughter of between half a million and a million people — or more — came to the surface in late March 1981 when Ralph McGehee, a former CIA officer, appealed to the Federal District Court in Washington, D.C., against the CIA's censorship of an article he had written for *The Nation*. McGehee, in his article, expressed the belief that the "captured" documents on El Salvador were fabricated by the CIA. As an example of a previous CIA fabrication operation, McGehee wrote of the CIA's work in Indonesia in 1965. McGehee's story is added here because it ties the CIA to the greatest wholesale slaughter of human beings since the Nazi extermination of the Jews.)

After describing the CIA's failed paramilitary operation to oust Indonesian President Sukarno in 1958, McGehee wrote: "What that massive military campaign failed to accomplish was achieved later by a simple CIA (Editor's Note: a nine-letter word is censored, probably "deception") operation." McGehee went on to describe the failed pro-Sukarno coup attempt of the night of September 30-October 1, 1965, in which six top military officers were assassinated. In the wake of the coup failure, McGehee wrote, "the Agency saw in those events the chance to destroy the PKI" (Editor's Note: the Indonesian Communist Party).

McGehee began the next page of his draft: "After taking over the government, the Indonesian army initiated no action against the PKI, since the PKI was not involved in the coup attempt." The rest of the page was completely censored. McGehee began the following page: "Indonesian military leaders (Editor's Note: several words are censored, probably referring to CIA involvement) began a bloody extermination campaign. In mid-November 1965 General Suharto (Editor's Note: Suharto has dominated Indonesia since 1965 and is today the country's President) formally authorized the 'cleaning out' of the Indonesian Communist Party and established special teams to supervise the mass extermination operation. A key part in stirring up a mood of butchery was played by media fabrications. Photos of the bodies of the dead generals — badly decomposed — were featured in all newspapers and T.V. broadcasts, with accompanying texts falsely claiming that the generals had been castrated and their eyes gouged out by communist women. This cynically fabricated campaign was designed to arouse panic about communist sadism and thus set the stage for the second largest holocaust of the twentieth century.

"The mass killings began in late 1965 in Central Java with the arrival there of paratroopers. Lists of targets compiled by the military were given to right-wing Muslim groups, who were armed with parangs and transported in army trucks to villages where they killed with bloody mutilation. Schoolchildren were asked to identify "communists," and many so identified were shot on the spot by army personnel along with their whole families. Many people were denounced as communists in personal disputes, and on the basis of one word or the pointing of a finger, people were taken away to be killed. The killing was on such a huge scale as to raise a sanitation problem in East Java and Northern Sumatra, where the smell of decaying flesh was pervasive and rivers were impassable because of the clogging of human bodies."

McGehee went on to write that the official Indonesian military estimate of those killed was "more than 500,000" and added that "other estimates run to many more than one million." McGehee continued:

"To conceal its role in the massacre of those innocent people the CIA in 1968 wrote a false account of what happened and published a book, *Indonesia — 1965: The Coup that Backfired*. That book is the only study of Indonesian politics ever released to the public on the Agency's own initiative. At the same time that the Agency wrote the book, it also composed a secret study of what really happened. (Editor's Note: here three-and-a-half lines are censored.) The Agency was extremely proud of its successful (Editor's Note: a nine-letter word is again censored, possibly 'deception') and recommended it as a model for future operations."

Reading McGehee's draft, it is quite obvious that the content of the page on which all but the first sentence is censored is the way the CIA linked the Indonesian Communist Party to the coup attempt in order to provoke the massacre that followed. If McGehee wins his legal appeal against censorship, the truth will be known. Meanwhile, one can speculate that the CIA censored McGehee's description of more fabrications of documents, perhaps including a famous "confession" by D. N. Aidit, the PKI Secretary General, in which he supposedly admitted PKI involvement in the coup attempt. The "confession" was said to have been taken from him just before he was executed in November 1965.

PART 5

THE AMERICAN INSTITUTE FOR FREE LABOR DEVELOPMENT AS A C I A FRONT

The next subject I want to talk about is the American Institute for Free Labor Development — the AIFLD. This extremely important organization is currently running the Salvadoran agrarian reform program. But first, the background.

In 1960, before going down to Ecuador on my first field assignment in the CIA, I took a special course given to officers who were involved in what the CIA calls "Labor Operations." I can tell you that these operations are vast and complicated and constitute an international complex of penetrations of trade union organizations through which the CIA attempts to manipulate the unions for political purposes. However, for this meeting, I will discuss only the AIFLD.

The AIFLD was established in 1961, supposedly as an educational institute. At the same time as it set up operations in Washington, it began to open field offices, and eventually it had offices in practically every Latin American capital city. Training was done both on the spot in Latin America through the local offices, and in Washington (and later, Front Royal, Virginia) for those specially selected for this training in the United States. Over the years the AIFLD has trained hundreds of thousands of Latin American workers both in Latin America and in the United States.

The real purpose of this "educational" institute, however, was to train cadres to organize new trade unions or to take over existing ones, in such a way that the unions would be controlled, directly or indirectly, by the CIA. At one point I was working in labor operations in Ecuador and was dealing directly with the CIA agent who headed the AIFLD office in Bogota, Colombia. We arranged for him to come to Quito to help us with certain problems that we were having with our labor operations.

The following extracts from *Inside the Company: CIA Diary* show how the CIA participated in setting up the AIFLD together with episodes from my experience in CIA operations through the AIFLD.

Quito — 15 June 1962

The other new program is more closely related to regular station operations and is Washington's answer to the limitations of current labor programs undertaken through AID as well as through ORIT and CIA stations. The problem is related to the controversy over the ineffectiveness of ORIT but is larger — it is essentially how to accelerate expansion of labor-organizing activities in Latin America in order to deny workers to labor unions dominated by the extreme left and to reverse communist and Castroite penetration. This new program is the result of several years' study and planning and is to be channeled through the American Institute for Free Labor Development (AIFLD), founded last year in Washington for training in trade-unionism.

The reason a new institution was founded was that AID labor programs are limited because of their direct dependence on the U.S. government. They serve poorly for the dirty struggles that characterize labor organizing and jurisdictional battles. ORIT programs are also limited because its affiliates are weak or non-existent in some countries, although expansion is also under way through the establishment of a new ORIT school in Mexico. Control is difficult and past performance is poor. The CIA station programs are limited by personnel problems, but more so by the limits on the amount of money that can be channeled covertly through the stations and through international organizations like ORIT and the ICFTU.

Business leaders are front men on the Board of Directors so that large sums of AID money can be channeled to AIFLD and so that the institute will appear to have the collaboration of U.S. businesses operating in Latin America. Nevertheless, legally, AIFLD is a nonprofit, private corporation and financing will also be obtained from foundations, businesses and the AFL-CIO.

The AIFLD is headed by Serafino Romualdi, IO Division's long-time agent who moved in as Executive Director and resigned as the AFL-CIO's Inter-American Representative. Among the Directors are people of the stature of George Meany, J. Peter Grace and Joseph Beirne, President of the Communications Workers of America (CWA) which is the largest Western Hemisphere affiliate of the Post, Telegraph and Telephone Workers International (PTTI). AIFLD, in fact, is modeled on the CWA training school of Front Royal, Virginia where Latin American leaders of PTTI affiliates are being trained. Day to day control of AIFLD by IO Division, however, will be through Romualdi and William Doherty, former Inter-American Representative of the PTTI and now AIFLD Social Projects Director. Prominent Latin American liberals such as Jose Figueres, former President of Costa Rica and also a long-time Agency collaborator, will serve on the Board from time to time.

The main purpose of AIFLD will be to organize anti-communist labor unions in Latin America. However, the ostensible purpose, since union organizing is rather sensitive for AID to finance, even indirectly, will be "adult education" and social projects such as workers' housing, credit unions and cooperatives. First priority is to establish in all Latin American countries training institutes which will take over and expand the courses already being given in many countries by AID. Although these training institutes will nominally and administratively be controlled by AIFLD in Washington, it is planned that as many as possible will be headed by salaried CIA agents with operational control exercised by the stations. In most cases, it is hoped, these AIFLD agents will be U.S. citizens with some background in trade-unionism although, as in the case of ORIT, foreign nationals may have to be used. The training programs of the local institutes in Latin America will prepare union organizers who, after the courses are over, will spend the next nine months doing nothing but organizing new unions with their salaries and all expenses paid by the local institute. Publicity relating to AIFLD will concentrate on the social projects and "adult education" aspects, keeping the organizing program discreetly in the background.

This month, in addition to training in Latin American countries, AIFLD is beginning a program of advanced training courses to be given in Washington. Spotting and assessment of potential agents for labor operations will be a continuing function of the Agency-controlled staff members both in the training courses in Latin America and in the Washington courses. Agents already working in labor operations can be enrolled in the courses to promote their technical capabilities and their prestige.

In Ecuador, the AIFLD representative from the U.S. who is now setting up the training institute – the first course begins in three weeks – is not an agent but was sent anyway in order to avoid delays. However, Gil Saudade arranged for Ricardo Vazquez Diaz, the Education Secretary of CEOSL, to be the Ecuadorean in charge of the local AIFLD training programs. Carlos Vallejo Baez, who is connected with the Popular Revolutionary Liberal Party, will also be on the teaching staff. Eventually Saudade will either recruit this first AIFLD representative or headquarters will arrange for a cleared agent to be sent.

Quito — 3 September 1962

Meanwhile the AIFLD program is continuing to progress with close coordination with CEOSL through Ricardo Vazquez Diaz. Next month Vazquez will conduct a seminar for labor leaders from which four will be selected for the three-month AIFLD course starting in October in Washington.

Two weeks ago a PTTI delegation was here to discuss organization and a low-cost housing program with their Ecuadorean affiliate, FENETEL, which is one of the most important unions in CEOSL. The PTTI is training FENETEL leaders at their school in Front Royal, Virginia, and the visit was also used to create publicity for the AIFLD seminar program. Included in the delegation was the new PTTI Inter-American Representative and a Cuban who is leader of the Cuban telephone workers' union in exile. This PTTI organization is without doubt the most effective of the International Trade Secretariats currently working in Ecuador under direction of IO Division.

Quito — 16 January 1963

Reorganization of CEOSL is moving ahead although termination of the old CROCLE agents by the Guayaquil base required a visit in November by Serafino Romualdi, Executive Director of AIFLD and the long-time AFL-CIO representative for Latin America. The struggle between the old CROCLE and COG agents, who favored retention of their unions' autonomy within CEOSL, and our new agents, who insisted (at our instruction) that CROCLE and COG disappear in favor of a new Guayas provincial federation, finally led to the expulsion a few days ago of the CROCLE and COG leaders from CEOSL. Those expelled included Victor Contreras who only last April became CEOSL's first President. Matias Ulloa Coppiano is now Acting Secretary-General of CEOSL and Ricardo Vazquez Diaz is Acting Secretary of Organization. Both are agents of Gil Saudade who originally recruited them through his Popular Revolutionary Liberal Party.

Ricardo Vazquez Diaz has been very effective in expanding the AIFLD education program along with Carlos Vallejo Baez. In recent months, courses have been held in Guayaquil and Cuenca as well as Quito. Other courses are being planned for provincial towns in order to strengthen the CEOSL organizations there.

Quito — 30 August 1963

Labor operations always seem to be in turmoil but now and then they produce a redeeming flash of brilliance. Ricardo Vazquez Diaz, one of the labor agents I took over from Gil Saudade, told me the other day that his mistress is the official shorthand transcriber of all the important meetings of the Cabinet and the junta and that she has been giving him copies so that he can be well-informed for his CEOSL work. He gave me samples and after Dean saw them he told me to start paying her a salary through Vazquez. From now on we'll be getting copies of the record of these meetings even before the participants. In the Embassy we'll make them available just to the Ambassador and the Minister Counsellor, and in Washington short summaries will be given limited distribution with the entire Spanish text available on special request. The Ambassador, according to Dean, is most interested in seeing how the junta and Cabinet members react to their meetings with him and in using these reports to plan his meetings with them. Eventually we'll try to recruit Vazquez's mistress, ECSIGH-1, directly, but for the moment I'll have to work this very carefully in order not to jeopardize the CEOSL operation. Vazquez claims he's told no one of the reports, which I believe, because, if he told anyone, it would be one of the other CEOSL agents who probably would have mentioned it to me. These reports are jewels of political intelligence — just the sort of intelligence that covert action operations should produce.

Quito — 8 September 1963

These labor operations are so messy they're forcing me to put practically all my other operations on ice for lack of time. No wonder Saudade had so few agents: they talk on and on so that one agent-meeting can fill up most of an afternoon or morning.

Our call for help from McClellan backfired. He sent a telegram to the junta threatening AFL-CIO efforts to stop Alliance for Progress funds and appeals to the OAS and U.N. if the junta doesn't stop its repression of trade unions. Three days ago the Secretary-General of the Administration denounced McClellan's telegram and showed newsmen documents from CROCLE and COG backing the junta and the colonel in charge of the railways. Now the junta is going to suspend the railway workers' right to organize completely. Somehow we have to reverse this trend and we asked for a visit from some other high-level labor figure from Washington, hopefully William Doherty, the former PTTI Latin American Representative and now with the AIFLD. Doherty is considered to be one of our more effective labor agents and Dean thinks he might be able to change the junta's attitude towards our organizations.

Quito — 15 October 1963

Even the AIFLD operation is beset with problems. The country program chief here isn't an agent and so we can't guide him (except through Washington) so that his program harmonizes nicely with ours. Doherty finally came to help straighten out the AIFLD program for us, but this isn't the end of it. He's going to arrange to have Emilio Garza, the AIFLD man in Bogota who is a recruited and controlled agent, come here for as long as is needed to make sure the AIFLD program is run the way Dean wants it run. Mostly it's a question of personnel assignments through which we want to favor our agents. Sooner or later all the AIFLD programs will be run closely by the stations — until now the expansion has been so fast that in many cases non-agents have been sent as AIFLD chiefs and can only be controlled through cumbersome arrangements of the kind we've had here.

Quito — 10 November 1963

Bill Doherty arranged for Emilio Garza, the Bogota AIFLD agent, to come to help us smooth out the problems between our CEOSL agents and the AIFLD operation. The agent was an excellent choice and I've already recommended that he be transferred to Ecuador when his assignment in Bogota ends. He's the most effective of the career labor agents that I've worked with.

Montevideo — 22 March 1964

The most important new activity in labor operations is the establishment last November of the Montevideo office of the American Institute for Free Labor Development. This office is called the Uruguayan Institute of Trade Union Education and its director, Jack Goodwyn, is a U.S. citizen contract agent and the Montevideo AIFLD representative. Alexander Zeffer, the station officer in charge of labor operations, meets Goodwyn under discreet conditions for planning, reporting and other matters. In addition to training locally at the AIFLD institute, Uruguayans are also sent to the ORIT school in Mexico and to the AIFLD school in Washington.

Montevideo — 2 May 1964

I don't envy Alex Zeffer for his labor operations. He is going to have to start again, practically from scratch, because the decision was finally made to withdraw support from the Uruguayan Labor Confederation (CSU). Last month the CSU held a congress and the leadership was unable to overcome the personality conflicts that have resulted in continuing withdrawals of member unions and refusals of others to pay dues. The real problem is leadership and when Andrew McClellan, the AFL-CIO Inter-American Representative, and Bill Doherty, the AIFLD social projects chief arrived last week they advised CSU leaders that subsidies channeled through the ICFTU, ORIT and the ITS are to be discontinued.

The situation is rather awkward because the CSU has just formed a workers' housing cooperative and expected to receive AIFLD funds for construction. These funds will also be withheld from the CSU and may be channeled through another non-communist union organization. Next week Serafino Romualdi, AIFLD Executive Director, will be here for more conversations on how to promote the AIFLD program while letting the CSU die. One thing is certain: it will take several years before a new crop of labor leaders can be trained through the AIFLD program and from them recruitments made of new agents who can set up another national confederation to affiliate with ORIT and the ICFTU.

Montevideo — 17 February 1966

Station labor operations continue to be centered on the Uruguayan Institute of Trade Union Education, which is the Montevideo office of the AIFLD. Jack Goodwyn, Director of the Institute, is working closely with Lee Smith, the station covert-action officer, in order to develop a pool of anti-CNT labor leaders through the training programs of the Institute. The most effective program, of course, is the one in which trainees are paid a generous salary by the Institute for nine months after completion of the training course, during which time they work exclusively in union-organizing under Goodwyn's direction. It is this organizational work that is the real purpose of the AIFLD, so that eventually our trade unions can take national leadership away from the CNT. Goodwyn's job, in addition to the training program, is to watch carefully for prospective agents who can be recruited by Smith under arrangements that will protect Goodwyn.

The goals will take a long time to reach and progress often seems very slow. Nevertheless Goodwyn has already achieved several notable successes in the social projects field, which are showcase public-relations projects such as housing and consumer cooperatives. Using a four-million-dollar housing loan offer from the AFL-CIO, to be guaranteed by AID, Goodwyn has brought together a small number of unions to form the Labor Unity Committee for Housing. Some of these same unions have also formed what they call the Permanent Confederation, which is the embryo of a future national labor center that will affiliate with ORIT and the ICFTU. Another housing project, also for about four million dollars, is being negotiated with the National Association of Public Functionaries — one of the two large unions of central administration employees. Goodwyn has also formed a consumer cooperative for sugar workers in Bella Union — the same region where the important revolutionary socialist leader, Raul Sendic, gets his support.

Montevideo — 9 June 1966

Jack Goodwyn has arranged for one of his AIFLD people to be named as the Uruguayan representative at the conference this month of the International Labor Organization in Geneva. The prestige appointment was made by the government, and Goodwyn's man is going as representative of the Uruguayan Labor Confederation (CSU). The PCU and other leftists are squealing because the CSU is completely defunct and the CNT in any case represents 90-95 per cent of organized labor. The appointment is indicative of how the government increasingly sees the advantage of cooperation and even promotion of the AIFLD and related trade-union programs. Private industry is similarly well disposed.

In Washington the Agency has arranged with Joseph Beirne, President of the Communications Workers of America (CWA), to have the CWA's training school at Front Royal, Virginia turned over to the AIFLD. This school has been used for years as the main center of the Post, Telegraph and Telephone Workers' International (PTTI) for training labor leaders from other countries. Now the school will be the home for the AIFLD courses which until now have been held in Washington. Not a bad arrangement: seventy-six acres on the Shenandoah River where the isolation and control will allow for really close assessment of the students for future use in Agency labor operations. Also this year the AIFLD is starting a year-long university-level course in "labor economics" which will be given at Loyola University in New Orleans. AIFLD hasn't been exactly cheap: this year its cumulative cost will pass the 15 million dollar mark with almost 90 per cent paid by the U.S. government through AID and the rest from U.S. labor organizations and U.S. business. Since 1962 the annual AIFLD budget has grown from 640,000 dollars to almost 5 million dollars while the ORIT budget has remained at about 325,000 dollars per year. Millions more have been channeled through AIFLD in the form of loans for its housing programs and other social projects.

Mexico City — 15 July 1967

The station covert-action operations section consists of Stanley Watson, the Deputy Chief of Station, and two case officers under Embassy cover plus one case officer under non-official cover. Operations underway provide for placing propaganda in the major Mexico City dailies, several magazines and television. Student operations are centered mostly in the National University of Mexico (UNAM), while labor operations are concentrated on support for and guidance of the Mexico City headquarters of ORIT. Station labor operations also include agents at the new ORIT school in Cuernavaca (built with CIA funds) for spotting and assessment of trainees for use in labor operations after they return to their country of origin. The Mexico programs of the American Institute for Free Labor Development (AIFLD) are also under station direction.

For additional information on how the CIA has worked through the AIFLD, I include the following extracts from the documentary film, *On Company Business*, describing the CIA's operations to promote the 1964 military coup in Brazil that overthrew the elected Goulart government.

The statements that follow are from interviews or newsreel footage of the following people:

Richard Martinez: Former CIA agent working in secret trade union operations in Brazil (interview)

George Meany: Then President of the American Federation of Labor–Congress of Industrial Organizations (AFL-CIO), and also President of the American Institute for Free Labor Development (AIFLD) (newsreel footage)

Philip Agee: (Interview)

Andrew McClellan: Inter-American Director of the AFL-CIO and long a key agent in the CIA's labor operations (interview)

William (Bill) Doherty: Executive Director of the AIFLD and long a key agent in the CIA's labor operations (interview)

Victor Reuther: Former European representative of the American Congress of Industrial Organizations and long a leader of the U.S. trade union movement (interview)

J. William Fulbright: Former Chairman of the U.S. Senate Foreign Relations Committee (newsreel footage)

Pedro Paulo Barauna: Former Brazilian army Colonel exiled under the Brazilian military dictatorship (interview)

Alan Francovich and Arturo Sandoval: Interviewers

Richard Martinez: I got a call from Washington, if I would interested in a position in Latin America. To me a young man coming out of a ghetto I felt it was a big opportunity. I didn't even know where Latin America was.

Alan Francovich: Who called you from Washington?

Richard Martinez: Ah, Sam Robles. See, Sam Robles and I had been friends here. Sam Robles was the secretary of the state AF of L-CIO, a very strong, very strong labor leader. And he was instrumental in my being called to Washington to be interviewed for this particular position in Brazil. My position was going to be administrator and organizer for the Postal, Telegraph, Telephone International, which later on I learned was one of these phony organizations out of the CIA. My boss was Wallace Leggy, who was one of John McCone's top hands. John McCone at that time was the head of the CIA.

George Meany (newsreel footage): In August of 1960 when we came to a full realization as to what had happened to the Cuban workers and the entire Cuban people under Castro, the AF of L-CIO appropriated twenty thousand dollars for the purpose of funding the establishment of a mechanism through which we could help to strengthen the free labor unions of Latin America and develop trade union leaders.

Philip Agee: The CIA's trade union operations are effected through a vast bureaucracy of people. These are the officers of the international trade unions, and of the national unions, especially in the United States, through which the CIA is able to infiltrate and manipulate the international unions. Ah, of course, Mr. Meany has been in the past one of the principal, if not the principal U.S. trade unionist through which these operations are effected.

Andrew McClellan: I'm Andrew McClellan. I'm the inter-American representative of the AFL-CIO and have been since 1964. Prior to that time I was the associate inter-American representative. And prior to that time I was inter-American representative of the International Union of Food and Allied Workers, based in Geneva and working in Latin America.

Bill Doherty: I'm the Executive Director of the American Institute for Free Labor Development. Prior to that time, as a matter of fact I've been the executive director now for some ten years, and I've been with the American Institute for Free Labor Development since its founding in 1962. For the period immediately prior to 1962 I was the inter-American representative of the Postal, Telegraph and Telephone International, which has headquarters in Switzerland, but I was their representative in the Western Hemisphere.

Alan Francovich: Did they tell you what you would be doing in the labor movement in Brazil?
Richard Martinez: The idea was to, ah, well, they didn't explain anything. You go there with the impression that you are going there to do a labor job, to represent the membership. This was my impression. They didn't tell me otherwise. So I started tackling the problems, combatting the management for better conditions, working conditions, higher salaries, lenient rules. What you do in the labor movement.
Apparently I was doing the wrong thing. Three months later I was, through a courier that was sent to Brazil, where I had to go travel for about four or five hours, go all over the city, to reach this guy who is just across the street from my office, but they wanted to make sure that there were any enemies following me. They instructed me that I was to return to Washington. That was in November, shortly before Thanksgiving.
Alan Francovich: What year?
Richard Martinez: That was in 1962, the same year that I started there, to be trained in clandestine activities. Leggy pointed out to me that we were organizing for 1964. And he was reorganizing his forces in D.C. He was the head of the whole PTTI operation then. And he said, Richard, look, we are organizing against Communists for 1964. So your job is to organize within the, your field as a communicator to organize against the Communists. Later on after I got trained in New York I felt well, it was a brainwash type of thing. I became a real, very fanatic. I was a real fanatic then.

Alan Francovich: There have been some people who accuse the AFL-CIO of collaborating with the CIA. What would be your response to that accusation?
Andrew McClellan: I think that is so reckless and so infantile, so juvenile to make such an accusation.
Alan Francovich: And you, Mr. Doherty?
Bill Doherty: Well, I'm in agreement. I don't know of anybody who wouldn't out-and-out deny such an accusation. It's just not true.

Philip Agee: In Latin America, one of the principal and most effective of the trade unionists, of the American trade unionists who worked with us was Bill Doherty. Now he had originally started in the Post, Telegraph and Telephone Workers International, coming up through the Communications Workers of America. Later on he was transferred into the American Institute for Free Labor Development. This was set up during the Kennedy period, and is a joint effort by American trade unionists, like

George Meany, and the heads of American-based multinational corporations which operate in Latin America. The cover for this type of activity is indeed education and social projects such as the development of cooperatives and housing. But the real reason is to create cadres of organizers who, after their training in the AIFLD is over, they can go back to their industries and spend one year or two years or even longer doing nothing but organizing.

Andrew McClellan: This is the 75th class that has graduated from Front Royal from the time that we started the programs in 1961. And this particular group has been studying democratic trade unionism. It is our hope that they will go back to their respective countries and put into practice some of the things they have learned while they were here at Front Royal.

Bill Doherty: Concluding our luncheon today, and wishing you not only in my name but in the name of President George Meany of the AFL-CIO, I'd like to give you a thought in Spanish that comes from one of the great political and one of the great literary geniuses of this century and of the past century, the true liberator of this country, from heaven who's embarrassed by the shame that now exists in Cuba because of the dictatorship of Fidel Castro. That great Cuban Jose Marti one time said: "El mundo se divide en dos ramas: los que aman y construyen, y los que odian y destruyen. Nosotros companeros sindicalistas libres, somos que amamos y construimos. Vayanse con Dios, companeros."

Victor Reuther: These institutes that were created by the AF of L-CIO as their major instrument and vehicles now for international work, and has on its boards of directors prominent American employers. For instance, the American Institute for Free Labor Development in Latin America has for many years had as chairman of its board one Peter Grace. And if one looks at the long list of corporations that initially contributed to the establishment of the AF of L's American Institute for Free Labor Development, it includes United Fruit, Anaconda Copper, and a whole string of U.S. corporations that have never voluntarily accepted their obligation to pay decent wages or provide good working conditions in the United States. They always had to be forced to do it through union organization and strike action, etc., and why suddenly these corporate interests now should be embraced as allies and be foisted on Latin American labor or any other American labor groups, any other Latin American labor groups, as people with credentials suitable for picking future trade union leaders and training them, this is beyond my imagination.

George Meany: They spend the first nine months after they get back instructing other people in our branch institutes in Latin America, and what they do after that nine months is over I cannot say. If they join some political party that's against the regime in power, I think it's stretching your imagination quite a bit to attribute that to what the AIFLD did while they were up here.

Richard Martinez: By May of 1964, I would call my leadership and I'd tell them, look, this is what we have to do. We have to get the people on our side because the Communists have a bigger membership than we do. So you have to go out there and pull the membership away from them, see. And this is where the idea of training our leadership to go to Front Royal came into being.

Alan Francovich: This is Peter Grace, and he says here, AIFLD men also helped drive Communists from control of British Guyana, they prevented the Communists from taking over powerful unions in Honduras and helped to drive the Communists from strong jugular unions in Brazil. Could you go back to that period and sort of describe what the atmosphere was in Latin America?
Bill Doherty: Well, we were living in the early sixties, I think, Andy, you would agree with me, in an era when we were in the streets battling for the lives of the free

trade unions against what was then a more powerful Communist trade union movement. But since then, in my estimation, it has lost an awful lot of its appeal and its attraction and its ability to maneuver.

Richard Martinez: I was doing just exactly what Bill Doherty had done for years and years in Brazil. Not only in Brazil, but all over the country, all over the Latin American countries. So, Bill Doherty, now heading the AIFLD, it was the same type of operation, going around buying people. So I would recommend maybe six, seven, eight people which were good potentials as labor organizers and I would put them on a plane and send them down to Front Royal. They would be paid there, they got their lodging, meals, the whole works. And then I would support their families in Brazil.

Alan Francovich: And was this part of the preparation for what happened in 1964?

Richard Martinez: That was the object of the whole thing.

Newsreel announcer: A half a world away troops are called out in the suburbs of Rio de Janeiro to quell rioting over President Joao Goulart's attempts to form a new Brazilian government after the resignation of Prime Minister Tancredo Neves and his cabinet. Food stores are looted as dealers hold back supplies of beans, rice and other staples because they feel government price controls are set too low. Order is restored but not before eleven persons are killed and a crippling general strike is called over the power struggle between the President and the Parliament of Brazil.

Victor Reuther: Says Mr. Doherty, "What happened in Brazil on April 1st did not just happen; it was planned, and planned months in advance. Many of the trade union leaders, some of whom were actually trained in our Institute, were involved in the revolution and in the overthrow of the Goulart regime."

Bill Doherty: Immediately prior to the military takeover in Brazil there was a group of students from Brazilian unions in training in Front Royal. This wasn't the first of the Brazilian groups that have been here nor has it been the last. We've had them continuously. They weren't in any kind of a course training for revolutionary activity or clandestine activities or in a regular collective bargaining course. It so happens that when many of those students went back home from that course, their unions were involved in this struggle against the attempt of the Communists to take over some of the unions. And that's precisely what I meant by the statement.

George Meany: I can say to you categorically now that it is not true. Under no circumstances have we ever received or solicited any money from the CIA.

J. William Fulbright: It doesn't say that the AFL-CIO received it. The 33 million doesn't go to the AFL-CIO. It goes to the AIFLD.

George Meany: Well, let me state that these unions you mention have stated just as categorically as I have that they do not receive and have not received CIA money.

Andrew McClellan: The Communists are going to accuse anything that is effective as being CIA, because I think the CIA, the Communists, the KGB have long been involved in an international struggle. The truth of the matter is that our books are now, and have always been open to the public. Our funds, our government funds, are appropriated by the Congress. The Congressional committees have completely, have total access to them.

Andrew McClellan: It was the women who started the marches for God and peace, the so-called "pots and pans" demonstration. They talked in terms of hundreds of thousands demonstrating in Rio and Sao Paolo. And I'll tell you it was the women that obliged the military to move in and take over. That happened in Chile ten years later. Almost the whole scenario was the same, which leads one to believe that there may have been some Brazilian advisors, some Brazilian advisors in Chile at the same time fomenting the revolution against Allende.

Pedro Paulo de Baruna: On the day before the coup, Castello Branco, who was then Chief of the Army General Staff, could not make up his mind. He wasn't sure that the coup would be successful. General Vernon Walters personally went to tell him that yes, he should join the coup because, in case it was needed, an American Naval Task Force was sailing close to the coast of Espiritu Santu, where the Marines would land to support the coup forces. And it was for this reason that Castello Branco decided to support the coup.

Newsreel announcer: Anti-Goulart demonstrations that greeted the now-deposed Brazilian President at Miami airport when he was enroute to take office in 1961 show the deep distrust that has finally led to his downfall and exile in Uruguay. Troops had to be called out in Brasilia to quell the bitter protests of thousands against the notoriously left-leaning Joao Goulart's taking office. A Russian trade show in Rio de Janeiro gave President Goulart, who paradoxically is a millionaire rancher, a chance to hobnob with some of his Soviet heroes. But it was his sympathy with nearer-at-hand Fidel Castro that the Brazilians really feared. Riotings against Goulart were frequent. Yet when the end of his regime came it was through a brief and bloodless military coup. What his successors can do with the almost totally wrecked economy he leaves behind him is a matter of concern to the entire Western hemisphere.

Arturo Sandoval: Did you have arms stashed right there in your office?
Richard Martinez: Yeah, they were right there in my closet.
Arturo Sandoval: What kind of weapons were they?
Richard Martinez: Shit, you name it, machine guns, all types of weapons.
Arturo Sandoval: Did your field workers participate at all in that coup?
Richard Martinez: Oh, yes.
Arturo Sandoval: What did they do?
Richard Martinez: They burnt out the Communist headquarters, they burnt up the whole damn building. My own people. All I knew was that the Communists had been put away in prisons, the military had brought in ships, put them in the bay and confined the Communists, put them in the ships, locked the doors and thrown the keys away.
Alan Francovich: So there were a lot of Communists in the labor movement then that you knew about put in jail?
Richard Martinez: Oh, yes, there were more of them than us. More.
Howard Dratch: And they were all jailed?
Richard Martinez: They were all thrown in jail.

Finally, I call your attention to remarks (from *On Company Business*) of the then-Secretary of State, Dean Rusk, taken from newsreel footage of the day, concerning the overthrow in Brazil. He says:

"Castro's course is not the path of the future. This was illustrated in Brazil, where tendencies moving in the Castro direction were called to a halt very quickly by those who believe in a constitutional democracy in that country, the Congress, the Governors, the Armed Forces."

Constitutional democracy? As everyone here knows, there hasn't been one day of constitutional democracy in Brazil since Dean Rusk made that statement. In fact it was a constitutional democracy which the U.S. government, through the CIA, overthrew.

So much for a little of the AIFLD's history. Today it is at work in El Salvador, running, for all practical purposes, the military junta's agrarian reform program. This involvement grew out of the AIFLD's earlier work there, notably its role in establishing the Salvadoran Communal Union (UCS), a peasant-farmer organization, in 1966. When the current military junta declared land reform as one of its objectives to break the power of the traditional oligarchy, the AIFLD jumped in to provide the technical knowhow.

Jose Viera, Secretary General of UCS, became Director of the Salvadoran government's Institute for Agrarian Transformation, and the AIFLD, which gets it money through the Agency for International Development (AID) contracts, called in Roy Prosterman to be the architect of the reform program. Other AIFLD officials involved in the Salvadoran project were Michael Hammer, whose AIFLD work in Latin America goes back 17 years, and Mark Pearlman, who joined the AIFLD in 1980.

Prosterman is a law professor who played a key role in the land reform program in Vietnam which was central to rural pacification during the war. His experience in Vietnam allowed him to repeat in El Salvador the efforts that had failed before. I'm sure most of you have noticed that the U.S. Department of State constantly mentions the current Salvadoran land reform program as one of the main justifications of its support to the junta.

Much has already been written on the failure, so far, of the agrarian reform — particularly its limited scope, lack of new titles to land supposedly redistributed, and creation of uneconomical small plots. It's a continuing argument. The AFL-CIO, which claims sponsorship of AIFLD, naturally thinks the program is a success — going so far as to claim the instant creation of a new Salvadoran "middle class" out of the former landless peasants. Yet even the AFL-CIO admitted in its newspaper on January 10, 1981, that there was "an air of despair and disillusionment over the program."

You may wonder why the American espionage and sabotage agency is involved in agrarian reform. The answer is that by involvement in agrarian reform, the CIA opens the door for their pacification operations in the countryside where guerrilla movements so often are successful in recruiting new people. In El Salvador, this means that the CIA, through the AIFLD presence in the agrarian reform program, is able to collect information on the ways new guerrillas are recruited among the peasants and which peasants are participating in recruitment and other programs of the guerrilla forces. The Agency will then pass this information to the Salvadoran security forces who can sweep in and assassinate all peasants believed, rightly or wrongly, to be loyal to the guerrillas.

This program of the AIFLD is one of the means by which the El Salvador junta and its paramilitary squads have been able to carry out summary executions of thousands of Salvadoran peasants over the last year or two. It should be recalled in this connection that in the 1960's following the perceived success of the AIFLD in Latin America, parallel institutes were set up by the CIA in Africa and Asia. The Asian institute worked in Vietnam on the rural pacification programs there through which tens of thousands of Vietnamese peasants were assassinated in the CIA's infamous "Phoenix Program."

The first I learned of AIFLD's involvement in the Salvadoran land reform program was when I received a copy of a letter from Constantine Menges of the Washington, DC, office of the Hudson Institute, to William Bowdler, then Assistant Secretary of State for Inter-American Affairs. I don't know how the letter went astray, but it has been widely used in the European press to denounce American interference with support from Social Democratic parties for the Salvadoran revolutionary movement. In any case, the Hudson Institute is a well-known research center and "think tank" with headquarters in New York. About 40% of its activities involve Pentagon and other government-related projects.

In his letter of 14 October 1980, Menges urged the Department of State to send people to Europe to convince the Social Democratic parties to withdraw their support from the Revolutionary Democratic Front and to back American efforts to prop up the military junta. Menges' letter was written not long before the meeting of the Socialist International in Madrid in which the matter of support for the Front would be discussed. He specifically mentioned the need to inform European Social Democrats on the Salvadoran agrarian reform program.

What was interesting to me was that of the four people recommended by Menges for conversations with the Europeans, two were associated with the AIFLD: Roy Prosterman and Michael Hammer. He described Hammer as having four years' experience in El Salvador and as "having played a major role in the agrarian reform this year."

When I first saw the Menges letter in November last year, and learned that the AIFLD was on the spot in El Salvador through technical assistance to the agrarian reform program, I naturally thought: "Well, there they are at it again." The next I heard was of the assassinations in early January of Hammer and Mark Pearlman, the AIFLD official mentioned before, along with Jose Viera, the Director of the Salvadoran Institute for Agrarian Transformation. Hammer had arrived back in El Salvador the day he was killed.

Apparently the three men were meeting in the restaurant of the Sheraton Hotel in San Salvador, and according to the Salvadorans who spoke to me, the normally heavy military security forces guarding the hotel suddenly were withdrawn that night, while the two assassins simply entered the hotel, walked into the restaurant, shot the three men and strolled leisurely out. It was only too obvious that the murders were committed in coordinated fashion between the security forces and the assassins.

In reports I read in the American press, including *Time* and *Newsweek*, there was no mention of the fact that the AIFLD, the employer of these two men, had been denounced many times as a CIA front. I'm not the only one who has made this revelation. As you saw in the film script, the subject came up during hearings of the United States Senate during the 1960's. Nevertheless, it seems that the American press, which one would think might comment on the AIFLD's relationship with the CIA, in this case participated in the cover-up by omitting to mention that connection in their reporting. It certainly has been interesting for me to contrast the government's official interest in the killing of the three nuns and a woman lay-worker with its attitude to the killing of the AIFLD people. In the case of the nuns, vigorous pressure was applied on the Salvadoran government to investigate and to punish those responsible. I have seen nothing about U.S. pressures to find the killers of Hammer and Pearlman. This leads me to conclude that the government in Washington would prefer to have no publicity regarding Hammer and Pearlman and their AIFLD connection — because of what I am now going to mention.

Something very curious happened in Washington on January 14, just days after the assassination of Hammer and Pearlman. As you may know, my passport was revoked in December 1979, and since then I have been trying to get it restored through the courts in the United States. I won my case in the Federal District Court over a year ago, but they would not give it back to me pending appeal. In June I won in the Court of Appeals but still did not get the passport back because the government took the case to the Supreme Court. These books I show you now are the arguments of both the government and my lawyers which were submitted to the Supreme Court last November and December. The oral arguments took place before the Justices of the Supreme Court on January 14.

During the Supreme Court hearing, the Solicitor General of the United States, who was arguing the government's case against me, was asked by one of the Justices whether, hypothetically speaking, the Secretary of State had the power to prevent an American citizen from travelling to El Salvador to denounce American policy. The Solicitor General replied: "I'm out of the record in answering this, but just recently two Americans have been killed in Salvador. Apparently they were some kind of undercover persons working under the cover of a labor organization." With that remark the courtroom began to buzz, and reporters went out to file the story.

I ought to mention that I had not denounced either Hammer or Pearlman as CIA-connected, and in fact the Solicitor General did not accuse me of that. Nevertheless, by trying to make the case against me stronger, he once again (and it was stupid on his part) confirmed that the American Institute for Free Labor Development is a front and cover for the CIA. Ironically, the murders were carried out, without any doubt, by the right-wing paramilitary squads that also have links with the CIA. Later you will see an interview with the former American Ambassador to El Salvador, Robert White, in which he too confirms that the nuns and Hammer and Pearlman were murdered by these right-wing assassination squads.

PART 6

THE C I A AND POLITICAL REPRESSION IN LATIN AMERICA

Now I would like to go into the CIA's links with local security services in Latin America generally, and with paramilitary assassination squads that have been a part of the scene in Latin America since the 1950's. I worked for some years with the security forces in both Ecuador and Uruguay and therefore had some experience and knowledge of these so-called liaison operations undertaken by the CIA throughout Latin America. The result, as you all know, is a direct connection between the CIA and some of the worst terrorism going on in the world, including disappearances, torture and outright assassination by these security services and the paramilitary squads — which in some countries are the same people.

A. The Subversive Control Watch List

You see there more excerpts from *Inside the Company* showing our work in Ecuador in the early 1960's to prepare and maintain what we called the LYNX list, also known as the Subversive Control Watch List. This was a file that might have from 50 to 500 names on it, and the people on this list were supposed to be the most important left-wing activists whose arrest we might like to effect through a local government, very quickly, when a crisis developed. Under the subject's name we would include his place and date of birth, wife's name, where they worked, and biographical data on the whole family, including schools the children attended and where the family spent its leisure time — all information necessary to make a quick arrest, including places the subject could possibly hide underground. In Ecuador we were paying teams to collect and maintain this type of information.

In July 1963, when a military coup occurred in Ecuador, largely as a result of our operations, we began passing the information from this Subversive Control Watch List to the government, which used it to arrest hundreds of Ecuadorians during the first weeks following the coup. The CIA probably did the same thing in Chile in 1973.

Information contained in the Subversive Control Watch List came from all the stations' intelligence collection sources, and it was far superior to anything the local security services could obtain for themselves. Certain pieces of information on the list might be passed on to local security forces, but normally the material was kept secret in the CIA station to be used in times of crisis.

Quito — 1960

ECJACK. About two years ago the Army established the Ecuadorean Military Intelligence Service (SIME) under Lieutenant-Colonel Roger Paredes, ECJACK, who then made contact with Noland. Paredes had been trained by the U.S. Army at Fort

Leavenworth some years earlier. In 1959, however, discouraged by the lack of support from his government for SIME, Paredes suggested to Noland that he might be more effective if he retired from the Army and worked full time with the station. At this point SIME was only a paper organization, and even today is still useless.

Paredes's suggestion to Noland came just at the time the station investigations and surveillance team was discovered to be falsifying reports and expenses. The old ECSERUM team was fired and Paredes retired from the Army to form a new team. He now runs a five-man full-time team for surveillance and general investigations in Quito and, in addition, he has two reporting agents in the important southern sierra town of Loja. These two agents are on the fringes of communist activities there.

Station direction of this operation is entirely through Lieutenant-Colonel Paredes, who uses the SIME organization as cover and as ostensible sponsor for the other agents in the operation. Another sub-agent is the chief of the identity card section of the Ministry of Government. As all citizens are required to register and obtain an official government-issued identity card, this agent provides on request the full name, date and place of birth, names of parents, occupation, address and photograph of practically any Ecuadorean. His main value is to provide this data for the station LYNX List, which is a list of about 100 communists and other activists of the extreme left whom the station considers the most dangerous. The LYNX List is a requirement for all Western Hemisphere stations, to be maintained in case a local government in time of crisis should ask (or be asked by the U.S. government) for assistance in the emergency preventive detention of dangerous persons. The ECJACK team spends part of its time updating addresses and place of employment of current LYNX List members and in getting the required information on new additions.

Quito — 13 May 1962

Because Arosemena continues to resist firing extreme leftists in his government — penetration in fact continues to grow — Noland recommended, and headquarters approved, expansion of the political operations financed through the ECACTOR project. Not only will continued and increased pressure be exerted through the regular agents in Quito, Cuenca, Riobamba, Ambato and Tulcan, but we have made two new recruitments of important Social Christian leaders in Quito. I am in charge of both these new cases.

The first new operation is with Carlos Roggiero, a retired Army captain and one of the principal Social Christian representatives on the National Defense Front. Roggiero is chief of the Social Christian militant-action squads, including the secret bomb-squad, and I have started training him in the use of various incendiary, crowd disperse-ment and harassment devices that I requested from TSD in headquarters. Through him we will form perhaps ten squads, of five to ten men each, for disrupting meetings and small demonstrations and for general street control and intimidation of the Communist Youth, URJE and similar groups.

The other new operation is with Jose Maria Egas, a young lawyer and also a leading Social Christian representative on the National Defense Front. Egas is a fast-rising political figure and a really spellbinding orator. Through him I will form five squads composed of four to five men each for investigative work connected with our Subversive Control Watch List — formerly known as the LYNX list. The surveillance team under Lt. Col. Paredes simply hasn't the time to do the whole job and is needed on other assignments. With the group under Egas's control we will have constant checking on residences and places of work so that if the situation continues to deteriorate and a moment of truth arrives, we will have up-to-date information for immediate arrests. If Egas's work warrants it, we may train him in headquarters and even extend the operation to physical surveillance.

Quito — 15 June 1962

Recently I read the report by a special inter-departmental team of experts from Washington called the Strategic Analysis Targeting Team (SATT), which in months past secretly visited all the Latin American countries. Their purpose was to review all

U.S. government programs in each country and to determine the gravity of the threat of urban terrorism and guerrilla warfare. We prepared a secret annex for the SATT Report, and among their recommendations were expansion of the Subversive Control Watch List program and updating of contingency planning in order to continue our operations from a third country – in case we lose our Embassy offices. Ecuador, in fact, shared with Bolivia and Guatemala the SATT Report's category as the most likely places for early armed insurgency. Emphasis on immediate expansion of Civic Action and labor programs is probably a result of the SATT Report.

Quito – 11 July 1963
Arosemena's out and a four-man military junta is in. . . .

The junta is composed of the officers who commanded the Army, Air Force and Navy plus a colonel who was Secretary of the National Defense Council. The Navy captain is the junta chief but Colonel Marcos Gandara of the Defense Council is said unanimously to be the brains and main influence. No question that these men are anti-communist and will finally take the kind of action we want to disrupt the extreme left before they get their serious armed operations underway.

Quito – 13 July 1963
No problem for the junta in consolidating power. Loyal messages were received from military units throughout the country, civil liberties have been suspended, and communist and other extreme leftists are being rounded up and put in jail, more than a hundred in Guayaquil alone. Communism is outlawed (the junta's first act), censorship has been imposed, there is a curfew from 9 p.m. to 6 a.m., and next year's elections are canceled.

It will take some days for formal U.S. recognition of the junta but we've already started passing data from the Subversive Control Watch List to Major de los Reyes here in Quito and to Colonel Lugo in Guayaquil which they are using with military colleagues in the arrests campaign. For the time being we'll keep working with these police agents, and after U.S. recognition of the junta and Dean's return, decisions will be made on new contacts in the government. The most likely liaison contacts are the Minister of Defense, Colonel Aurelio Naranjo, who was chief of the Cuenca garrison and leader of the movement that forced Arosemena to break with Cuba; the Minister of Government, Colonel Luis Mora Bowen; and the junta leader, Colonel Marcos Gandara.

Quito – 31 July 1963
The first three weeks of junta rule have been rather mild as military dictatorships go, in fact after all the crisis and tension in recent months one can even note a feeling of euphoria. Today the junta was recognized by the U.S. but all along we've kept busy getting information to Major de los Reyes and Colonel Lugo. Goes to show how important station operations can be at a time when conventional diplomatic contacts are suspended. Even so, the most important communist leaders from our viewpoint, Echeverria, for example, have eluded all efforts to catch them. Very possibly some have even left the country.

Right now there are about 125 political prisoners in Quito, including not only communists but Velasquistas and members of the Concentration of Popular Forces. The junta policy is to allow them to go into exile, although some will be able to stay in Ecuador depending on their political antecedents – judgment of which, in most cases, is based on information we're passing to Colonel Luis Mora Bowen, the Minister of Government. Processing these prisoners, and others in Guayaquil and elsewhere is going to take a long time because of interrogations and follow-up. Although Dean is working closely with the Minister of Government in processing the prisoners, he hopes to use these cases to start a new unit in the Ministry of Defense that will be solely dedicated to anti-communist intelligence collection – basically this is what we had previously set up in the police. In fact the Ministry of Defense will be better because politics sooner or later will come back into the Ministry of Government and the police, while the military unit should be able to remain aloof from normal politics, concentrating on the extreme left.

B.   Liaison Operations with Local Services

Throughout Latin America in the 1960's, and I don't think it's any different today, the CIA maintained intimate working relationships with the local military and police security services. This work included all kinds of support given by the CIA to these services, not the least of which was money, training, equipment, information, guidance and encouragement. In return, the CIA received valuable services such as identification photographs of certain people, control of the travel of targets of interest, tapping telephones, support when making illegal entries for bugging — and other benefits. In Central America in the 1960's there was no exception to this kind of relationship with the local security services.

The following extracts from *Inside the Company* provide background information on the CIA's liaison operations with other security services, and details of my work with these services in Latin America in the 1960's. You will notice that the CIA officer who replaced me in Montevideo in 1966 had recently trained the bodyguards for the President and the Somoza family in Nicaragua. You will notice the use of the Agency for International Development from the 1950's to the 1970's for training police all over the world, and the CIA's use of these training programs, called Public Safety Missions, as cover for CIA officers.

Liaison Operations

From the standpoint of pure doctrine all liaison operations are considered compromised, since even the existence of a liaison relationship implies the giving of something by the CIA: at the very least the identity of a CIA officer. It is always hoped that the virtues of liaison operations with other intelligence services outweigh their defects, but the judgment is sometimes hard to make. The two most basic principles of liaison operations from the counter-intelligence point of view are: first, there is no such thing as a friendly intelligence service, and, second, all liaison services are penetrated by the Soviets or by local revolutionary groups. Thus any operations undertaken jointly by the CIA with a liaison service are by definition compromised from the start. It is for this reason that some CIA intelligence reports (FIR's) include the NOFORN or NO FOREIGN DISSEM indicators which restrict reports to U.S. officials only. The indicators are used so that foreign liaison services will not receive information from sensitive sources in the course of normal exchange programs.

Why get involved with other services? Basically, liaison operations are conducted because they are useful. They extend a station's limited manpower however shaky the extension may be. They give the CIA a foot in the door for penetration of the liaison service. And they may also result in a local service taking action, such as an arrest or raid, at station request.

In non-communist countries it is the policy of the Agency to assist local security services to improve their capabilities if, of course, these services want the help and their government is not openly hostile to the U.S. By giving money, training and equipment to local services like the police, the CIA is able to receive information that might otherwise not be available because, for example, of the shortage of station officers. Travel control, for instance, involves obtaining airline and ship passenger lists from the companies or from local immigration services. Often it is easier to obtain them from a liaison service than from five or ten different companies. Telephone tapping is often possible only through a local service, especially when many lines are to be monitored. Mails can be opened much more easily by a local service than by the lengthy process of unilateral agent recruitment in post offices. Above all, if flaps (scandals) occur, the local service, not the CIA, will take the rap.

Usually a Chief of Station will handle the contact with the chief of a local service. Some stations may have whole sections of liaison officers at the working level both in operational planning and in information exchange. The general rule, of course, is to expose the absolute minimum of station officers to a local service and, if possible, only those officers engaged in liaison operations. Officers engaged in unilateral operations, that is, operations undertaken without the knowledge of the local government, should be protected against compromise with the local service.

Some local services are so pitifully backward that they need overt U.S. government assistance. Thus the International Cooperation Administration (ICA) [predecessor of AID] technical assistance missions in many countries include Public Safety Missions made up of U.S. technicians who work with police departments. They seek to improve the local service's capability in communications, investigations, administration and record keeping, public relations and crime prevention. The Public Safety Missions are valuable to the CIA because they provide cover for CIA officers who are sent to work full time with the intelligence services of the police and other civilian services. Station officers under other cover may work with military intelligence and, at times, officers under cover as businessmen, tourists or retired people may be assigned to work with local services.

CIA assistance to local services through Public Safety Missions or other forms of cover are not only designed to help improve the professional capability of the local service. Operational targeting of the local service is guided by CIA liaison officers so that the local service performs tasks that are lacking in the overall station operational program. In other words local services are to be used for the benefit of the CIA, and this includes keeping the local service away from station unilateral operations.

The personal relations between CIA liaison officers and their colleagues in local services are very important, because the CIA liaison officers are expected to spot and assess officers in the local service for recruitment as penetration agents. Liaison officers make money available to officers of the local service and it is expected that the local colleague will pocket some of the money even though it is supposed to be strictly for operations. The technique is to get the local police or intelligence officer used to a little extra cash so that not only will he be dependent on the station for equipment and professional guidance but also for personal financing.

Security officers such as police are often among the poorest paid public servants and they are rarely known to refuse a gift. Little by little an officer of a local service is called upon to perform tasks not known to anyone else in his service, particularly his superiors. Gradually he begins to report on his own service and on politics within his own government. Eventually his first loyalty is to the CIA. After all, that is where the money comes from. Penetration operations against local services are often of very considerable importance because of the place of security services in local political stability. Reporting from these agents is sometimes invaluable during situations of possible *coup d'etat*.

Finally, CIA stations may undertake unilateral operatons through officers of liaison services who have been recruited as penetration agents. That is the final goal. Recruited liaison officers may also report on efforts by their services to uncover unilateral station operations. This, too, is a happy situation.

Quito — 1960

ECAMOROUS. The main station activity in security preparations for the Inter-American Conference is the training and equipping of the intelligence department of the Ecuadorean National Police. The intelligence department is called the Department of Special Services of the National Police Headquarters, and its chief is Police Captain Jose Vargas, ECAMOROUS-2, who has been given special training here and in headquarters. Weatherwax, our case officer under Public Safety cover, works almost exclusively with Vargas, who has been in trouble recently for being the leader of a secret society of pro-Velasco young police officers. Secret societies in the police, as in the military, are forbidden.

In spite of all our efforts, Vargas seems incapable of doing very much to help us, but he has managed to develop three or four marginal reporting agents on extreme leftist activities in his home town of Riobamba, a sierra provincial capital, and in Esmeraldas, a coastal provincial capital. Reports from these sources come directly to Vargas, and from him to the station, because there is little interest in this type of information further up the line in the Ecuadorean government. On the contrary, with Araujo as the minister in charge of the National Police, intelligence collection by a police officer is a risky activity.

Intelligence needs during the Inter-American Conference will have to be satisfied largely by the station directly through unilateral operations but before information of this kind is passed to Vargas it will have to be disguised to protect the source. Although strictly speaking ECAMOROUS is a liaison operation, the police intelligence unit is completely run by the station. Vargas is paid a salary by Noland with additional money for his sub-agents and expenses. Some technical equipment such as photogear and non-sensitive audio equipment has been given to Vargas by the station, and we have trained his chief technician, Lieutenant Luis Sandoval.

Vargas is young and rather reckless but very friendly, well-disposed and intelligent. Although he is considered to be excellent as a long-term penetration of the National Police, he could be worked into other operations in the future. His first loyalty is undoubtedly to the station, and when asked he is glad to use his police position as cover for action requested by the station.

ECOLE. This is the station's main penetration operation against the Ecuadorean National Police other than the intelligence side, and it also produces information about the Ecuadorean Workers Confederation (CTE). The principal agent, Colonel Wilfredo Oswaldo Lugo, ECOLE, has been working with the U.S. government since hunting Nazis with the FBI during World War II. Since 1947 he has been working with the Quito station, and in the police shuffle and purge during Velasco's first weeks in office, Lugo was appointed Chief of the Department of Personnel of the National Police Headquarters.

In contrast with the fairly open contact between Noland and Weatherwax and Captain Vargas, the intelligence chief, contact between Noland and Lugo is very discreet. The agent is considered to be a penetration of the security service and in times of crisis his reporting is invaluable, since he is in a position to give situation reports on government plans and reactions to events as reflected in orders to police and military units.

Over the years Colonel Lugo has developed several agents who report on communist and related activities. Two of these agents are currently active and are targeted against the CTE. Their reporting is far inferior to PCE penetration agents such as Cardenas, Luis Vargas and Basantes, but they are kept on the payroll as insurance in case anything ever happens to the better agents. Noland also pays a regular monthly salary to Colonel Lugo.

Montevideo — 1964

AVBALSA. Liaison with the Uruguayan military intelligence service is in charge of Gerry O'Grady, the Deputy Chief of Station, who meets regularly with Lieutenant-Colonel Zipitria, the deputy chief of the service. Holman also occasionally meets Zipitria and when necessary Colonel Carvajal, the military intelligence service chief. For some years the Montevideo station has tried to build up the capabilities of his liaison service through training, equipment donation and funding but with very little success. Even now, their main collection activity is clipping from the local leftist press. The main problem with this service is the Uruguayan military tradition of keeping aloof from politics, as is shown by Carvajal's reluctance to engage the service in operations against the PCU and other extreme-left political groups. On the other hand the Deputy Chief, Zipitria, is a rabid anti-communist whose ideas border on a fascist-style repression and who is constantly held in check by Carvajal. For the time being the station is using the Deputy Chief as a source of intelligence on government police towards the extreme left and on rumblings within the military against the civilian government. Hopefully Zipitria will some day be chief of the service.

AVALANCHE. The main public security force in Uruguay is the Montevideo Police Department – cryptonym AVALANCHE – with which liaison relations date to just before World War II when the FBI was monitoring the considerable pro-Nazi tendencies in Uruguay and Argentina. In the late 1940s, when the CIA station was opened, a number of joint operations were taken over from the FBI including the telephone-tapping project. Although police departments exist in the interior departments of Uruguay, the technical superiority and other capabilities of the Montevideo police almost always produce decisions by Ministers of the Interior that important cases be handled by AVALANCHE even when outside Montevideo.

As in Ecuador, the Minister of the Interior is in charge of the police, and station liaison with civilian security forces begins with the Minister, currently a Blanco politician named Felipe Gil whom Holman meets regularly. Holman also meets regularly, or whenever necessary, Colonel Ventura Rodriguez, Chief of the Montevideo Police; Carlos Martin, Deputy Chief; Inspector Guillermo Copello, Chief of Investigations; Inspector Juan Jose Braga, Deputy Chief of Investigations; Commissioner Alejandro Otero, Chief of the Intelligence and Liaison Department; Colonel Roberto Ramirez, Chief of the Guardia Metropolitana (the anti-riot shock force); Lieutenant-Colonel Mario Barbe, Chief of the Guardia Republicana (the paramilitary police cavalry); and others. Of these the most important are the Minister, Chief of Police, Chief of Intelligence and Liaison and Chief of the Guardia Metropolitana, who supervises the telephone-tapping operation.

As in Argentina, the political sensitivity of an AID Public Safety Mission for improving police capabilities has precluded such a Mission in Uruguay and restricted police assistance to what overall demands on station manpower allow. But whereas in Argentina a non-official cover operations officer has for some years been ostensibly contracted by the Argentine Federal Police to run telephone-tapping and other joint operations, in Uruguay these tasks have been handled by station officers under official cover in the Embassy. Until January all the tasks relating to AVALANCHE were handled by the Deputy Chief of Station, but Holman took over these duties when Wiley Gilstrap, the Deputy, was transferred to become Chief of Station in San Salvador and replaced by O'Grady, whose Spanish is very limited. The station long-range plans continue to be the establishment of an AID Public Safety Mission that would include a CIA officer in order to release station officers in the Embassy for other tasks. However, such a development will have to wait until a strong Minister of the Interior who will fight for the Public Safety Mission appears on the scene. On the other hand Uruguayan police officers are being sent by the station for training at the Police Academy, which has changed its name to the International Police Academy and is moving from Panama to Washington.

Of the activities undertaken by the police on behalf of the station, the most important is the AVENGEFUL telephone-tapping operation. Other activities are designed to supplement the station unilateral collection program and to keep the police from discovering these operations. Apart from telephone tapping these other activities are effected through the Department of Intelligence and Liaison.

Travel Control. Each day the station receives from the police the passenger lists of all arrivals and departures at the Montevideo airport and the port where nightly passenger boats shuttle to Buenos Aires. These are accompanied by a special daily list of important people compiled by I & E personnel, including those traveling on diplomatic passports, important political figures, communists and leftists and leaders of the Peronist movement. On request we can also obtain the lists of travelers who enter or leave at Colonia, another important transit point between Montevideo and Buenos Aires. Daily guest lists from the hotels and lodgings in Montevideo are also available. The main weakness in travel control is at the Carrasco airport, which is the main airport for Montevideo but is in the Department of Canelones just outside the Department of Montevideo, and there is considerable rivalry between the Montevideo and the Canelones police. More important, however, is the lucrative contraband movement at the airport which jealous customs officials protect by hampering any improvement of police control. Thus station efforts to set up a watch list and a document photography operation at the airport have been unsuccessful.

Name Checks. As a service to the Embassy visa office, information is requested constantly from the police department, usually on Uruguayans who apply for U.S. visas. Data from the intelligence and criminal investigations files is then passed by the station to the visa office for use in determining whether visas should be granted or denied.

Biographical Data and Photographs. Uruguay has a national voter registration that is effectively an identification card system. From the AVALANCHE service we obtain full name, date and place of birth, parents' names, address, place of work, etc., and identification photos of practically any Uruguayan or permanent resident alien. This material is valuable for surveillance operations of the AVENIN and AVBANDY teams, for the Subversive Control Watch List and for a variety of other purposes.

License Plate Data. A further help to station analysis of visitors to the Soviet and Cuban embassies are the names and addresses of owners of cars whose license plate numbers are photographed or copied at the observation posts. The police make this information available without knowing the real reason. The same data is also used to supplement reporting by the two surveillance teams.

Reporting. The Intelligence and Liaison Department of the Montevideo Police Department is the government's (and the station's) principal source of information on strikes and street demonstrations. This type of information has been increasing in importance during the last few years as the PCU-dominated labor unions have stepped up their campaigns of strikes and demonstrations in protest against government economic policies. When strikes and demonstrations occur, information is telephoned to the station from I & E as the events progress. It includes numbers of people involved, degree of violence, locations, government orders for repression, and estimates of effectiveness, all of which is processed for inclusion in station reporting to headquarters, the Southern and Atlantic military commands, etc. At the end of each month I & E also prepares a round-up report on strikes and civil disturbances of which the station receives a copy.

While contact between the various officers in the police department and the station is no secret to the Chief of Police – they are described as "official" liaison – the station also maintains a discreet contact with a former I & E chief who was promoted out of the job and now is the fourth- or fifth-ranking officer in Investigations. This officer, Inspector Antonio Piriz Castagnet, is paid a salary as the station penetration of the police department, and he is highly cooperative in performing tasks unknown to his superiors. The station thus calls on this agent for more sensitive tasks where station interest is not to be known by the police chief or others. Piriz also provides valuable information on government plans with respect to strikes and civil disorder, personnel movements within the police and possible shifts in policy.

The overall cost of the AVALANCHE project, apart from AVENGEFUL telephone tapping, is about 25,000 dollars per year.

AVENGEFUL. The station telephone-tapping operation is effected through the AVALANCHE liaison service (the Montevideo Police Department) with a history dating back to World War II when the FBI was in charge of counter-intelligence in South America. This is currently the most important joint operation underway between the station and an Uruguayan service. Connections are made in telephone company exchanges by company engineers at the request of the police department. A thirty-pair cable runs from the main downtown exchange to police headquarters where, on the top floor, the listening post is located.

The chief technician, Jacobo de Anda, and the assistant technician and courier, Juan Torres, man the LP, which has tables with actuators and tape-recorders for each of the thirty pairs. Torres arranges for lines to be connected by the telephone company engineers and he delivers the tapes each day to another courier, AVOIDANCE, who takes them around to the transcribers who work either at home or in safe site offices. This courier also picks up the transcriptions and old tapes from the transcribers and passes them to Torres who sends them to the station each day with yet another courier who works for the Intelligence Department of the police. The police department thus arranges for connections and operates the LP.

The courier AVOIDANCE is a station agent known only to Torres among the police department personnel involved. Each of the transcribers is unknown to the police department but copies of all the transcriptions, except in special cases, are provided by the station to the police intelligence department. Each operations officer in the station who receives telephone coverage of targets of interest to him is responsible for handling the transcribers of his lines: thus the Soviet operations officer, Russell Phipps, is in charge of the two elderly Russian *emigres* who transcribe (in English) the Soviet lines; the CP officer, Paul Burns, is in charge of the transcriber of the PCU line; and the Cuban operations officer is in charge of the transcribers of the Cuban lines. Most of the transcribers are kept apart from one another as well as from the police department.

The station, which provides technical equipment and financing for the operation, deals directly with the Chief of the Guardia Metropolitana, who is the police department official in overall charge of the telephone-tapping operation. He is usually an Army colonel or lieutenant-colonel detailed to run the Guardia Metropolitana, the paramilitary shock force of the police. Currently he is Colonel Roberto Ramirez. Usually he assigns lines to be tapped as part of his operations against contraband operations which also provides cover for the station lines which are political in nature. Torres and de Anda work under the supervision of the Chief of the Guardia Metropolitana although approval in principle for the operation comes from the Minister of the Interior (internal security) and the Chief of the Montevideo Police Department. The station encourages the use of telephone tapping against contraband activities not only because it's good cover but also because police contraband operations are lucrative to them and such operations tend to offset fears of political scandal depending upon who happens to be Minister of the Interior at any particular time.

Only seven lines are being monitored right now. They include three lines on Soviet targets (one on the Embassy, one on the Consulate and another that alternates between a second Embassy telephone and the Soviet Commercial Office), two on Cuban targets (one on the Embassy and one on the Commercial Office), one on a revolutionary Argentine with close associations with the Cubans, and one line assigned to the headquarters of the Communist Party of Uruguay.

Security is a serious problem with the AVENGEFUL operation because so many people know of it: former ministers and their subordinates, former police chiefs and their subordinates, current officers in the Guardia Metropolitana and the Criminal Investigations and Intelligence Departments. Copies of the transcriptions prepared for the police intelligence department are considered very insecure because of the poor physical security of the department despite continuous station efforts to encourage tightening. Regular denunciations of telephone tapping by the police appear in the PCU newspaper, *El Popular*, but without the detail that might require shutting down the operation.

Telephone tapping in Montevideo, then, is very shaky with many possibilities for serious scandal.

Montevideo — 15 August 1965

Horton is anxious to build up the capabilities of the police intelligence department — making it a kind of Special Branch for political work along the lines of British police practice. He wants me to spend more time training Otero, Chief of Intelligence and Liaison, and to give him more money for furniture, filing cabinets and office supplies. As soon as possible Horton wants Otero put in for the International Police Academy and for additional training by headquarters at the conclusion of the Academy course. Before leaving Washington Horton obtained AID approval for a CIA officer to be placed under Public Safety cover, and after we get approval from the Chief of Police and get the officer down here we will have him working full-time with Intelligence and Liaison.

Physical surveillance and travel control are the kinds of operations that we plan to emphasize from the beginning. Expansion of AVENGEFUL will come later, perhaps, along with recruitment operations against targets of the extreme left, but these changes will follow Otero's training in Washington. In travel control we will start by trying to set up the often-delayed passport photography and watch-list operation at the Montevideo airport.

The AID Public Safety program is moving along well. Vehicles, communications, riot-control equipment and training are the main points of emphasis. Until our Public Safety cover officer arrives, however, we plan to keep the police intelligence work strictly in our office. It's going to be a long and difficult job and I won't have time to do it adequately because of other work. Somehow we have to make them start thinking seriously on basic things like security and decent filing systems.

Montevideo — 3 January 1966

Another important weapons robbery occurred the other night — possibly the work of the Tupamaros. They got away with eighty-six revolvers, forty-seven shotguns, five rifles and ammunition, all taken from a Montevideo gun shop. Commissioner Otero leaves in three weeks for Washington. Headquarters decided to train him at the International Police Services School, which is a headquarters training facility under commercial cover, instead of at the AID-administered International Police Academy. AID cover for the training, however, is retained.

Montevideo — 13 January 1966

Otero left today for training at the International Police Services School in Washington. Horton and I went to police headquarters to bid farewell and we took advantage of the meeting with Colonel Ubach, the Chief of Police, to propose bringing down one of our officers to work full-time with police intelligence, using the AID Public Safety mission as cover. Ubach isn't terribly quick mentally, but he agreed, as he does to everything else we propose. Now we'll get approval from Storace, the Minister of the Interior, and advise headquarters to select someone. Once this matter is settled we'll begin working on the Minister, the Chief, and others in order to take the intelligence department out of the Investigations Division, preferably on an equal bureaucratic level as Investigations or at least with some autonomy. If approved we'll try to maneuver Inspector Piriz in as Intelligence Chief because he's much more experienced, mature and capable than Otero who suffers from impatience and is disliked by colleagues. Piriz, moreover, has already been on the payroll for some years and his loyalty and spirit of cooperation are excellent. While Otero is away I'll work closely with his deputy, Sub-Commissioner Pablo Fontana.

Montevideo — 20 March 1966

Frank Sherno, the regional technical officer stationed in Buenos Aires, sent us a portable Recordak document-copying machine which I hope to set up at the Montevideo airport as part of an improved travel-control operation. With this machine we can photograph all the passports from communist countries and that of anyone else on our watch list. Recently I've begun to work on this with Jaureguiza, another Police Commissioner who is in charge of general travel control and the Montevideo non-domiciled population. Jaureguiza has agreed to obtain a convenient room at the Montevideo airport near the immigration counters to install the machine. When this is settled Sherno will come to set it up and train the operators. Hopefully we can get this done before Otero gets back from his training in Washington because he'll want to control it and his abrasive personality would hinder getting it started. By now he has finished the police training course at the International Police Services School and is undergoing special intelligence training by headquarters' OTR officers.

Montevideo — 10 August 1966

At last my replacement is here and I'll be able to leave by the end of the month. He is Juan Noriega, a former Navy pilot, who recently finished his first tour at the Managua station where he was responsible for training the bodyguards for the President and the Somoza family.

Montevideo — 24 August 1966
I've turned over all my operations to Noriega and in a few days will be flying home. In two and a half years our station budget has gone up to almost a million and a half dollars while several new additions have been made to the station case officer complement. In a couple of weeks Bill Cantrell arrives to work full-time with Otero's police intelligence department.

Through assistance programs to local security forces around the world, CIA officers became directly involved in the institutionalization of torture as an interrogation method, especially in Latin America. There cannot be any doubt that CIA officers are working with the Salvadoran security services in joint efforts to repress the revolutionary movement. Late last year an American named Thomas Bracken was killed in El Salvador, and when his death was announced it was revealed that he was serving as a "private advisor" to the Salvadoran National Police. The Salvadoran Minister of Defense was quoted in the Mexico City daily, *El Dia* (28 December 1980), as confirming that the Salvadoran government "consulted with the American Embassy before contracting him." The obvious probability is that Bracken's services were arranged by the CIA.

The following extract from *On Company Business* provides an intimate view of the involvement of American security advisors in torture by "friendly" security services. The main commentary is by A. J. Langguth, formerly the *New York Times* Bureau Chief in Saigon, who wrote a book on this subject (*Hidden Terrors*, Pantheon Books, New York, 1978).

The following statements are from interviews or newsreel footage of the following people:

A. J. Langguth: Former Saigon Bureau Chief of the *New York Times* and author of *Hidden Terrors* (interview)
Angela Seixas: Brazilian political activist imprisoned and tortured by Brazilian security forces, later exiled (interview)
Philip Agee: (interview)
Agency for International Development (technical assistance to foreign police): Speaking on death of Daniel Mitrione (newsreel footage)
Hugo Vilar: Uruguayan political leader exiled under his country's military dictatorship (interview)
Manuel Hevia: Cuban exile formerly employed by the U.S. Public Safety Mission (police assistance) in Montevideo, Uruguay. His chief was Daniel Mitrione. (newsreel footage)
Juan Ferreira: Uruguayan exiled under his country's military dictatorship and son of Wilson Ferreira, former Uruguayan Presidential candidate, also exiled (interview)
Tupamaro guerrilla in Uruguay: (audio tape)

Langguth: The police program began on a large scale under Dwight Eisenhower. He felt there was a need to train the police to help with the fighting of communism after the second World War. He recruited for the purpose a man named Byron Engle who was, by the time he came into this program, a member of the CIA.
After the Bay of Pigs, Engle's program was much expanded. Police from around the world were brought and trained by U.S. advisors. The training was to make them more efficient, but a third of the training was given over in one way or another to make them aware of the communist menace and go back into their countries to fight communism.

Angela Sexias: Immediately when you are arrested you have to tell them your house, they force you, they try to force you to tell what, where you live, other addresses you know, where you meet, because that's where they get their information from. And the situation is so difficult. They do not put infiltrators, they have not courage nor possibility of actually infiltrating the left, it's too dangerous. So the only way they get their information is through torture.

Langguth: Whenever one could get the information about a specific, high-ranking official in torture, not one of these men off the street, but a man who based his career on his ability to extract information from political prisoners, in the cases that I investigated I found that they had been trained at a United States base.

Angela Sexias: Well, they started asking some questions, I didn't say anything. They started immediately torturing me. After the doctor left. And I mean it's the same story of so many people. It's torture, electric shocks and beatings, and telephones and finally it's a few hours like that.

Langguth: Many of the people I spoke with, exiles, political exiles in Europe, had been tortured with U.S. Army field telephones. They were simple, they were easy to operate and we had sent them in large numbers as part of our military assistance.
You hook up wires to the telephone and you put one wire perhaps on a man's penis and another in his mouth. When they are put in the mouth the torturer uses a rubber glove. This is done with a certain degree of surgical precision. There is no embarassment among the torturers, I was told, about the handling of genitals, although when women are tortured oftentimes the higher-ranking officials will find an excuse to come by and watch this torture.

Angela Sexias: I decided that I would confirm everything that they wanted. I was in such a condition, and they certainly wouldn't settle for less. And I didn't want to go through any more torture. Ideologically I was weak enough to say, if they know, why not.

Langguth: What we brought to it, what we, the United States, through our efficient system brought was the sense that you used only the amount of torture appropriate to get information and the reason torture persists is that although they cant among the police officers that torture is not an effective way to get information, of course, it is.

Angela Sexias: Torture is a necessity of the system, not because some minds, sick minds think of it, but because the resistance continues to grow. It's a sporadic thing, small in form, but it's always there. Torture is the answer to that.

Philip Agee: We were unsuccessful in our efforts to weaken the left in Uruguay during the period when I was in Uruguay in 1964-1966. Our job in the face of the growth of the strength of the left during that period was to promote repression. It was the only alternative we had. In 1966 we brought in a CIA officer who set up his office in the police department under the cover of the Public Safety mission of AID. This officer was to work exclusively with the police intelligence, trying to improve its capabilities. This officer was still there in 1970 at the time that the American Public Safety mission chief, Dan Mitrione, was kidnapped and executed by the Tupamaros.
Langguth: Mitrione was the small-city cop in Richmond, Indiana. He had advanced to the position of chief of police. And had heard about Byron Engles' program in Washington, applied, and of course, he was exactly the sort of person they were looking for to send abroad: diligent, hardworking.
AID Public Safety spokesman: Dan exemplified the highest principles of the police profession, that of social service. He served in Brazil for seven years, at the International Police Academy in Washington for two, and in Montevideo for one. There are

200 million people in Latin America. In many of these countries the communist ter- rorists are trying to tear the fabric of democracy apart. Some of these countries, Uru- guay among them, realize that the best protection against this is the development of a democratic policeman, asked the United States to help. And this is what Dan was doing in Uruguay.

Langguth: Mitrione was a tough professional by 1969. He had spent nine years in the program. He had been in Brazil where there had been a great deal of repression and refinement of torture as an interrogation technique. He went to Uruguay to get information.

Hugo Vilar: Some time ago this photograph was seen throughout the world, a photograph released by a commisar of the armed forces of our country. Here you can see an almost naked prisoner with a hood. Nearly all of the prisoners are hooded. This measure is taken so that they cannot identify their torturers.

Manuel Hevia: Daniel Mitrione, efficient looking, congenial in manner. He was a perfectionist. He supervised every detail. He insisted on checking everything. During the training sessions he directed and personally participated in each stage. This ques- tion of perfectionism. He insisted on an economy of effort. He used to say, "Precise pain in the precise place at the precise time. You must be careful. You should avoid excesses." Another phrase of his, "Remember that the death of the prisoner consti- tutes a failure of the technician." Because he considered himself a technician.

Langguth: One of the pieces of equipment that was found useful was a wire so very thin that it could be fitted into the mouth between the teeth and by pressing against the gum increase the electrical charge. And it was through the diplomatic pouch that Mitrione got some of the equipment he needed for interrogations, including these fine wires.

Manuel Hevia: Several street beggars were picked up whose disappearance would attract no attention. This was a technique that Mitrione had developed or rather perfected in Brazil. Using these beggars, experiments were conducted with the differ- ent forms of interrogation, letting the students see the effect of different voltages on different parts of the human body, male and female. All these unhappy people died without really knowing why they were undergoing this pain. Without even having the cowardly solution of answering any questions because they were not asked any. They were simply guinea pigs.

Langguth: In Los Fresnos, Texas, the CIA ran for the police program a school in the construction of bombs. Students came from around the world, particularly Latin America, and they were instructed in the manufacture of plastique homemade bombs. Dan Mitrione sent students from Uruguay to that school. The idea was that you had to be particularly trustworthy and you were pledged not to talk about the activities, but the courses were run by CIA personnel.

Juan Ferreira: The death squads were very active in 1972 to 1973 and this was denounced in the Uruguayan congress before the congress was dissolved, and it was mainly denounced when the Tupamaros kidnapped one of the main leaders, one of the main heads of the death squads, called Nelson Bardesio. He was a CIA agent. He con- fessed he was a CIA agent. He was trained in the United States. He was paid by the Central Intelligence Agency of the United States. The way they hide his work was he was a photographer. He had a laboratory, but he was organizing all these death squads. He participated in a lot of assassinations and bombings.

Langguth: Nelson Bardesio was sent to Buenos Aires to train with the Argen- tinian police. From that trip he brought back to Montevideo charges of plastique ex- plosives. That kind of plastique material for bombs was used against political figures on the left by the police, who went around Montevideo in police cars at night, bomb- ing political opponents.

Philip Agee: Every CIA station during that period, and I would expect today, was required to maintain what was called a Subversive Control Watch List. This was a list of the most important left-wing politicial activists, in the city or the country. And the list would include not only their names, but the name of their mother, the name of their father, of their children, of their wife, their address where they lived, the address where they worked, the places they would go with their friends, clubs they might belong to, where they would take their leisure activities, everything we might need to know to take sudden action against that person. These lists would be usually maintained in the CIA offices and kept up to date. But whenever necessary they were turned over to the local police or the local military authorities for action on the part of those authorities.

Juan Ferreira: The Uruguayan death squads started acting in Buenos Aires and some of our best friends and aides were kidnapped and assassinated. The prominent leaders who were kidnapped and assassinated were Senator Zelmar Michelini, a very popular leader in Uruguay, and Hector Guitteirez Ruiz. They were both kidnapped and assassinated that same night and that same night they went after us. When we started living in Argentina we had to register in the police headquarters. And for the first three or four weeks we lived in a street called Suipacha. Then we moved to an apartment where we lived, where my parents lived, for two years, and I lived for the last eight months. And the only place we had the old address registered was the police headquarters. And it was to our old address where they went after us.

Hugo Vilar: The murder of these political leaders of Uruguay is part of an entire international campaign which includes the murder of the Chilean Generals Schneider and Prats, the attempt against Bernard Leighlin in Europe, the murder of Orlando Letelier, the former Chilean Ambassador, in Washington, the killing of Torres, the former president of Bolivia, and the murder of tens and scores of patriots from Uruguay, Bolivia, Argentina, Chile and Brazil which has occurred in their own country or in other countries, in Latin America or elsewhere.

Manuel Hevia: Mitrione's presence and actions in Uruguay do not represent the excesses of a single individual. He went to Uruguay to accomplish a mission, to fulfill a task, to coordinate a part of the advisory program the CIA undertook in Police Headquarters in Montevideo. Starting in Mitrione's time there was a qualitative increase in the tortures, beatings, and kickings, the brutality which persists. But he introduced the refinements of modern technology.

Tupamaro: Well now, tell me something about the CIA.

Dan Mitrione: Well, you know, you're not going to believe me. No matter what, I have to convince you that I know nothing about the CIA. Absolutely nothing about the CIA.

Tupamaro: How do you think the Uruguayan Government will behave now?

Dan Mitrione: I hope they bargain with you.

Tupamaro: Yes. We hope it too. We don't like this.

Dan Mitrione: The only thing I regret about all this – I don't like one thing – and that is too many innocent people suffer, my wife and children, there is no reason for them to be suffering.

Tupamaro: I'm sorry about them too. I'm sorry about all of the families of our friends who are in prison being tortured or killed. There are many, really, many innocent people have to suffer.

Langguth: The government of Uruguay, bolstered by the new policy of Richard Nixon not to deal with revolutionaries, resisted every attempt to exchange political prisoners for Mitrione's life. The result was that a deadline was set some ten days after his capture for release of the one hundred and fifty political prisoners or Mitrione would be killed. The government did not respond to the warning. Mitrione's body was found the following day in an abandoned car in a side street in Montevideo.

Ron Ziegler, White House spokesman: The kidnapping and murder of U.S. AID official Dan Mitrione by criminal terrorists in Uruguay is a despicable act. This callous murder emphasizes the essential inhumanity of the terrorists. The American people join the president in condemning this cold-blooded crime against a defenseless human being. Mr. Mitrione's devoted service to the cause of peaceful progress in an orderly world will remain as an example for free men everywhere.

C.   CIA Links to Terrorism and Paramilitary Squads

In *Inside the Company* I described the terrorist activities of the paramilitary organization of the Social Christian Movement in Ecuador. The leader of this party was President of Ecuador when I was assigned to that country. I trained some of these squads in the use of incendiary devices and in all kinds of dirty operations to break up meetings and to generally terrorize organizations on the left. At that time they were not engaged in outright assassination of people on the left, but I mention this to show that the CIA, as a matter of practice, has had its connections with the paramilitary organizations. In Chile, during the early 1970's, the CIA did the same through its connections with the right-wing terrorist organization known as Patria y Libertad.

Terrorism was an effective political weapon in Ecuador during the 1960's. Bombings of churches by the Social Christian paramilitary squads were attributed to the left through falsified propaganda left at the sites. The bombings would be followed by CIA-financed marches and rallies in which speakers would whip up anti-Cuban and anti-Communist emotions in the huge crowds — all in the name of loyalty to the Church. These operations provided the provocation for a military revolt forcing the break in diplomatic relations between Ecuador and Cuba — over the objections of the President at that time, Carlos Julio Arosemena.

The next extract is from *On Company Business*. Richard Helms, former Director of the CIA, is describing the CIA's terrorist campaigns against Cuba in the 1960's when he was Director. Notice what he says in this newsreel footage of his testimony in the United States Congress. He mentions the invasions of Cuba which the CIA was constantly running, and goes on to say:

Under government aegis we had task forces that were striking at Cuba constantly. We were attempting to blow up power plants. We were attempting to ruin sugar mills. We were attempting to do all kinds of things in this period. This was a matter of American Government policy.

And then he goes on to describe some of the CIA's attempts to assassinate Fidel Castro.

The following statements are taken from interviews or newsreel footage of the following people:

David Atlee Phillips: Former Chief of the CIA's Latin American Division (interview)
Richard Helms: Former CIA Director (newsreel footage of testimony in the U.S. House of Representatives)
Representative Dodd: Member of the U.S. House of Representatives (newsreel)
McGeorge Bundy: President Kennedy's Advisor for National Security Affairs (newsreel)
Television reporter: (newsreel)
John McCone: CIA Director during the 1950's (newsreel)
Victor Marchetti: Former CIA official and co-author of *The CIA and the Cult of Intelligence*, Alfred A. Knopf, New York, 1974 (interview)
Robert Maheu: Former FBI Agent and former CIA agent involved in plots to assassinate Castro (newsreel)
Chicago police spokesman: (newsreel)

David Phillips: When the Bay of Pigs failed, of course, I was sitting in the building on that night when everyone knew that it was a failure and Robert Kennedy came in in his shirtsleeves and he had been sent there by his brother to clean that place out. He wanted to find out what had gone wrong. And to do something about it. The result, however, was that Bobby Kennedy fell in love with the concept of clandestine operation. And we now know, there's one question that's not been answered: did President Kennedy and Bobby Kennedy know that there were assassination plans against Fidel Castro. It's an unanswered question. The one thing that I'm absolutely sure of is that not only they knew but they wished for the continuance, in that long period after the Bay of Pigs in which there were many actions taken against Cuba. To put it precisely there was one point when Bobby Kennedy said, "When are you fellows going to get off your bottoms and do something about Fidel Castro?"

Richard Helms: There were found a suit, a wet suit and clam shell, various things that were on the shelf of the agency that were regarded as things that might be used in possibly killing Castro or being used against him, which never came off the shelf, were never used. If that's a plot, to have created this, then I will back up and say that we ought to enumerate every single item that conceivably had to do with the invasions of Cuba which were constantly running. Under the government aegis. We had task forces that were striking at Cuba constantly. We were attempting to blow up power plants. We were attempting to ruin sugar mills. We were attempting to do all kinds of things in this period. This was a matter of American government policy. This wasn't the CIA. If those things taper over into assassination plots, maybe so.

Rep. Dodd: Why didn't you want to tell the Warren Commission, or why didn't you tell the Warren Commission about the efforts to get rid of Fidel Castro or to overthrow the Cuban government?

Richard Helms: Mr. Dodd, you are singling me out as to why I didn't march up and tell the Warren Commission when these operations against Cuba were known to the Attorney General of the United States, the Secretary of Defense, the Secretary of State, the Assistant to the President for National Security Affairs, the President of the United States himself, although he at that point was dead. I mean, all kinds of people knew about these operations high up in the government. Now why am I singled out as the fellow who should have gone up and identified a government operation to get rid of Castro? And it was a government-wide operation, supported by the Defense Department, supported by the National Security Council, supported by almost everybody in high position in the government.

McGeorge Bundy: As far as I ever knew, or know now, no one in the White House, or at the cabinet level, ever gave any approval of any kind to any CIA effort to assassinate anyone. I told the Committee in particular that it is wholly inconsistent with what I know of President Kennedy and his brother Robert that either of them would ever have given any such order or authorization or consent to anyone through any channel.

Reporter: You had been in the agency during the time when most of the allegations of CIA assassination plots occurred. Sir, what did you tell the Commission to your knowledge of the assassination?

John McCone: Well, I had no knowledge of it whatsoever. And as you know I stated that there was a lack of feasibility. There obviously was discussions of the question of whether such matters had been planned, but I had to plead ignorance because none were brought to my attention. And therefore I knew nothing of them.

Victor Marchetti: No president in his right mind is going to say, dear director, I hereby order you to assassinate Fidel Castro. In fact he would probably do the exact opposite. He will issue what is known in the trade as a non-order, or a non-directive. He will say, we are having terrible problems down here in Cuba and it's quite obvious to all of us that the key to us is Fidel Castro. Now if we could get rid of that person maybe we could work out some kind of an arrangement. But, of course, we can't do anything like that, that would be wrong. And I don't know what we are going to do about it. We're just going to have to make the best of it as we go along.

Now he is saying this, say, at a luncheon with McNamara and Rusk and maybe Helms or McCone, or whoever was director, it went over from McCone to Helms. Now these men are astute enough to know that what the president is really telling them is, get rid of Castro. But I am not going to put it in writing and I have already made a statement for the record that I am against it, in the event anything ever goes wrong, I will be able to say, didn't I tell you that would be wrong.

Rep. Dodd: Could you tell this committee who the individuals were involving Mafia chieftains or organized crime?

Richard Helms: As far as I am aware on that particular situation it was William K. Harvey, who was in touch with John Roselli and it was Harvey and Roselli who were attempting to find, if I understood it correctly, some channel from Florida into Havana. Ah, I also understand that there was a question of poison pills which were supposed to be transported to Havana. There was never any evidence that they were transported there or ever left the United States. There was never any evidence that this plot ever left the Florida mainland. And there, if it was an, indeed, an assassination plot it was misadvertised to me, because I understood that it was an effort to see if the connection could be made between the Mafia in Florida and the Mafia in Havana. And to the best of my knowledge, the connection never was made.

Robert Maheu: Some time in 1960, during the period where in some previous years I had been doing work for the CIA, I was approached by my project officer, who asked me if, in connection with a planned invasion in Cuba, I would contact a Mr. John Roselli. We started having meetings in Miami. During one of those meetings in Miami, I was introduced to a Mr. Sam Gold, who subsequently turned out to be Mr. Giancanna.

Victor Marchetti: In any dirty job, such as paramilitary activities, assassinations, sabotage and the like, which were known as special ops, almost invariably the agency, direct involvement of the agency officer, the career officer, ends in the planning stage. And sometimes even before that, just policy, decision-making. The dirty work will be carried out by either contract agents or the one-time agents, gangsters, mercenaries, whoever happens to be, whatever assets are available at that moment.

Robert Maheu: We were entirely, it was important in connection with the invasion of Cuba at that time to dispose of Mr. Castro and to the word dispose you can add anything you want.

Rep. Dodd: It is likely that at the very moment President Kennedy was shot, a CIA officer was meeting with a Cuban agent in Paris and giving him an assassination device to use against Castro. Now I read this, and again I read from the same report that we read from earlier, they're calling it an assassination device. Are we getting semantical here again?

Richard Helms: I believe it was a hypodermic syringe they had given him. It was something called Blackleaf Number 40 and this was in response to AMLASH's request that he be provided with some sort of a device providing he could kill Castro. He returned this device to the case officer and the case officer brought it back to Washington and that was the end of the plot.

Rep. Dodd: OK, but for purposes of discussion, the officer gave this Cuban, this agent in Paris, a device with the material you describe and I presume the material injected into a human being would kill him. Is that correct?

Richard Helms: I would think so, yes.

Rep. Dodd: So the agent gave the Cuban agent this device to kill somebody.

Richard Helms: I'm sorry that he didn't give him a pistol. It would have made the whole thing a whole lot simpler and less exotic.

Rep. Dodd: Well, whether it's a pistol or a needle, if AMLASH is a political plot to destabilize the government, what in blazes are you giving an agent a device that will kill Castro if it's not an assassination plot?

Richard Helms: Well, if you want to have it that way, you just have it that way.

Rep. Dodd: Well, I don't want, it's not what I want . .

Richard Helms: Well, I think it is what you want, Mr. Dodd.

Rep. Dodd: Mr. Helms, I am reading here from reports that were prepared at your request by the Inspector General. I'm not fabricating this, I'm taking it right out of . .

Richard Helms: Oh, I understand that.

Rep. Dodd: I'm quoting.

Richard Helms: I understand that.

Rep. Dodd: But it's not a question of what I want, it's a question of what this committee would like to know, and the committee is not satisfied, I don't believe, at this point, as to exactly what the characterization of AMLASH was.

Richard Helms: Now, I've told you what I believe the characterization of AMLASH to be.

Rep. Dodd: But how does that jive with this?

Richard Helms: If you want, it's because he gave him a gun, or a hypodermic syringe or whatever the case may be at his request because he had aims on Castro, if that is your definition of assassination plot, then have it that way. That's quite satisfactory with me.

Alan Francovich: Don't you open yourself to blackmail? In other words, if you are involved in a covert operation and you're using elements, like for instance the Mafia, in an assassination attempt against Castro, isn't that really a very dangerous thing to get involved in?

David Atlee Phillips: That it is. It's very, very tricky. Um . . the Mafia. Aren't you getting into trouble when you use them during World War II, as we now recently, we used them in New York City. I had only known that we used them in Marseilles on the docks there. Of course it's a tricky business. It's a part of the evaluation that a good intelligence officer and a good policy-maker would make in deciding to use any person or any instrument or any political organization, there's no question. But it's very tricky.

Victor Marchetti: In the setup that the agency has, where the dirty work is done by contact people or one-time hirees and so forth, obviously if anything goes wrong they can be disavowed. If the person turns bad, turns sour, and may want to get out and may possibly have some credibility, and/or evidence, well then stronger action is called for and you can have the ultimate termination of the agent.

Chicago Police spokesman: When the police arrived they found Mr. Giancanna laying on the floor, dead. He had been shot numerous times in the upper part of his body and throat — approximately six shots, believed to be fired from a twenty-two-caliber weapon.

Reporter: Is there anything to support the theory that Giancanna's killing may have been, in some way, connected with his involvement with an alleged CIA plot to assassinate Fidel Castro?

Chicago Police spokesman: We know nothing about that. We have nothing to lead us to believe that at all.

Returning to the current Salvadoran crisis, I have given you a copy of the widely circulated "dissent channel" document written by unidentified U.S. government officials in November 1980. Those who participated in drafting this policy statement — in fact it is an argument against the Carter policy towards El Salvador, and still more, against the Reagan policy — were from the Department of State, Department of Defense, National Security Council, CIA and other agencies active in El Salvador and Central America. The entire document follows because it contains valuable and well-reasoned arguments against escalation of the military conflict and in favor of approaches to a negotiated settlement.

Of particular importance to me, when I first read the "dissent channel" document, was the acknowledgement of U.S. government links to the paramilitary assassination squads in El Salvador, Guatemala and Honduras. Under the heading "Current U.S. Role in El Salvador," i.e., late 1980, and the sub-heading "Strengthening counter-insurgency capabilities of armed forces through:" — the document reports the United States is "seeking to bring under unified command the paramilitary units operating in the country, [and] establishing and/or improving communications and cooperation among armed forces and paramilitary organizations in Guatemala, El Salvador and Honduras."

The U.S. government connection for these activities, though not stated in the document, must surely be the CIA and, perhaps, the Defense Attache's office or the military assistance mission. In any case, if you believe the document is genuine, as I do, then here is the proof that the links exist, and the substance of these relations is obviously guidance and support for really horrendous repression.

I should mention that the Department of State has denounced the "dissent channel" paper as non-official and even as a forgery, following a report by a leading *New York Times* columnist who attached considerable credence and importance to the document. When I first read it, I looked for any sign that it might have been forged. I know the official style from hundreds, maybe thousands, of State Department documents I have read in the past. All the language used in the document seemed appropriate to me, and of those forgeries of Eastern services that I have seen, none would suggest to me that they would be capable of writing a 29-page document like this without at least some errors that would cast doubt on its validity.

Finally, I include excerpts from an interview with Robert White, American Ambassador to El Salvador until he was fired by Reagan in February 1981. In this interview Ambassador White, who certainly read the CIA's intelligence reports, states that Cuban assistance to the Salvadoran revolutionaries is minimal — and he confirms the atrocities of the security services and paramilitary organizations.

Surely Ambassador White would have known of the "captured documents" which at the time of the interview were being surfaced by the Reagan administration through the *New York Times* (de Onis article of February 6, 1981). The Ambassador's statement that "until now Cuban support has not been crucial to the attack capability of the guerrillas" makes a sham of the whole Reagan-Haig campaign against El Salvador. The interview is reprinted from *U.S. News & World Report*, January 26, 1981.

Q: How much are the Cubans and Russians involved in backing the Marxist guerrillas in El Salvador?

White: Whether Cuba existed or not, you would still have a revolutionary situation in El Salvador. Cuba has helped the Salvadoran guerrilla movement with training, propaganda and weapons. But up until now, Cuban support has not been crucial to the attack capability of the guerrillas.

Q: To look briefly at the other side of the civil war in El Salvador: who comprises the right wing and sponsors the right-wing murders?

White: The right wing is a group of extremely rich people, most of whom live in Miami and in Guatemala City. They fund these killings through direct payments to death squads. There has always existed a relationship between this group of extremely rich people and the security forces. Now, the majority of the officer corps has broken with the far right, but there still is a small group that maintains those links and who does the bidding of these people in Miami and Guatemala. The leader of this extreme-right group is a man called Major Robert D'Abuisson, who lives in Guatemala City. He is barred from entering the United States. It is also interesting to note that the first edition of the right-wing San Salvador daily, *El Diario de Hoy*, published after the murder of the two AIFLD officials, gave a totally false version of the killings, designed to exonerate the right and blame the left.

Q: In recent weeks a number of Americans have been murdered in El Salvador — seven, perhaps eight. Who is responsible for these killings?

White: It's impossible to produce proof of culpability for each person killed here. But there is a pattern. Let's just take the last few months: first, the execution of the six leftist leaders in broad daylight on a busy downtown street. A large group of men park their vehicles, go into a Jesuit school, search the premises and walk out again — none is masked or disguised or anything like that. They take the six people away, torture and execute them. Then the case of the four American nuns. The nuns are working with the poor. The poor are obviously the ones who side most with the revolutionaries, because they are desperately poor and desperately want a change. And so certain members of the security forces consider that working with the poor in itself is a revolutionary activity. The nuns are killed, and abundant evidence points to some involvement by the security forces. In the most recent case, we have two men park their car, walk into the lobby of the Sheraton Hotel at 11:30 at night and kill three men who are identified with land reform. Two of them are Americans. The killings were done clearly by professional hit men. Now, if you take that altogether, I don't believe a reasonable man can come up with any other conclusion than that right-wing hit squads enjoy some kind of relationship with some people in the security forces who — at least until now — have given them some kind of immunity.

Q: You're suggesting that the right wing was responsible for killing the Americans?

White: Absolutely. That's exactly what I'm suggesting.

So there you have the points I wish to make today:

First, the historical practice of the U.S. government, through the CIA, in falsifying documentation that will "prove" a particular point like the Soviet or Cuban hand involved in a local revolutionary situation when such proof does not otherwise exist.

The second point was the establishment and use of the American Institute for Free Labor Development over the years as a CIA front, and its current use in El Salvador in the so-called agrarian reform program — as confirmed by the Solicitor General of the United States.

The third point is the CIA's historical connections with the local security services in Latin America and with the paramilitary terrorist and assassination squads, and their connections to these groups in El Salvador today.

A lot more on these topics ought to be coming out in the media right now.

PART 7

CRITIQUE OF STATE DEPARTMENT WHITE PAPER

(Editor's Note: The following analysis is based on a series of interviews and discussions with Philip Agee.)

Getting a copy of the White Paper was not easy. As soon as I heard that the Department of State had distributed it, I telephoned friends in New York and asked them to send a copy. With some difficulty they got one and sent it Air Mail Express on February 26. For days I waited in vain for it to arrive. On March 6, by chance, a friend called from Bonn saying he had a copy of the White Paper and asked if I'd like to see it. The American Embassy, with some reluctance, had loaned it to him for the weekend. After copying it, I began this analysis. Like magic, the copy from New York then arrived, but with the envelope torn apart and the "Express" indication marked out. It was in a Deutsche Bundespost plastic bag for damaged material, although it had been mailed in a heavy manila envelope very carefully and tightly sealed with tape. Two weeks from New York to Hamburg Air Mail Express? A convenient delay somewhere in the postal system? Who knows.

The 180-page White Paper consists of 19 documents said to have been captured by the Salvadoran security forces from the guerrillas, with an analysis prepared by the Department of State, which I will call the Short Analysis (published in the press on February 20). Another analysis, which I will call the Long Analysis (published on February 24), was also prepared by the State Department from the White Paper documents.

Each of the 19 documents consists of a machine copy of the Spanish original (all but 6 typewritten), an English translation, a glossary giving the supposed meanings of names and code words used in the document, and a short introduction describing the document. The Spanish originals total 46 pages, and they vary between one and four pages in length.

My original preoccupation with the circumstances in which these documents were captured was not relieved by reading the White Paper. Nowhere is there any description of how the documents were obtained beyond the simple claim that they were captured from the guerrillas "between November 1980 and January 1981" (the Short Analysis) or "recovered from the Communist Party of El Salvador (PCS) in November 1980 and from the People's Revolutionary Army (ERP) in January 1981" (Long Analysis). In the introductory comments attached to each document, nothing at all is said about whether the document came from the PCS or the ERP. The reader has no idea, when reviewing each document, when it was captured, where, in what battle, from whom, or any of the other circumstances that one would expect to find in the introductory comment.

Initial press reports varied on how the documents were obtained.

Newsweek, for instance, reported on March 2 that "U.S. officials said Salvadorans found many of the papers hidden in the walls of a guerrilla 'safe house' in San Salvador last December and January" — as if they had missed some documents on the first seizure and went back and found more the next month. *Time* reported on March 23 that the Salvadoran National Police found them when raiding "a small grocery store in San Salvador. Hidden behind a hollow wall, they found a plastic garbage bag and a large suitcase, both filled with papers."

In mid-March the State Department surfaced for the Mexico City press a man who said he got the documents from the Salvadoran security forces. He is Jon Glassman, a State Department official who was working in the Political Section of the U.S. Embassy in Mexico City. Glassman said, according to the Mexican daily *Uno Mas Uno* (13 March 1981), that he was sent to El Salvador on January 16 by the then-Assistant Secretary of State for Inter-American Affairs, William Bowdler, to gather information on the quantity and types of weapons the guerrillas were using in the general offensive begun a few days earlier.

In November, Glassman said, the Salvadoran security forces had captured some 20 documents in a gallery belonging to the brother of Shafik Handal, Secretary General of the PCS. The Salvadorans gave these documents to the U.S. Military Attache in San Salvador, who sent them to the Pentagon for analysis. (These would be the documents captured, according to the White Paper, from the PCS in November.)

Glassman met with the Minister of Defense and the Army General Staff who gave him copies of the November documents.

I could see in them promises but not fulfillment of arms shipments. I could see the thing in terms of rifles, but not global quantities. I thought that other security bodies could have recent captures of documents or also captures that they might not have given to the General Staff. I went to the National Guard, the Treasury Police and the National Police.

At the National Police, according to *Uno Mas Uno*, Glassman learned that on January 9 or 10 various "safe houses" of the ERP had been discovered and that in one of them a plastic bag containing some eighty documents had been captured.

Back at the Embassy, Glassman studied the documents, concluded that code words such as "Esmeralda" meant Cuba and "Lagos" meant Nicaragua and that both were transshipping points for arms to El Salvador. Returning to the Minister of Defense, Glassman reported his dramatic discovery and asked the Minister to review his files for any more captured documents. "Then the General Staff looked and found about ten documents that they hadn't given to me before." In that packet Glassman found what he considered to be a direct connection between the guerrillas and the Cuban Department of Special Operations.

There are several problems with Glassman's story. First, the CIA and Military Attache offices in the American Embassy in San Salvador are surely in daily contact with the security and military people whom Glassman visited and who "captured" the documents. These CIA and military officers would have to be plain fools not to understand the importance of the documents and to exploit them the moment they were "captured." This is especially so for one document, from the November seizure, sent by the Military Attache to Washington, that purports to describe an extremely successful trip of the PCS Secretary General to Vietnam, Ethiopia, Cuba and the socialist countries of Europe. This one document alone, if legitimate, would unquestionably have been published by the Salvadorans and the vast U.S. propaganda apparatus.

If you believe the Glassman story, no one in San Salvador or Washington did anything with the sensational November "capture" until February, after the fortuitous Glassman trip to El Salvador in January. This failure to act, when taken with Glassman's account of being sent to El Salvador to do just what CIA officers would have been doing continuously for years, and then being handed the "ERP documents" just days after they were "captured," then getting the additional ten documents that "prove" the Cuban connection — all this strains the imagination.

The Salvadorans may well have captured some documents, but the most sensational in this White Paper are, I believe, fabricated — including the arms shopping report and one showing a guerrilla link with the Cuban Department of Special Operations. Keeping in mind that the CIA is perfectly capable of fabricating documents, my belief is that fabricated documents were inserted with the genuine ones, probably with cooperation from Salvadoran security officials. Glassman may then have been sent to San Salvador to "find" the treasure that the CIA had prepared.

Such an operation would be nothing new for the CIA, as I have shown from cases I knew of, and participated in, in the 1960's. As I will show, most of the names of the guerrilla leaders were known publicly, and important events, such as unity agreements among the guerrilla organizations, were published by the guerrillas through communiques at the time they occurred. It was left for the CIA to "prove" the links with Cuba, Nicaragua, the Soviet Union and other socialist countries through falsification of documents. Only then, having "proved foreign intervention," could Washington justify increased support for the repressive Salvadoran junta, sending military "advisors," and eventually combat troops if needed, in order to change the outcome of a liberation struggle that the guerrillas were winning — and, in spite of U.S. intervention — will likely win in the end.

The continued absence of specific information regarding the circumstances of capture renders all the documentation highly suspect from an analyst's point of view. It goes without saying that if one is going to build a case on captured documents, as clearly the U.S. government is trying to do, the circumstances of capture should be the very first information on which to base their authenticity. Thus the reader must take on absolute faith the White Paper's claim that "United States Government analysts assess the documents as fully genuine." What analysts? The White Paper doesn't say.

Other problems undermining the White Paper involve errors in translations. Certain documents are described as "excerpts" and include no name of writer or date in the Spanish original. Yet the introductory remarks to these documents includes names of authors and dates. Other problems involve unsupported suppositions, e.g., that a certain "Simon" mentioned in several documents is the code name of Shafik Handal, the PCS Secretary General. Still more damaging are statements in the State Department analyses that find no support whatsoever in the documents.

We should remember that the 46 pages of Spanish originals are acknowledged in the Short Analysis as "only a very small portion of the total documents recovered." However, the Long Analysis attributes the White Paper findings to "this mass of captured documents." The U.S. press backed up the State Department's emphasis on "mass," describing the "captured" documents as a "bale of battle plans, letters and other documents" (*Newsweek*, March 2), and "an 18-inch high stack of documents" (*Time*, March 9). *The New York Times*, for its part, reported from Paris that the diplomatic mission headed by Lawrence Eagleburger, Assistant Secretary of State for European Affairs, presented 16 pounds of evidence to officials in the various European capitals they visited.

Nowhere in the U.S. press have I seen a word of skepticism concerning the authenticity of these documents, despite the CIA's long history of falsifying documents for similar purposes, which I described at my press conference on February 20 — almost none of which, as far as I know, was carried in principal newspapers in the United States. *Time*, on March 9, went so far as to say "hardly anyone outside the communist world seemed to question the report." If the editors of *Time* had been reading the Mexico City press and, I would expect, the press of many other capitals, they would have found many responsible journalists questioning the authenticity of these documents. I can think of no other reason for Glassman's unusual press interview in Mexico City to defend the White Paper.

Curiously, the White Paper does not contain one of the two "captured documents" on which Juan de Onis relied for his February 6 *New York Times* article. The missing document supposedly showed agreement by the ruling party of Mexico, the PRI, to give considerable political support to the Salvadoran revolutionary movement. The Mexicans, as one would expect, made a stinging denunciation of American foreign policy along with their denial. That strong reaction may have caused the State Department officials to omit that document from the White Paper after they had originally surfaced it through de Onis.

I believe that after considering my critique of the White Paper, it will be easy to conclude with me that: (1) The State Department's analyses are not supported in important places by the original documents; (2) The State Department's analyses are inaccurate and sloppy; (3) The State Department, by distortions and inventions, has made the White Paper a propaganda exercise rather than a statement of facts; and (4) at least some of the documents appear to have been falsified.

In analyzing the White Paper it is necessary to compare the original documents in Spanish, first with the English translation, and then with the interpretations given in the Short and the Long analyses. By way of general observations, before discussing the documents and the chronology of events as presented in the analyses, I want to mention two items: first, the Long Analysis mentions in several places that the Soviet Union was behind military support for the Salvadoran liberation movement.

This special report presents definitive evidence of the clandestine military support given by the Soviet Union.

The situation in El Salvador presents a strikingly familiar case of Soviet, Cuban and other Communist military involvement in a politically troubled Third World country. By providing arms, training, and direction to a local insurgency. . . .

In all of the documents, even if you believe them, the only support actually given by the Soviet Union was an airline ticket for the PCS Secretary General from Moscow to Hanoi. The only other specific Soviet support mentioned in the documents was an agreement in principle to give military training to thirty Salvadoran communists who were studying in the USSR in 1980, but there is no evidence the training actually took place. Both the Short and the Long analyses mention that the Soviets agreed in principle to provide air transport for 60 tons of weapons from Vietnam, and this appears in Document E. However, the analyses fail to mention that this "agreement in principle" would have to be approved by higher authority. Moreover, according to the document, the final approval for air transport was not given, and the Cubans (more on this below) decided to bring the arms from Vietnam by ship. Document E shows that on July 22, the Soviets turned down a request for arms by the Salvadoran guerrilla leaders in May, but the rejection is overlooked in the analyses. There is absolutely no other evidence in the documents of Soviet support to the Salvadoran guerrillas unless you believe that Soviets were behind support given to the Salvadorans by Cuba, Nicaragua and socialist countries — and this is not said in the documents.

My second observation is that the State Department's Long Analysis alleges that of some 800 tons of weapons promised by socialist countries to the Salvadoran guerrillas, nearly 200 tons of those arms were actually delivered secretly to El Salvador. Nowhere in the documents is it established that 200 tons actually arrived in El Salvador.

Another distortion in the introductory section of the Long Analysis relates to the Communist Party of El Salvador. The analysis states:

El Salvador's extreme left, which includes the long-established Communist Party of El Salvador and several armed groups of more recent origin, has become increasingly committed since 1976 to a military solution. A campaign of terrorism — bombings, assassinations, kidnappings, and seizures of embassies — has disrupted national life and claimed the lives of many innocent people.

In actual fact the PCS did not opt for armed struggle until its Seventh Congress in April 1979 (interview with Shafik Handal, PCS Secretary General in *Granma*, Havana, June 1, 1980). Moreover, PCS members held high positions in the Salvadoran government from the overthrow of the Romero regime in October 1979 until early January 1980. Thus it is highly inaccurate to imply that the PCS was committed to a military solution since 1976.

Other glaring inaccuracies can be found in the Long Analysis. For example:

During 1980, previously fragmented factions of the extreme left agreed to coordinate actions in support of a joint military battle plan developed with Cuban assistance. As a precondition for large-scale Cuban aid, Salvadoran guerrilla leaders, meeting in Havana in May, formed first the Unified Revolutionary Directorate (DRU) as their central executive arm for political and military planning and, in late 1980, the Farabundo Marti People's Liberation Front (FMLN), as the coordinating body of the guerrilla organizations. A front organization, the Revolutionary Democratic Front (FDR), was also created to disseminate propaganda abroad. For appearances sake, three small non-Marxist-Leninist political parties were brought into the front, though they have no representation in the DRU.

The documents contain no suggestion that coordination achieved by the guerrilla organizations through their unity agreement was a "precondition for large-scale Cuban aid."

Concerning the Revolutionary Democratic Front (FDR), the Long Analysis states:

Three small non-Marxist-Leninist political parties – including a Social Democratic Party – work with guerrilla organizations and their political fronts through the Democratic Revolutionary Front (FDR), most of whose activities take place outside El Salvador.

The fact is that the FDR was established in April 1980 at a rally attended by approximately 100,000 people, according to the highly respected *Latin America Weekly Report* of April 25 and other press reports. Some 50 different organizations joined the FDR, including the University of El Salvador and the Central America University, along with trade unions and political organizations affiliated with the guerrilla groups. It is no news that inside El Salvador the FDR's work has been difficult, what with savage repression of opposition political activities by Salvadoran security forces and the paramilitary assassination squads, culminating with the murders of the entire FDR leadership in San Salvador in late November 1980. With this kind of repression and martial law in effect since the FDR was formed, it is easy to understand how dangerous operating in El Salvador must be. But it is a gross distortion for the State Department to imply that the FDR, which preceded the DRU, was a creation of the guerrilla organizations. The three non-Marxist political parties that joined the FDR hardly joined for "appearances sake" when you realize that every one of their members was facing assassination because of FDR membership.

The White Paper then describes "a chronology of events" beginning in December 1979, but it is careful to add that, in addition to the White Paper documents, other information from other sources has also helped to fill out the chronology. What this "other evidence" and "other sources" are is left to the reader of the White Paper to imagine. But the deficiencies of the analyses, only as directly relating to the documents, are sufficient to destroy the White Paper as a whole.

The chronology begins with Document A, which is said to be a copy of a typed letter written in Havana on December 16, 1979, to Fidel Castro and signed by: Shafik Handal for the PCS; D. Fuentes, as First Political-Military Officer of the Armed Forces of National Resistance (FARN); and by Marcial, as First Responsible for the People's Liberation Forces (FPL). For the State Department analysis, the importance of this letter lies in the thanks given by the guerrilla leaders both to Castro and the Communist Party of Cuba for their help and influence in bringing the guerrilla organizations to an agreement whereby they would operate in unity and coordination. (Previously the three groups operated separately, which was a source of overall weakness.) The clear implication in the letter is that the three guerrilla organizations owed their unity to enlightenment by the Cubans, which the State Department interprets as the beginning of "external support."

I believe this document is a fabrication. The unity agreement reached in December 1979 among the three guerrilla organizations became public knowledge when they formed the Political-Military Coordinating Body (CPM) in January 1980 in El Salvador. The glossary attached to this document fails to mention (although other glossaries do) that "Marcial" is the well-known nom de guerre of Salvador Cayetano Carpio, the leader of the FPL. Notice, for what will come later, that Handal signs this document in his true name and not with a nom de guerre. As for D. Fuentes, who supposedly signed for the FARN (also known as RN) the translation has a question mark after D. Fuentes, presumably to indicate that the Department of State does not know who he is. I have learned from the FDR representative in Paris that the name of the First Political-Military Officer of the RN in December 1979 was Ernesto Jovel, that his position was well known publicly, and that his nom de guerre was "Neto." In September 1980 Jovel was killed in an air crash, and we will see his nom de guerre in Document H as "Neto." The FDR representative told me that there is no known "D. Fuentes" in the RN leadership, either as true name or nom de guerre. And obviously, Jovel would have signed the letter "Neto" if not in his true name.

In my research, I found no indication that any of the three men was in Havana in December 1979 or that any agreement among their organizations was reached there.

My feeling that this document is falsified is also based on the way the writers, who lead organizations long involved in struggles against each other as well as against the Salvadoran government, acknowledge an apparently sudden enlightenment by Fidel Castro and the Cuban Communist Party as what enabled them to overcome their long and debilitating divisions. Handal, in the *Granma* interview, attributed their December 1979 unity agreement to the successful example of the Nicaraguan Sandinistas, who overcame their differences and went on to defeat Somoza. In addition, the second paragraph addresses Castro as "companero, hermano, y amigo." In language usage among revolutionaries in Latin America, "companero" is normal, but in such a formal letter "hermano" and "amigo" would not be used. "Hermano" is a term too familiar and informal for a letter of this kind. "Amigo" is still worse, because among revolutionaries the word "amigo" is used to refer to non-revolutionaries who sympathize with revolutionary movements and sometimes give them their support. Latin American revolutionaries told me that Fidel Castro would never be addressed as "amigo."

Another question arising from this document is that the writers say they are attaching a copy of their agreement. The State Department analyst gives no reason why the attached agreement is not included in the White Paper, or whether it was with the copy when it was "captured." One would think that the unity agreement would be even more important than the letter itself. Finally, one must assume that the "captured" copy of the letter was a carbon copy retained by one of the three men who signed it. And one might expect that only the original that went to Fidel Castro would have been signed by all three men, with the copy retained by one of the three having only the signatures of the other two. For example, if this were Handal's copy it would only have the signatures of Fuentes and Marcial — although I admit this reasoning is highly speculative.

The White Paper chronology goes on to Document B, which is two pages of hand-written notes. The analyst says these are notes on a trip to Mexico by a member of the Political Commission of the PCS named "Logan" and dated April 26, 1980. However, the document itself contains no indication of a trip to Mexico, or that the notes were written by "Logan" or that he is a member of the PCS Political Commission. Nor is there any date on the document.

As to content, this document's importance for the White Paper analyses is that one note says that "petitions" were presented to representatives of East Germany, Bulgaria, Poland, Vietnam, Hungary and Cuba at a meeting in the Hungarian Embassy. The State Department's Short Analysis translates "petitions" as "requests," adding "presumably for arms." Both analyses say that the USSR was also at this meeting, but the document does not show them present. The document says that later on there was a meeting with a Soviet. There is no indication that the meeting was held in Mexico City as stated in the analyses. Moreover, a telephone call to the Mexican Consulate in Hamburg revealed that Vietnam does not even have an embassy or diplomatic representation in Mexico City. This meeting, if it did occur, must have been in some country other than Mexico.

There are other errors in the translation of this document. There is a sentence translated "They talked about the advantage of mentioning everything to David" when in fact the original Spanish translates as "They talked about the advantage of talking over everything in David." This probably refers to the city David, Panama, and not to someone named "David." Another bad translation is in the middle of the second page of the document, where a phrase is translated "they want to agree on a party 'Perl.'" In the glossary to this document "Perl" is said to mean "Perla-Cuba" (Cuba is known as the Pearl of the Antilles). However, it is clear that the Spanish notes say "They want to agree from party to party." Finally, there is no comment in the analyses that the bottom line of the first page of the notes and the bottom three lines of the second page of the notes seem to have been written by a second person. The document could have been written by anyone, and its interpretation in the White Paper suffers from invention, poor analysis and poor translation.

The White Paper chronology continues with Document C, two pages of handwritten notes. The analyses say that these notes were written by PCS Secretary General Shafik Handal at a meeting of the PCS Political Commission on April 28, 1980. We must again take much on faith because nowhere in the document is there any mention of a meeting of the Political Commission, nor is any date contained in the two pages of notes, nor is there any mention of Handal (or his supposed nom de guerre, "Simon"). In fact, in looking at the notes it seems that the last third, or half, of the second page was written by someone other than the person who wrote the first page and half of the second. There are two very different handwritings involved in these notes.

The importance of Document C, by attributing these notes to Handal, is the connection shown between the PCS and Cuba and other socialist countries. The Long Analysis emphasized the following extract from these notes:

Speed up reorganization and put the party on a war footing.

But the Spanish notes do not say "war footing" but "estado de pelea," which if literally translated would mean "a state of quarrel, dispute or struggle." If the writer of these notes had meant a "war footing" he would have written "estado de guerra." But the propagandist who wrote the analysis could not resist exaggerating. After "war footing" the analysis proceeds:

He added, I'm in agreement with taking advantage of the possibilities of assistance of the socialist camp. I think their attitude is magnificent. We are not yet taking advantage of it.

In fact the person who wrote the notes did *not* add that statement after having mentioned putting the party in a state of struggle, because this last statement appears in the notes *before* the mention of putting the party in a state of struggle. In addition, the original notes say "we are not taking advantage of it." There is no "yet" in the original notes, but by adding the "yet" the analyst adds an element of probability to the "possibilities" mentioned by the writer.

The Long Analysis goes on:

In reference to a unification of the armed movement, he asserts that the idea of involving everyone in the area has already been suggested to Fidel himself.

The Short Analysis, however, converts the suggestion to Fidel to "as suggested *by* Fidel." Moreover, there is no indication in the notes that the person writing was referring to "unification of the armed movement."

The Analysis goes on:

Handal alludes to the concept of unification and notes "Fidel thought well of the idea."

In the notes themselves, the unification question related to the trade union movement and joint regional political action, not to the military struggle.

The matter of armed struggle is in fact mentioned at the beginning of these notes: "We have created the FAL," i.e., the Armed Forces of Liberation, which is the PCS military wing. According to my research the PCS did not form the FAL until the summer of 1980, long after the supposed April date of these notes. Also, the names "Felipe" and "Rene" contained in the notes are said in the glossary to mean "The People's Liberation Forces — FPL" (Felipe) and "National Resistance — RN" (Rene). There is no clue in the notes or in the analyses how anyone came to believe these names were code words for the two guerrilla organizations. In later documents both names appear again and are not said in glossaries to mean either of the two organizations. One might expect that if Handal was writing these notes and mentioned FAL as such, he would also have mentioned FPL and RN in that form rather than with code words, or to be consistent he would have used a code word for the FAL.

The next part of the chronology is based on Document D, which is said to be a report by an unidentified "Eduardo" on a trip from May 5 to June 8, 1980. He went to Honduras, Guatemala, Costa Rica, Cuba, Nicaragua, back to Costa Rica and back to Honduras before returning to El Salvador. The trip dates are contained in the document, but the White Paper introductory comment identifies "Eduardo" as a member of the PCS "Political Commission." Nowhere in the document is he so identified, and the introductory comment fails to give his last name or any other identifying information.

The importance of this document for the White Paper is that it supposedly shows the leaders of the PCS, the RN, the FPL and the People's Revolutionary Army (ERP) meeting together in Havana to form a new unified guerrilla command called the Unified Revolutionary Directorate (DRU). The document also shows the leaders meeting three times with Fidel Castro, twice with the Directorate of Special Operations of the Cuban Ministry of the Interior (DOE), once with a member of the Cuban Department of Analysis and once with the Cuban Chief of Communications. These meetings, according to the document, took place in Havana between May 19 and June 1, 1980. Besides pointing out the importance of the entry of the ERP into the already existing coalition of the other three guerrilla organizations, the White Paper analyses emphasize the Cuban assistance in framing the guerrillas' military plans and in communications support.

There are several reasons why I believe this document is falsified. I should point out that the ERP did join the other three organizations in May 1980, and together they established the Unified Revolutionary Directorate (DRU). They put out their own communique announcing the formation of the DRU in San Salvador on June 17. (See text in *El Dia*, Mexico City, June 19 and 20; also *Granma*, Havana, June 29.) In the communique the guerrillas mentioned their earlier unity agreement of December 1979, and they gave May 22 as the date of the latest unity agreement and formation of the DRU. The "captured" document, however, shows the date of the unity agreement as May 21.

The document mentions that the first meeting with Castro took place in the "Palace." But Castro's office is not in a building called the "Palace." His office is in the building housing the Central Committee of the Communist Party of Cuba, which is referred to as the "sede" (seat) of the Central Committee or of the Party. But never as the "Palace." The meeting might have occurred in the Palace of the Revolution (a museum), where Castro sometimes receives visitors, but the meeting is an "interview" according to the document, and not a reception. In this supposed meeting the document notes that there was filming and photography. There was also a press conference of the leaders one week later on May 31. Keeping in mind that this unity agreement was extremely important, you would think that the press conference would have been reported. In a review of the Cuban and other Latin American press, as well as *Latin America Political Report* (published in London), I found no report at all of any Salvadoran unity meeting in Havana or of any press conference by Salvadoran leaders on May 31. The first press reports on the unity meeting appeared in mid-June when the DRU issued its own communique in San Salvador.

The document also shows a "courtesy visit" by Castro to the guerrilla leaders the day after their first interview with him. Then the document shows another visit from Castro to the guerrillas (wherever they were) for the signing of the unity documents. If one believes this document, one gets the impression that Castro was shepherding and supervising the entire unity process. Yet according to the document, the agreement among the four organizations resulted from just two days' conversations (20 and 21 May) with the implication that the guerrilla leaders came to Havana simply to sign the unity document. Although Document D is effective, if you believe it, in establishing the Cuban tutelary role in the unity process, it is doubtful that the four guerrilla leaders would travel to Havana to formalize their agreement. Obviously, they could reach their agreements and formalize them in El Salvador itself. If they needed more secure conditions for discussions, these were no doubt available in Nicaragua, a lot closer to home than Havana.

There are other problems with this document. For example, the name "Rene" is again interpreted in the glossary as a code word for the RN guerrilla organization. Before "Rene" is mentioned, however, the RN is mentioned by those letters, RN. Although the document may be an informal outline of these meetings, one would assume that if it was important enough in one part of the report to use the code word, the writer would not have used the true initials. The glossary also interprets the name "Hercules" as a code word standing for the ERP guerrilla organization, and in the entry under May 21 the report notes the "incorporation of the Hercules." The very next entry notes the "entry of E." E would probably mean the ERP, although this is not in the glossary. But again, why would a member of the PCS Political Commission use a code word on one line of the report and the letter signifying the true name of the same organization on the next line?

The report also mentions two meetings of the guerrilla leaders in Havana with one "Humberto" and later a supper in "Humberto's house" in

Managua after the meetings in Havana. The glossary says that "Humberto" is Humberto Ortega, the leader of the Sandinistas, without giving any support for this interpretation. An entry in the report also mentions a trip by "Simon" on May 30 without saying where he went. The glossary again interprets, without giving reasons, "Simon" as the code name for Shafik Handal, the PCS Secretary General. The document also mentions a meeting with "Felipe," but the Document D glossary gives no explanation for what "Felipe" means, whereas in Document C "Felipe" supposedly is a code word for the FPL (People's Liberation Forces). While the analyst seems clever enough to interpret "Rene," "Hercules" and "Simon" as code words, nothing is said of such other names appearing in the same report as "Eduardo," "Aldana," "J.J.," "Ron," "Manuel," "German," "Aurelio," "Orlando," "Vladimir," "Carmen," "Ovidio," "Hugo," "Luis Enrique," "Jose" and "Benito." The analyst also interprets "toy market" as "weapons market" without explaining why. Another odd thing about this document is that of "Eduardo's" seven stops on a month-long trip, the only dates given are for the time spent in Havana.

Discrepancies in the analyses also exist. For example, in the Short Analysis, in reference to the Salvadoran's meeting in Havana with "Humberto," the analyst writes:

One "Humberto" is also present and consulted on unity arrangements.

In fact there is no indication whatsoever in the document that the meeting in Havana with "Humberto" had anything to do with consultations on "unity arrangements." The Long Analysis, in referring to this document, begins:

From May 5 to June 8, 1980, Salvadoran guerrilla leaders report on meetings in Honduras, Guatemala, Costa Rica and Nicaragua.

In fact the document does not say that they were reporting on meetings during that one-month period. Rather the document is supposedly the report of *one* presumed PCS leader who travelled to those countries during that period.

The document has several errors in translation, such as the courtesy visit by Castro to the guerrillas (original Spanish) translated as a courtesy visit by the guerrillas to Castro. Finally, as one might expect the author of this document to round out his fantasy, the guerrillas supposedly met in Managua, after their trip to Havana, with representatives of the German Democratic Republic and the USSR, while also arranging a secure Managua headquarters and getting other types of support from the Sandinista government. The supposed departure of Handal ("Simon") from Havana on May 30 serves as a tie to the next document as the White Paper chronology continues.

Document E is the first one surfaced through Juan de Onis and the *New York Times* on February 6, 1981. This is probably the most important document of all, and there are good reasons to believe that it was falsified.

The document is supposedly a four-page typewritten report of a trip by a Salvadoran guerrilla leader during June, July and August 1981 to the USSR, Vietnam, Ethiopia, the German Democratic Republic, Czechoslovakia, Hungary, Bulgaria and Cuba. The report shows the numbers and types of weapons and other military support obtained by the Salvadoran guerrilla leader on his trip. The White Paper analyst, without giving reasons, says that the guerrilla leader who made the trip is Shafik Handal, the PCS Secretary General. The code word "Simon" is not in this document, nor is Handal's name.

In the White Paper introduction to Document E, the analyst erroneously writes that the trip was from June 9 to July 3, whereas the report itself shows the Salvadoran first meeting with a Soviet in Moscow on June 2. He flies from Moscow to Havana on July 23 and stays there until August 5. On July 3, when the analyst believes the trip has ended, the Salvadoran arrives in Ethiopia.

Another error in the Long Analysis has the Salvadoran meeting "again" in Moscow on July 22 with Mikhail Kudachkim of the CPSU Central Committee. The Salvadoran had, according to the document, met with Kudachkim the month before, but the July 22 meeting was with a CPSU official named Brutents, not with Kudachkim.

As a first comment on Document E, I find it very hard to believe that an experienced political leader, who has lived for many years under great repression in El Salvador, would take a report such as this back to El Salvador, where the danger would be great that the document would be captured. However, my belief that this is falsified is based on something the State Department analyst failed to mention either through inattention or on purpose.

This document, although not seen as such by the White Paper analyst, is written as though it were an internal Cuban government report on the Salvadoran's trip. The entire report is written in the third person when referring to the traveller, i.e., the traveller is referred to as "the comrade" who travelled here and there and spoke with this and that person. However, the writer of this report also mentions "our," and it is quite clear that he means "Cuban." For example, when discussing the transportation of arms from Vietnam, the report states that the "comrade" requested air transport from the Soviet Communist Party — which failed to give a reply other than that they agreed "in principle." Then the report says:

In the (USSR) Embassy here (Cuba) on July 28, (the comrade) requested that a cable be sent urging a reply (about the air transportation of arms), and on August 5, before leaving here, it had not arrived, which was communicated to the Ambassador of V. (Vietnam) together with *our* decision to bring it by ship.

The report goes on to observe that if a favorable reply arrives concerning air transportation, they would take advantage of it, but that it would require "our coordination with the V." Further along, in discussing the arms supposedly promised by Ethiopia, the report reads that the Ethiopian support was "confirmed through a cable from our embassy there," and adds "the same cable says this cargo would leave in *our* ship on August 5."

Clearly "our embassy" can only refer to the Cuban Embassy in Addis Ababa, since the PCS has no embassies. Even if "our embassy" means the PCS representative in Ethiopia, the word "representative" would be used, and not "embassy." Moreover, the PCS has no ships capable of carrying tons of weapons across the oceans from Ethiopia and Vietnam.

I found it interesting that of only two paragraphs of the 19 documents that were not translated in the English versions, one was the lines quoted above: "The same cable that says that this cargo would leave on our ship on August 5." It is possible that the analyst was confused over "our ship" and decided to leave these lines out of the translation thinking that no one would read the originals carefully. But in the end, one cannot escape the fact that this document was written to appear to be an internal Cuban report on the Salvadoran's trip, based on conversations with the Salvadoran after he returned to Havana — presumably a report prepared for use in the Department of Special Operations of the Cuban Ministry of the Interior.

Now one has to ask oneself the question of why the Cubans would have given Handal a copy of their internal report giving the details of his trip and types and quantities of all the pistols, mortars, ammunition, rocket launchers and other military equipment, when Handal already had the information, having given it to the Cubans for this report. It is also clear that this report would have been written after "the comrade" left Havana, presumably to return to El Salvador. This is seen in the reference quoted above, "August 5, before leaving here," which clearly shows that the information would have been obtained in conversations with the Salvadoran, who then left Havana before the Cuban official wrote this report from his notes or from a tape recording of the conversations. Thus there would have been no way for the Salvadoran to carry the report with him on his departure from Havana. The entire report, then, is a poorly conceived fantasy that attempts too hard to demonstrate military support from too many countries.

I cannot understand why the White Paper analyst and Juan de Onis failed to understand that this was meant to be an internal Cuban report, except that if they had described it as such, they would have been unable to explain how the report could have made its way to a "document cache" in El Salvador.

This document also raises the question of whether the U.S. government ever got copies of the original "captured" documents or worked from machine copies of them. The White Paper does not clarify this point. However, the translation of Document E contains the translator's comment in parentheses in the Bulgaria section: "numerals cut off at the edge of page." I would conclude from this that the translator worked only with a machine copy, as contained in the White Paper itself, and the State Department analysts may well have had only copies. If so, what happened to the originals and, if they were available, why didn't the translator refer to the original of this page in order to complete the translation rather than being satisfied with translating a document that was laid badly onto the copy machine? One should recall that the Short Analysis contains the affirmation that "U.S. government analysts assess the documents as fully genuine."

This is indeed a farfetched claim if, as Document E suggests, the analysts never saw originals.

There are other reasons why such an arms shopping trip by Handal would be unlikely. In the first place, Handal was only just beginning to set up a PCS military arm. The PCS's reluctance to enter the armed struggle until 1979 was the very reason many members left the party and joined active guerrilla groups. Other guerrilla leaders, some with as much as ten years experience in military operations, were parties to the May unity agreement. From the way Document E reads, "the comrade" made the trip by himself. Handal is not a military man. Thus the other guerrilla leaders in the May unity agreement surely would have insisted that one of them make the shopping trip, or at least accompany Handal — rather than dispatching Handal alone just a few days after the agreement to search for mortars and rockets and other sophisticated weaponry that he didn't know anything about. That Handal made this trip is even more unlikely, considering past resentments of the other guerrilla groups toward the PCS, when you take the CIA's estimate of PCS membership in 1980 (*National Basic Intelligence Factbook*) of 220-225 people — compared with the CIA's estimate of the other organizations: "more than 2000 members." Surely other leaders, representing guerrillas in action, and knowing military equipment needs, would have made the shopping trip rather than the leader of 225 latecomers to the armed struggle. And if you believe Document C as Handal's notes, you find that just a month before this shopping trip began, Handal's military group (the FAL) hadn't even gone into action.

If Document E concerning Handal's arms shopping trip is falsified, then Document F must also be falsified. This is supposedly a report listing the same quantities of armaments and other military equipment from Vietnam, Ethiopia and other socialist countries. It is signed by "Ana-Maria" who, in the glossary of this document and several others, is said to be in reality Ana Guadalupe Martinez, a well-known leader of the ERP guerrilla organization. The White Paper introduction to this document says that it is a report on a meeting of the DRU on September 30, 1980, but the document is dated September 1, 1980, not September 30. There is nothing in the report that suggests that it is a report on a meeting of the DRU, nor is there any evidence that "Ana-Maria" is the nom de guerre of Ana Guadalupe Martinez. Moreover, at the end of this document before the name "Ana-Maria" the report ends with "The Political Commission of COCEN," and in the glossary COCEN is said to mean Central Committee. The analyst has converted "Political Commission of the Central Committee" to the "Unified Revolutionary Directorate (DRU)." The political catchword or slogan then used by the DRU ("United to combat until the Final Victory") is nowhere to be found in this document.

There is another reason to doubt the authenticity of this document. It seems to have been so badly fabricated that the person who faked it was confused over the revolutionary slogans of the four guerrilla organizations. At the end of this document the writer has put "Revolution or Death! the People Armed Will Win!" Under the slogan comes the name "Ana-Maria."

If "Ana-Maria" is indeed the ERP leader Ana Guadalupe Martinez, she would never have put the slogan "Revolution or Death! the People Armed Will Win!" because this is not the slogan of the ERP. This slogan is the slogan used by the Popular Liberation Forces (FPL), whereas the ERP slogan is "Struggle to Win or to Die." It is inconceivable that a leader of the ERP, even if working within the Unified Revolutionary Directorate, would attach the slogan of a rival guerrilla organization to one of her own reports. Anyone who wants to check the slogans of the four guerrilla organizations can find them at the end of the joint communique released by the DRU in June 1980 and published in the weekly edition of *Granma* in Havana on June 29, 1980, and in *El Dia*, Mexico City, June 19 and 20, 1980. You can also find the DRU slogan at the end of the same communique.

Another problem with Document F is that in transferring the information from Document E, an error in dates was made. According to Document E, the weapons from Vietnam would be ready for shipment during the first five days of September, whereas in Document F it says that on September 5 they will be in "Esmeralda" (said by the White Paper analyst to mean Cuba). Also, it is clear following the listing of weapons coming from Vietnam that the person typing the report began the listing for what was coming from Ethiopia and then went back and inserted under the Vietnam section — but on the same line as "Ethiopia" — the words "60 tons." If the typist had put "60 tons" before beginning the "Ethiopia" section, the two items would not be on the same line. It appears that the typist inserted the "60 tons" for emphasis, after having finished the report, or having gone on to the section on "Ethiopia." Also, the typist of Document F changed the date of departure for Cuba of the Ethiopian shipment from August 5 to August 15.

The White Paper's Long Analysis continues with Document G, a description of a visit by leaders of the Salvadoran guerrillas to Nicaragua, where they supposedly met with one of the leaders of the Sandinista Front. According to the Spanish original (and also the translation), the visiting Salvadorans were the Joint General Staff for military operations (Estado Major General Conjunto — EMGC). The Short Analysis properly reflects the positions of these visitors. The Long Analysis, however, says that the visitors were "representatives of the DRU." Anyone who reads the original document, or its translation for that matter, can see that the EMGC is a different group from the DRU. The person who wrote the Long Analysis simply got the two organizations confused. Analyst's confusion aside, however, the importance of this document for the White Paper is that it supposedly shows that the Sandinistas agreed to give U.S.-manufactured weapons of their own, and that these would be replaced with weapons manufactured in communist countries when they arrived in shipments bound for the Salvadorans. One of the weaknesses of this document is that in none of the others was there any commitment by a communist country to supply weapons of its own manufacture — with the sole exception of a vague Czech commitment in Document E. But in the Long Analysis emphasis is given to a deliberate effort to supply the Salvadoran guerrillas only with weapons of U.S. manufacture, i.e., those from Ethiopia and Vietnam.

There are other problems with Document G. For example, the Long Analysis says that the Salvadoran guerrilla leaders "complain that the Sandinistas appear to be restricting their access to visiting world dignitaries." (The trip was during the celebrations of the first anniversary of the overthrow of Somoza.) What is actually said in the original document, and also in the translation, is that the EMGC met with DRU representatives who were already in Managua before the EMGC arrival. During this conversation the DRU representatives said that the Sandinistas required them to coordinate their visits to Embassies and different organizations — something quite different from "restricting access to visiting world dignitaries." The Long Analysis also says that Bayardo Arce, the Sandinista leader with whom they met, arranged a meeting for them with the Sandinista military commission. In fact, in the report Arce simply tells the EMGC that the meeting with the military commission had already been agreed.

The Long Analysis, referring to Document G, also has an outright fabrication. It says:

> The DRU representatives also meet with visiting Palestine Liberation Organization leader Yasir Arafat in Managua on July 22, 1980. Arafat promises military equipment, including arms and aircraft.

In Document G the EMGC does note that it had a meeting with Arafat on July 22. There is not a word about military equipment, arms or aircraft being promised by Arafat.

Other difficulties with the authenticity of this document is that it says the General Staff was in Nicaragua an entire week wasting time before it met with the representatives of the DRU, that is, the DRU office which would have been set up in Managua (according to Document D) after the May unity agreement. It seems inconceivable that the guerrilla General Staff would wait for an entire week before having a meeting with the DRU representative in Managua. Moreover, it is evident in the document that the Salvadoran General Staff was kept waiting for ten days before Bayardo Arce finally went to see them, and it is clear that they did not meet with any other Sandinista leader in the meanwhile. If one compares this treatment with the full support and facilities allegedly given by the Sandinistas in Document D (and emphasized in the White Paper analyses), one concludes that the Sandinista support was in fact quite limited. Moreover, it seems highly unlikely that the Sandinistas would keep the highest Salvadoran guerrilla military leadership waiting for ten days, or that Arce would be the only Sandinista leader who would speak with them — even in a period of celebration.

The Long Analysis goes on to say:

> On July 27, the General Staff delegation departs from Managua for Havana, where Cuban specialists add the final touches to the military plans formulated during the May meetings in Havana.

In the original document, the General Staff intended to go to Havana on July 27, but the last entry is July 23, and there is no indication that they actually went. Also, the document reflects their intention to go to Havana "to finish polishing the project," but there is no indication that this meant "military plans formulated during the May meetings in Havana." Finally, there is no reference in the original document that they made arrangements for the Havana trip such as obtaining tickets and visas.

The Long Analysis chronology goes on to say:

In mid-August 1980, Schafik Handal's arms-shopping expedition begins to bear fruit. On August 15, 1980, Ethiopian arms depart for Cuba.

The only support for this allegation is the reference in Document F (the one in which the ERP leader wrote the FPL slogan instead of her own), wherein it is said that the arms from Ethiopia "were to leave for Havana on August 15." None of the documents state that Ethiopian arms actually departed from that country for Cuba, as the Long Analysis would have one think. The Long Analysis then says:

Three weeks later the 60 tons of captured U.S. arms sent from Vietnam are scheduled to arrive in Cuba.

This statement is based on the same Document F which says, "They will be in Esmeralda on September 5." But recall that Document E (on which Document F was based) only said that the arms shipment from Vietnam would be ready for shipment during "the first five days of September," not that they would arrive in Cuba on September 5. The White Paper analyst simply followed the error of the person who fabricated Document F because it fit better with the overall false scenario.

The Long Analysis then says:

As a result of a Salvadoran delegation's trip to Iraq earlier in the year, the guerrillas receive a 500,000 Dollar logistics donation.

The donation is in fact mentioned in Document H, if one agrees with the analyst that the letter "I" stands for Iraq, or if one accepts the legitimacy of Document J (more of this document below), which mentions 200,000 Dollars from Iraq assigned for internal logistics purposes. In the case of Document J, Iraq is spelled out. But the documents contain no mention of a "Salvadoran delegation's trip to Iraq earlier in the year."

There is a more serious problem, though, with Document H, which purports to be a report of a meeting of the DRU on September 24, 1980. In the beginning of the document there is a section giving the names of those who attended. The top line has "Hugo — Rene," the second line has "Ana Maria — Marcial," and the third line has "Jonas — Eduardo." It seems that these names are set on separate lines because they are representatives or leaders of the three guerrilla organizations in the DRU at that time. (Earlier in September, the RN withdrew from the DRU.) Yet the writer seems confused over the organizations to which "Ana Maria" and "Marcial" belong, because the Document H glossary shows "Ana Maria" (as in other glossaries) as the code name for Ana Guadalupe Martinez, the ERP leader, whereas "Marcial," as in other glossaries, is said to be the code name for Salvador Cayetano Carpio, the leader of the FPL guerrilla group. But the confusion does not end there. In previous glossaries "Rene" is said to be the code word for the RN guerrilla group which, as I said, had withdrawn from the DRU before the date of this meeting. In Glossary H there is no reference to "Rene" as meaning the RN group, as there was on previous documents. If this document were genuine, "Rene" would probably refer to ERP leader Joaquin Villalobos, whose nom de guerre, "Rene Cruz," is well known. Further undermining the analyst's contention in other glossaries that "Rene" is the code name for RN, the first paragraph of Document H relates the accidental death of the First Responsible of the RN, and refers to him as Comrade "Neto," which is the well-known nom de guerre of Ernesto Jovel, the principal leader of the RN. It was widely reported at that time that Ernesto Jovel was killed in an airplane crash. Thus, "Ana Maria" should be on the same line as "Rene," if "Ana Maria" is the ERP leader, and not on the line with "Marcial," the FLP leader. And if "Rene" stands for RN, he would not have been present at this meeting.

The Long Analysis continues:

> By mid-September substantial quantities of the arms promised to Handal are well on the way to Cuba and Nicaragua. The guerrilla logistics coordinator in Nicaragua informs his Joint General Staff on September 26 that 130 tons of arms and other military material supplied by the communist countries have arrived in Nicaragua for shipment to El Salvador. According to the captured documents, this represents one-sixth of the commitments to the guerillas by the communist countries.

This statement is based on Document I, which purports to be a report of a meeting of the Joint General Staff (EMGC). Document I is another fragment and we are told nothing of the rest of the report. The introductory comment to Document I asserts that this report is dated September 26, 1980, but no date is to be seen on the original document. Nevertheless, in the translation September 26 is inserted under the title of the document, whereas it is not to be found on the original. Those present at the meeting, which takes place in El Salvador, are said to be "Ramon," "Vladimir," and "Jonas," and none of these are identified in the glossary. But the glossaries of Documents K, Q and R identify "Vladimir" as the "DRU logistics representative in Nicaragua" and not as a member of the EMGC.

In Document I there is no reference to a "guerrilla logistics coordinator in Nicaragua." Nor that the 130 tons of arms were "supplied by the communist countries." The document does mention that 130 tons are in storage in "Lagos" (supposedly meaning Nicaragua), and that these 130 tons are "one-sixth of all the material obtained with which the DRU will count on concentrated in Lagos." It is from this passage that the White Paper analyst extrapolated the conclusion in the beginning of the analysis that one of "the key stages in the growth of the communist involvement" was:

> The series of contacts between Salvadoran Communist leaders and key officials of several Communist states that resulted in commitments to supply the insurgents nearly 800 tons of the most modern weapons and equipment.

The analyst is inventing, or assuming, that the 780 tons were coming from communist countries, because all or part of the armaments mentioned here could have come from any country of the world. There is no mention in Document I that these arms were coming from "communist countries." What the State Department analyst failed to say, because it did not fit his overall scenario, is that in Document I, when the 130 tons in "Lagos" are mentioned, it is also stated that the guerrillas have been able to bring into El Salvador only 4 tons of the 130 supposedly in Nicaragua. Also conveniently not mentioned in the analysis is that according to this report, the Joint General Staff had virtually failed to function. In the past forty days the Joint General Staff had met only five times, and for the meeting which is the subject of this report, the three people who met had not even made arrangements for a place to hold their meeting. According to the report, they began the meeting by looking around for a cafe in which they could hold their revolutionary discussions.

The Short Analysis describes this meeting: "Guerrilla Logistics Committee informs its Joint General Staff," while the Long Analysis says: "The Guerrilla Logistics Coordinator in Nicaragua informs his General Staff." If one accepts the interpretation in the other glossaries that "Vladimir" is the logistics coordinator in Nicaragua, that leaves a two-person "General Staff" holding a fifth meeting in forty days with no security preparation, no guards, not even a place to meet. Moreover, the document makes no mention of any "report" by "Vladimir" on the logistics situation.

Finally, the English translation of the report ends with "End of Excerpt," whereas the original Spanish document has a paragraph of 16 additional lines that were not translated. I frankly find Document I very difficult to believe.

The Long Analysis continues:

In September and October the number of flights to Nicaragua from Cuba increased sharply. These flights had the capacity to transport several hundred tons of cargo.

There is no "captured" document to support this claim, possibly, I would suspect, because the Salvadoran guerrillas were too busy fighting the military junta to monitor the frequency of air traffic between Cuba and Nicaragua. But if U.S. intelligence agencies monitored a "sharp increase" capable of transporting "several hundred tons," and if this White Paper is to be believed, they should have given at least some details on this increase and the cargo-carrying capacity of the aircraft. Given the inventions and distortions already discussed, it is asking a lot to expect people to believe unsupported claims such as this one.

The White Paper Analysis continues:

At the end of September, despite appeals from the guerrillas, the Sandinistas suspend their weapons deliveries to El Salvador for one month after the U.S. government lodges a protest to Nicaragua on the arms trafficking.

This statement rests on Document J, another unexplained fragment.

The introduction to Document J describes the document as dated September 30, 1980, and as an excerpt from a letter from "Fernando" to "Frederico." Neither of the two is identified in the glossary, and only the name "Fernando" appears at the end of the document. "Frederico" appears nowhere in the document, nor does the original have a date. As in previous documents "Simon" is said to be Shafik Handal, PCS Secretary General, but with no supporting evidence.

There are some problems in the translation of Document J, such as "concrete mines" being translated as "contact mines," "ask Hugo for information" translated as "he requested information from Hugo," and "the house will be taken away" translated as "was taken away." In addition, the document mentions a work plan which includes "construction of 120 millimeter cannons." I am not an expert on artillery pieces, but this sounds to me like a rather ambitious project for home construction.

The purpose of this document, if it is faked, is to show that U.S. pressure forced the Sandinistas to stop the weapons deliveries despite the Salvadorans need for them. The Long Analysis continues:

When the shipments resume in October, as much as 120 tons of weapons and materiel are still in Nicaragua and some 300-400 tons are in Cuba.

This is based on Document K, which is a three-page handwritten letter from "Vladimir" (interpreted as the DRU logistics representative in Nicaragua) to the DRU leadership in El Salvador concerning the flow of arms from Nicaragua to the guerrillas. The original Spanish document merely says that additional shipments due to arrive in "Esmeralda" will bring the total there to 300-400 tons, but the document does not say if or when they actually arrived. Also, the translation mentions a 150-ton arrival in "Esmeralda," but on the Spanish original the numbers are all but illegible and could be interpreted differently.

The Short Analysis has this letter (Document K) addressed to the Joint General Staff, but in fact it was addressed to the Unified Revolutionary Directorate (DRU).

There is no indication in this document that "shipments resumed in October." The document deals with plans to ship weapons during the month of November, and the supposed logistics chief recognized that it would be almost impossible to transport the 109 tons that the Nicaraguans wanted to ship during November.

The Short Analysis, under the heading "September-October 1980," states: "Guerrillas begin preparations for infiltrating weapons and equipment into El Salvador by land, air and sea," citing Documents J, L, M, N and O. With respect to the time period September-October: Document J has no date, but in this document "last September 27" is mentioned as the date of the meeting. Document L consists of three pages of barely legible handwritten notes with lists of arms and no date whatsoever. It could refer to arms shipments at any time during the ten-year history of the Salvadoran guerrilla war. Document M is also undated, and consists of general ideas concerning logistics. It could date from any time following the formation of the

Joint General Staff (EMGC). Document N is also undated and consists of three pages of handwritten notes concerning arms and shipments. The translation of these notes includes the conversion of Tegucigalpa (the Honduran capital) to "Costa Rica," and the adding of certain words that are not on the original document. There is no indication that these notes pertain to the September-October 1980 period. Document O is an unsigned typed page with the heading "Short report sent by Comrade Jonas Montalvo (ERP)." It could date from any time following the formation of the DRU in May (the DRU is mentioned), until before the November U.S. elections (the election campaign is mentioned). The final paragraph mentions that logistics problems have to be solved in El Salvador and not outside the country. Of interest in this document is that this supposed ERP leader says that the Christian Democratic parties of Central America are fearful of a Reagan victory in the elections, as are the Panamanians, Venezuelans, Nicaraguans and Cubans.

The Long Analysis, continuing:

Because of the difficulty of moving such large quantities overland, Nicaragua – with Cuban support – begins airlifting arms from Nicaragua into El Salvador. In November, about 2.5 tons of arms are delivered by air before accidents force a brief halt in the airlift.

None of the documents mention this supposed airlift or any of the other information contained in that quote, nor is there any information to support the alleged delivery of 2.5 tons, or that accidents forced the airlift to stop. And, of course, the analysis gives no evidence to support the allegation of "Cuban support" to the airlift. A check of press reporting on El Salvador and Nicaragua during October, November and December showed no reports of aircraft accidents connected with any arms shipments. On the other hand, in Document K, the supposed DRU logistics representative in Nicaragua wrote on November 1: "We still have to work on how to resolve the air route."

The Long Analysis goes on to mention a guerrilla radio station, "Radio Liberacion," that supposedly began broadcasting to El Salvador from Nicaragua on December 15, 1980. The Long Analysis says:

References to the Sandinistas sharing the expenses of a revolutionary radio station appear in the captured documents.

The Short Analysis, in mentioning the Salvadoran guerrilla radio, says that it was set up "with the help of Cubans and Nicaraguans." The reference to the radio is in Document P, purportedly a letter from the DRU in El Salvador to DRU representatives in Nicaragua dated October 29, 1980. In this letter the need for setting up the radio in "Lagos" is discussed along with the observation that "collaboration and assistance of the Island and the Laguenos should be requested." However, the same document discusses two other radio projects, both of which are planned for operation in El Salvador itself, and reveals that the ERP already had a shortwave radio in Mexico and another radio already in El Salvador. (In my press research, I found that the ERP had a clandestine radio operating as early as January 1980.) The White

Paper fails to mention these other two radio projects, i.e., the existing ERP station in El Salvador and the other in Mexico, in order to concentrate attention on Salvadoran use of Nicaraguan territory, and to convert a plan to request Cuban and Nicaraguan assistance into a statement that the assistance was actually given.

Another problem relating to Document P (not so serious but possibly reflecting the analyst's confusion already apparent in embellishments, misinterpretations, exaggerations and fabrications), appears in the short introductory comment to this document. It says, "undated October 29, 1980."

The paragraph of the Long Analysis just preceding its discussion of the guerrilla radio station reads:

In December Salvadoran guerrillas, encouraged by Cuba, begin plans for a general offensive in early 1981. To provide the increased support necessary, the Sandinistas revive the airlift into El Salvador. Salvadoran insurgents protest that they cannot absorb the increased flow of arms, but guerrilla liaison members in Managua urge them to increase their efforts as several East European nations are providing unprecedented assistance.

The latest dates on documents in the White Paper are from November, so there is not a word to support guerrilla planning in December for an early 1981 offensive, nor for any encouragement by Cuba, nor for any airlifts by the Sandinistas to El Salvador. The Logistics matter mentioned in the above-quoted paragraph related to November documents, not December.

There is not a word to support the assertion that the guerrillas operating in El Salvador could not absorb the "increased flow of arms." In fact in Document S, which purports to be a letter from the DRU in El Salvador to its logistics representative in Nicaragua — and written no earlier than November 18 — the guerrillas in El Salvador express serious concern over any suspension of shipments from Nicaragua at that time.

The Short Analysis, in discussing logistics problems, says: "Beginning in November the FSLN sends to El Salvador more arms than the guerrillas can receive and distribute," citing Documents Q and R to support this statement. In fact Documents Q and R discuss problems of coordination between those on the shipping end and those on the receiving end of the system. There is no mention that more arms are coming "than the guerrillas can receive and distribute." This fabrication simply exaggerates the importance to the guerrillas in El Salvador of supposed shipments coming through Nicaragua. And the Long Analysis conveniently shifts the date from November to December to make it appear to coincide with the offensive that the Salvadoran guerrillas started in January.

If you believe the documentation, the guerrillas in El Salvador, far from having received massive shipments during November, mention in Document R (letter dated November 10 from the DRU in El Salvador to their logistics representative in Nicaragua) that "what has been received as a result of the successful arrival are 472 F. : 4 RP-2-M.30 and other types." If that means that under the logistics plan then in operation, 472 rifles (F. might stand for the Spanish word "fusil") plus ammunition arrived, it hardly constitutes an arms flow too massive for the guerrillas to handle.

There are problems with the translation and analysis of Document Q. This is a three-page handwritten document purporting to be a report to the DRU in El Salvador by one of the guerrillas who went to Nicaragua to discuss logistics problems. The translation of the second paragraph has "presented by him," "I insisted that," and "all" — none of which appear in the Spanish original. In the same translation "participation" (original) becomes "previous consultation" (translation) and "this consideration" (original) becomes "my arguments" (translation). Later in the translation, in a listing of weapons and ammunition, what appears in the original document as "88,460 cartridges for rifles" becomes "88,460 cartridges for each rifle." This translation also includes "2 tons" and "3 tons," both of which figures are totally illegible in the original. Finally, the translation of Document Q is signed "Respectfully, Rodrigo" and this appears nowhere at the end of the Spanish Document Q.

With respect to Document R, the translator failed to follow the numbers and letters of the paragraphs of the original. Parts of the original that are largely illegible appear in the translation. A phrase "this shows that with a good job of reconnaissance" appears in the translation but not in the original. There is no way to tell if the "captured" versions of Documents R and S are carbons, since the originals would have gone to Nicaragua.

The translation of Document S, purported to be a letter from the DRU to its logistics representative in Nicaragua, has at the top "El Salvador, Wednesday 19 November 1980" but none of this appears on the original.

The Long Analysis goes on to describe two incidents in January 1981, widely reported in the press, as evidence for the air shipment of arms into El Salvador:

On January 24, 1981, a Cessna from Nicaragua crashes on takeoff in El Salvador after unloading passengers and possibly weapons. A second plane is strafed by the Salvadoran Air Force, and the pilot and numerous weapons are captured. The pilot admits to being an employee of the Nicaraguan national airline and concedes that the flight originated from Sandino International Airport in Managua. He further admits to flying two earlier arms deliveries.

With reference to the Cessna one has to ask the question why the analyst believes weapons were "possibly" unloaded, when he says that passengers were unloaded as a fact. One would think that if observers saw passengers being unloaded they would also have seen weapons or at least crates of some sort also being unloaded. One can suspect that the analyst read a report of a Cessna crash and added it to the White Paper with the "weapons" possibility in order to emphasize the air supply route. As for the second airplane, the analyst failed to point out that the pilot is Costa Rican, as is the registry of the aircraft, and in fact the plane had left Costa Rica two days before it was captured in El Salvador.

The Long Analysis continues:

Air supply is playing a key role, but infiltration by land and sea also continues. Small launches operating out of several Nicaraguan Pacific ports traverse the Gulf of Fonseca at night, carrying arms, ammunition, and personnel. During the general offensive on January 13, several dozen well-armed guerrillas landed on El Salvador's southeastern coast on the Gulf of Fonseca, adjacent to Nicaragua.

In the absence of more than one known arms shipment by air, we can only take it on faith that "Air supply is playing a key role." As for infiltration by sea, the January 13 incident (the only one so far reported) is presented in the Long Analysis as fact, whereas in reality it is nothing more than fantasy. On January 14 the President of the Salvadoran Junta announced (according to *Inforpress Centroamericana*) that "at least 100 foreign guerrillas have disembarked in the last 24 hours on the beaches of El Cuco." He added, "the invaders came in 5 launches with capacity for 20 or 30 men whom the Salvadoran army have surrounded and expect to annihilate from one moment to another." At the same time, the U.S. Ambassador, Robert White, also charged that some 100 guerrillas had landed in El Salvador from boats from Nicaragua, and he was also reported in the press as having said that he personally had prior information about the invasion by Nicaragua. The "invasion" was immediately treated by the State Department as demonstrating open intervention by Nicaragua, and White was quoted in the Mexican press (*El Dia*, January 16) as saying that because of this incident "the nature of the struggle has changed since there is foreign support for a small group of dedicated revolutionaries." According to *El Dia* the Salvadoran Junta announced that it had killed more than 50 of the "invaders," and that the others had dispersed in rural areas. When they were captured alive, the government official said, they would be shown to the press. No captured Nicaraguans and none of the bodies of the 50 "killed" were ever displayed. The Salvadoran Ministry of Defense, meanwhile, said it had captured a foreign-built launch, but this, according to its identification markings, turned out to be a fishing boat from Honduras. *El Dia* went on to cite news dispatches from El Salvador describing the "invaders" (whom no one ever saw dead or alive) as "black and tall like Nicaraguans, Panamanians or Cubans," and the admission of one Salvadoran military official that "all of us Central Americans look alike." As the 100 Nicaraguan invaders turned into phantoms, the *International Herald Tribune* (January 21, 1981) reported that, "U.S. officials in San Salvador now say Mr. White overemphasized the supposed invasion and no longer thinks the evidence about it as compelling as the day he spoke." The White Paper, a month later, describes the "invasion" as undisputed fact.

The Long Analysis continues:

Overland arms shipments also continue through Honduras from Nicaragua and Costa Rica. In late January, Honduran security forces uncover an arms infiltration operation run by Salvadorans working through Nicaragua and directed by Cubans. In this operation a trailer truck is discovered carrying weapons and ammunition destined for Salvadoran guerrillas. Weapons include 100 U.S. M-16 rifles and 81mm mortar ammunition. These arms are a portion of the Vietnamese shipment: a trace of the M-16's reveals that several of them were shipped to U.S. units in Vietnam where they were captured or left behind. Using this network, perhaps five truckloads of arms may have reached the Salvadoran guerrillas.

What the Long Analysis fails to point out about this captured shipment is the following information from the February 12, 1981 issue of *Inforpress Centroamericana*, the serious and respected weekly newsletter published in Guatemala City. The shipment originated in Costa Rica and passed overland through Nicaragua, later to be captured in Honduras. According to *Inforpress*, the American Ambassador in Honduras said Nicaragua could not be blamed for the shipment "because possibly it passed through that country and the authorities did not realize it." There is no indication in the official Honduran military communique of the incident (also reported by *Inforpress*) that there was any Cuban involvement in this system. The White Paper analyst seemed unable to resist just one more fabrication of the "Cuban hand." One has to wonder why, if the analyst mentioned 100 U.S. M-16 rifles captured in this incident, he only mentioned that "several" were traced to Vietnam — instead of giving the exact number — especially since no M-16's appear on the Vietnam weapons list (Documents E and F). In addition the analyst gave no clue for why he concluded that "perhaps five truckloads of arms may have reached Salvadoran guerrillas," as opposed to 2, 6, 15 or 500.

One should recall from the beginning of the Long Analysis, the statement:

from the documents it is possible to reconstruct chronologically the key stages in the growth of the Communist involvement (including) the covert delivery to El Salvador of nearly 200 tons of arms, mostly through Nicaragua.

There is absolutely nothing in the documents to support this figure of 200 tons. During the months of this supposed "massive" foreign supply of arms to El Salvador's guerrillas, only two shipments were intercepted: one, the light plane whose trip originated in Costa Rica with a stop in Managua before arrival in El Salvador; the other, the van that also was bringing arms from Costa Rica, *not* Nicaragua. These two cases would appear to weaken the claims of authenticity for documents relating to the storage of arms in Nicaragua (Lagos), in particular Documents I and K.

If the arms were being sent by air from Cuba to Nicaragua, as the White Paper would have us believe, it hardly seems likely that the Nicaraguans would then ship them south to Costa Rica, and from there north all the way back across Nicaragua to Honduras, for eventual shipment west to El Salvador. And even if one believes these documents, there is no way to reach a figure of 200 tons of arms actually delivered in El Salvador. By fabricating this figure, not to mention all the other problems discussed above, the White Paper analyst simply destroys the credibility of his argument.

One should also compare the assertion in the Long Analysis that "the availability of weapons and materiel significantly increases the military capabilities of the Salvadoran insurgents," with the statement of the American Ambassador, Robert White, who was serving in El Salvador during the period covered by this White Paper, in his interview of January 1981 in *U.S. News & World Report*: "Up until now Cuban support has not been crucial to the attack capability of the guerrillas."

CONCLUSIONS

1. There is no evidence in the documents presented in this White Paper to support the belief that the Soviet Union has given significant support to the Salvadoran guerrilla movement, or the conclusion that "El Salvador has been progressively transformed into a textbook case of indirect armed aggression by communist powers through Cuba."

2. The most sensational of these documents show indications of having been falsified, particularly: Document B referring to the May 1980 guerrilla unity agreement being reached in Havana; Documents E and F referring to the supposed arms shopping trip by the Salvadoran Communist Party General Secretary to socialist countries; and Document A referring to an alleged Cuban role in the guerrilla unity agreement supposedly reached under Fidel Castro's direction in Havana in December 1979. The CIA could have fabricated all 19 of these documents, perhaps working with Salvadoran security officials, and then arranged for them to be inserted among documents that actually had been captured. Such an operation would not be the first time the CIA has done it.

3. Inaccuracies, fabrications, embellishments and false claims made in the White Paper analyses convert the White Paper (which in normal practice would be a statement of facts on an important public issue) into little more than a blatant propaganda exercise. This is especially so with respect to supposed Soviet and Cuban direction of arms supply to Salvadoran guerrillas. As everyone knows, the principal foreign power introducing foreign arms into the Salvadoran civil war is the United States itself. The White Paper's claim of "incontrovertible" evidence is an insult.

As a last thought, I want to mention a press report of March 6, 1981 from the newspaper *Uno Mas Uno* of Mexico City. The Guatemalan government, according to the report, announced on March 5 that they had captured "important documents of political-military organizations that proved the 'important role' of support to Guatemalan insurgents played by Cuba and Nicaragua." Anxious not to be left out of the game, the Guatemalan regime claims the documents prove that various guerrilla organizations, previously operating independently in Guatemala, had reached a unity agreement in Nicaragua and had sent a copy of their statement of agreement to Fidel Castro. The government statement went on to say that Nicaragua had already sent 1800 carbines and 10,000 rounds of ammunition to Guatemala, and that in Cuba there were 243 camps for military training of Guatemalan revolutionaries.

I can't wait to see Glassman's White Paper on the "captured" Guatemalan documents.

APPENDIX A

U. S. STATE DEPARTMENT WHITE PAPER

NOTE: Both versions of the Short Analysis were accompanied by identical sets of documents, glossaries, official translations, and lists of leftist opposition groups in El Salvador.

The Revised Version of the Short Analysis was released after Philip Agee presented his critique.

COMMUNIST INTERFERENCE IN EL SALVADOR
[WHITE PAPER – LONG ANALYSIS]

Special Report No, 80 – February 23, 1981
United States Department of State, Bureau of Public Affairs, Washington, D.C.

CONTENTS
Summary
I. A Case of Communist Military Involvement in the Third World
II. Communist Military Intervention: A Chronology
III. The Government: The Search for Order and Democracy
IV. Some Conclusions

Summary
This special report presents definitive evidence of the clandestine military support given by the Soviet Union, Cuba, and their Communist allies to Marxist-Leninist guerrillas now fighting to overthrow the established Government of El Salvador. The evidence, drawn from captured guerrilla documents and war materiel and corroborated by intelligence reports, underscores the central role played by Cuba and other Communist countries beginning in 1979 in the political unification, military direction, and arming of insurgent forces in El Salvador.

From the documents it is possible to reconstruct chronologically the key stages in the growth of the Communist involvement:

– The direct tutelary role played by Fidel Castro and the Cuban Government in late 1979 and early 1980 in bringing the diverse Salvadoran guerrilla factions into a unified front;

– The assistance and advice given the guerrillas in planning their military operations;

– The series of contacts between Salvadoran Communist leaders and key officials of several Communist states that resulted in commitments to supply the insurgents nearly 800 tons of the most modern weapons and equipment;

– The covert delivery to El Salvador of nearly 200 tons of those arms, mostly through Cuba and Nicaragua, in preparation for the guerrillas' failed "general offensive" of January 1981;

– The major Communist effort to "cover" their involvement by providing mostly arms of Western manufacture.

It is clear that over the past year the insurgency in El Salvador has been progressively transformed into another case of indirect armed aggression against a small Third World country by Communist powers acting through Cuba.

The United States considers it of great importance that the American people and the world community be aware of the gravity of the actions of Cuba, the Soviet Union, and other Communist states who are carrying out what is clearly shown to be a well-coordinated, covert effort to bring about the overthrow of El Salvador's established government and to impose in its place a Communist regime with no popular support.

I.   A Case of Communist Military Involvement in the Third World
The situation in El Salvador presents a strikingly familiar case of Soviet, Cuban, and other Communist military involvement in a politically troubled Third World country. By providing arms, training, and direction to a local insurgency and by supporting it with a global propaganda campaign, the Communists have intensified and widened the conflict, greatly increased the suffering of the Salvadoran people, and deceived much of the world about the true nature of the revolution. Their objective in El Salvador as elsewhere is to bring about – at little cost to themselves – the overthrow of the established government and the imposition of a Communist regime in defiance of the will of the Salvadoran people.

The Guerrillas: Their Tactics and Propaganda. El Salvador's extreme left, which includes the long-established Communist Party of El Salvador (PCES) and several armed groups of more recent origin, has become increasingly committed since 1976 to a military solution. A campaign of terrorism – bombings, assassinations, kidnappings, and seizures of embassies – has disrupted national life and claimed the lives of many innocent people.

During 1980, previously fragmented factions of the extreme left agreed to coordinate their actions in support of a joint military battle plan developed with Cuban assistance. As a precondition for large-scale Cuban aid, Salvadoran guerrilla leaders, meeting in Havana in May, formed first the Unified Revolutionary Directorate (DRU) as their central executive arm for political and military planning and, in late 1980, the Farabundo Marti People's Liberation Front (FMLN), as the coordinating body of the guerrilla organizations. A front organization, the Revolutionary Democratic Front (FDR), was also created to disseminate propaganda abroad. For appearances sake, three small non-Marxist-Leninist political parties were brought into the front, though they have no representation in the DRU.

The Salvadoran guerrillas, speaking through the FDR, have managed to deceive many about what is happening in El Salvador. They have been aided by Nicaragua and by the worldwide propaganda networks of Cuba, the Soviet Union, and other Communist countries.

The guerrillas' propaganda aims at legitimizing their violence and concealing the Communist aid that makes it possible. Other key aims are to discredit the Salvadoran Government, to misrepresent U.S. policies and actions, and to foster the impression of overwhelming popular support for the revolutionary movement.

Examples of the more extreme claims of their propaganda apparatus – echoed by Cuban, Soviet, and Nicaraguan media – are:

– That the United States has military bases and several hundred troops in El Salvador (in fact, the United States has no bases and fewer than 50 military personnel there);

– That the government's security forces were responsible for most of the 10,000 killings that occurred in 1980 (in their own reports in 1980, the guerrillas themselves claimed the killings of nearly 6,000 persons, including noncombatant "informers" as well as government authorities and military).

In addition to media propaganda, Cuba and the Soviet Union promote the insurgent cause at international forums, with individual governments, and among foreign opinion leaders. Cuba has an efficient network for introducing and promoting representatives of the Salvadoran left all over the world. Havana and Moscow also bring indirect pressure on some governments to support the Salvadoran revolutionaries by mobilizing local Communist groups.

II.   Communist Military Intervention: A Chronology

Before September 1980 the diverse guerrilla groups in El Salvador were ill-coordinated and ill-equipped, armed with pistols and a varied assortment of hunting rifles and shotguns. At that time the insurgents acquired weapons predominantly through purchases on the international market and from dealers who participated in the supply of arms to the Sandinistas in Nicaragua.

By January 1981 when the guerrillas launched their "general offensive," they had acquired an impressive array of modern weapons and supporting equipment never before used in El Salvador by either the insurgents or the military. Belgian FAL rifles, German G-3 rifles, U.S. M-1, M-16, and AR-15 semiautomatic and automatic rifles, and the Israeli UZI submachinegun and Galil assault rifle have all been confirmed in the guerrilla inventory. In addition, they are known to possess .30 to .50 caliber machineguns, the U.S. M-60 machinegun, U.S. and Russian hand grenades, the U.S. M-79 and Chinese RPG grenade launchers, and the U.S. M-72 light antitank weapon and 81mm mortars. Captured ammunition indicates the guerrillas probably possess 60mm and 82mm mortars and 57mm and 75mm recoilless rifles.

Recently acquired evidence has enabled us to reconstruct the central role played by Cuba, other Communist countries, and several radical states in the political unification and military direction of insurgent forces in El Salvador and in equipping them in less than 6 months with a panoply of modern weapons that enabled the guerrillas to launch a well-armed offensive.

This information, which we consider incontrovertible, has been acquired over the past year. Many key details, however, have fallen into place as the result of the guerrillas' own records. Two particularly important document caches were recovered from the Communist Party of El Salvador in November 1980 and from the Peoples' Revolutionary Army (ERP) in January 1981. This mass of captured documents includes battle plans, letters, and reports of meetings and travels, some written in cryptic language and using code words.

When deciphered and verified against evidence from other intelligence sources, the documents bring to light the chain of events leading to the guerrillas' January 1981 offensive. What emerges is a highly disturbing pattern of parallel and coordinated action by a number of Communist and some radical countries bent on imposing a military solution.

The Cuban and Communist role in preparing for and helping to organize the abortive "general offensive" early this year is spelled out in the following chronology based on the contents of captured documents and other sources.

Initial Steps. The chronology of external support begins at the end of 1979. With salutations of "brotherly and revolutionary greetings" on December 16, 1979, members of the Communist Party of El Salvador (PCES), National Resistance (FARN), and Popular Liberation Forces (FPL) thank Fidel Castro in a letter for his help and "the help of your party comrades . . . by signing an agreement which establishes very solid bases upon which we begin building coordination and unity of our organizations." The letter, written in Havana, was signed by leaders of these three revolutionary organizations.

At an April 1980 meeting at the Hungarian Embassy in Mexico City, guerrilla leaders made certain "requests" (possibly for arms). Present at this meeting were representatives of the German Democratic Republic, Bulgaria, Poland, Vietnam, Hungary, Cuba, and the Soviet Union.

In notes taken during an April 28, 1980 meeting of the Salvadoran Communist Party, party leader Shafik Handal mentions the need to "speed up reorganization and put the Party on a war footing." He added, "I'm in agreement with taking advantage of the possibilities of assistance from the socialist camp. I think that their attitude is magnificent. We are not yet taking advantage of it." In reference to a unification of the armed movement, he asserts that "the idea of involving everyone in the area has already been suggested to Fidel himself." Handal alludes to the concept of unification and notes, "Fidel thought well of the idea."

Guerrilla Contacts in Havana. From May 5 to June 8, 1980, Salvadoran guerrilla leaders report on meetings in Honduras, Guatemala, Costa Rica, and Nicaragua. They proceed to Havana and meet several times with Fidel Castro; the documents also note an interview with the German Democratic Republic (G.D.R.) Chairman Erich Honecker in Havana. During the Havana portion of their travels, the Salvadoran guerrilla leadership meets twice with the Cuban Directorate of Special Operations (DOE, the clandestine operations/special forces unit of the Cuban Ministry of Interior) to discuss guerrilla military plans. In addition, they meet with the Cuban "Chief of Communications."

During this period (late May 1980), the Popular Revolutionary Army (ERP) is admitted into the guerrilla coalition after negotiations in Havana. The coalition then assumes the name of the Unified Revolutionary Directorate (DRU) and meets with Fidel Castro on three occasions.

After the Havana meetings, Shafik Handal leaves Havana on May 30, 1980 for Moscow. The other Salvadoran guerrilla leaders in Havana leave for Managua. During the visit of early June, the DRU leaders meet with Nicaraguan revolutionary leaders (Sandinistas) and discuss: (1) a headquarters with "all measures of security"; (2) an "international field of operations, which they (Sandinistas) control"; and (3) the willingness of the Sandinistas to "contribute in material terms" and to adopt "the cause of El Salvador as its own." The meeting culminated with "dinner at Humberto's house" (presumably Sandinista leader Humberto Ortega).

Salvadoran Communist Party Leader's Travels in the East. From June 2 to July 22, 1980, Shafik Handal visits the U.S.S.R., Vietnam, the German Democratic Republic, Czechoslovakia, Bulgaria, Hungary, and Ethiopia to procure arms and seek support for the movement.

On June 2, 1980, Handal meets in Moscow with Mikhail Kudachkin, Deputy Chief of the Latin American Section of the Foreign Relations Department of the CPSU Central Committee. Kudachkin suggests that Handal travel to Vietnam to seek arms and offers to pay for Handal's trip.

Continuing his travels between June 9 and 15, Handal visits Vietnam where he is received by Le Duan, Secretary General of the Vietnam Communist Party; Xuan Thuy, member of the Communist Party Central Committee Secretariat; and Vice Minister of National Defense Tran Van Quang. The Vietnamese, as a "first contribution," agree to provide 60 tons of arms. Handal adds that "the comrade requested air transport from the USSR."

From June 19 to June 24, 1980, Handal visits the German Democratic Republic (G.D.R.), where he is received by Hermann Axen, member of the G.D.R. Politburo. Axen states that the G.D.R. has already sent 1.9 tons of supplies to Managua. On July 21, G.D.R. leader Honecker writes the G.D.R. Embassy in Moscow that additional supplies will be sent and that the German Democratic Republic will provide military training, particularly in clandestine operations. The G.D.R. telegram adds that although Berlin possesses no Western-manufactured weapons – which the Salvadoran guerrillas are seeking – efforts will be undertaken to find a "solution to this problem." (NOTE: The emphasis on Western arms reflects the desire to maintain plausible denial.)

From June 24-27, 1980, Handal visits Czechoslovakia where he is received by Vasil Bilak, Second Secretary of the Czech Communist Party. Bilak says that some Czech arms circulating in the world market will be provided so that these arms will not be traced back to Czechoslovakia as the donor country. Transportation will be coordinated with the German Democratic Republic.

Handal proceeds to Bulgaria from June 27 to June 30, 1980. He is received by Dimitir Stanichev, member of the Central Committee Secretariat. The Bulgarians agree to supply German-origin weapons and other supplies, again in an apparent effort to conceal their sources.

In Hungary, from June 30 to July 3, 1980, Handal is received by Communist Party General Secretary Janos Kadar and "Guesel" (probably Central Committee Secretary for Foreign Affairs Andras Gyenes). The latter offers radios and other supplies and indicates Hungarian willingness to trade arms with Ethiopia or Angola in order to obtain Western-origin arms for the Salvadoran guerrillas. "Guesel" promises to resolve the trade with the Ethiopians and Angolans himself, "since we want to be a part of providing this aid." Additionally, Handal secures the promise of 10,000 uniforms to be made by the Hungarians according to Handal's specifications.

Handal then travels to Ethiopia, July 3 to July 6. He meets Chairman Mengistu and receives "a warm reception." Mengistu offers "several thousand weapons," including: 150 Thompson submachineguns with 300 cartridge clips, 1,500 M-1 rifles, 1,000 M-14 rifles, and ammunition for these weapons. In addition, the Ethiopians agree to supply all necessary spare parts for these arms.

Handal returns to Moscow on July 22, 1980 and is received again by Mikhail Kudachkin. The Soviet official asks if 30 Communist youth currently studying in the U.S.S.R. could take part in the war in El Salvador. Before leaving Moscow, Handal receives assurances that the Soviets agree in principle to transport the Vietnamese arms.

Further Contacts in Nicaragua. On July 13, representatives of the DRU arrive in Managua amidst preparations for the first anniversary celebration of Somoza's overthrow. The DRU leaders wait until July 23 to meet with "Comrade Bayardo" (presumably Bayardo Arce, member of the Sandinista Directorate). They complain that the Sandinistas appear to be restricting their access to visiting world dignitaries and demanding that all contacts be cleared through them. During the meeting, Arce promises ammunition to the guerrillas and arranges a meeting for them with the Sandinista "Military Commission." Arce indicates that, since the guerrillas will receive some arms manufactured by the Communist countries, the Sandinista Army (EPS) will consider absorbing some of these weapons and providing to the Salvadorans Western-manufactured arms held by the EPS in exchange. (In January 1981 the Popular Sandinista Army indeed switched from using U.S.-made weapons to those of Soviet and East European origin.)

The DRU representatives also meet with visiting Palestine Liberation Organization (PLO) leader Yasir Arafat in Managua on July 22, 1980. Arafat promises military equipment, including arms and aircraft. (A Salvadoran guerrilla leader met with FATAH leaders in Beirut in August and November, and the PLO has trained selected Salvadorans in the Near East and in Nicaragua.)

On July 27, the guerrilla General Staff delegation departs from Managua for Havana, where Cuban "specialists" add final touches to the military plans formulated during the May meetings in Havana.

Arms Deliveries Begin. In mid-August 1980, Shafik Handal's arms-shopping expedition begins to bear fruit. On August 15, 1980, Ethiopian arms depart for Cuba. Three weeks later the 60 tons of captured U.S. arms sent from Vietnam are scheduled to arrive in Cuba.

As a result of a Salvadoran delegation's trip to Iraq earlier in the year, the guerrillas receive a $500,000 logistics donation. The funds are distributed to the Sandinistas in Nicaragua and within El Salvador.

By mid-September, substantial quantities of the arms promised to Handal are well on the way to Cuba and Nicaragua. The guerrilla logistics coordinator in Nicaragua informs his Joint General Staff on September 26 that 130 tons of arms and other military material supplied by the Communist countries have arrived in Nicaragua for shipment to El Salvador. According to the captured documents, this represents one-sixth of the commitments to the guerrillas by the Communist countries. (NOTE: To get an idea of the magnitude of this commitment, the Vietnamese offer of only 60 tons included 2 million rifle and machinegun bullets, 14,500 mortar shells, 1,620 rifles, 210 machineguns, 48 mortars, 12 rocket launchers, and 192 pistols.)

In September and October, the number of flights to Nicaragua from Cuba increased sharply. These flights had the capacity to transport several hundred tons of cargo.

At the end of September, despite appeals from the guerrillas, the Sandinistas suspend their weapons deliveries to El Salvador for 1 month, after the U.S. Government lodges a protest to Nicaragua on the arms trafficking.

When the shipments resume in October, as much as 120 tons of weapons and materiel are still in Nicaragua and some 300-400 tons are in Cuba. Because of the difficulty of moving such large quantities overland, Nicaragua – with Cuban support – begins airlifting arms from Nicaragua into El Salvador. In November, about 2.5 tons of arms are delivered by air before accidents force a brief halt in the airlift.

In December, Salvadoran guerrillas, encouraged by Cuba, begin plans for a general offensive in early 1981. To provide the increased support necessary, the

Sandinistas revive the airlift into El Salvador. Salvadoran insurgents protest that they cannot absorb the increased flow of arms, but guerrilla liaison members in Managua urge them to increase their efforts as several East European nations are providing unprecedented assistance.

A revolutionary radio station – *Radio Liberacion* – operating in Nicaragua begins broadcasting to El Salvador on December 15, 1980. It exhorts the populace to mount a massive insurrection against the government. (References to the Sandinistas sharing the expenses of a revolutionary radio station appear in the captured documents.)

On January 24, 1981, a Cessna from Nicaragua crashes on takeoff in El Salvador after unloading passengers and possibly weapons. A second plane is strafed by the Salvadoran Air Force, and the pilot and numerous weapons are captured. The pilot admits to being an employee of the Nicaraguan national airline and concedes that the flight originated from Sandino International Airport in Managua. He further admits to flying two earlier arms deliveries.

Air supply is playing a key role, but infiltration by land and sea also continues. Small launches operating out of several Nicaraguan Pacific ports traverse the Gulf of Fonseca at night, carrying arms, ammunition, and personnel. During the general offensive on January 13, several dozen well-armed guerrillas landed on El Salvador's southeastern coast on the Gulf of Fonseca, adjacent to Nicaragua.

Overland arms shipments also continue through Honduras from Nicaragua and Costa Rica. In late January, Honduran security forces uncover an arms infiltration operation run by Salvadorans working through Nicaragua and directed by Cubans. In this operation, a trailer truck is discovered carrying weapons and ammunition destined for Salvadoran guerrillas. Weapons include 100 U.S. M-16 rifles and 81mm mortar ammunition. These arms are a portion of the Vietnamese shipment: A trace of the M-16s reveals that several of them were shipped to U.S. units in Vietnam where they were captured or left behind. Using this network, perhaps five truckloads of arms may have reached the Salvadoran guerrillas.

The availability of weapons and materiel significantly increases the military capabilities of the Salvadoran insurgents. While attacks raged throughout the country during the "general offensive" that began on January 10, it soon became clear that the DRU could not sustain the level of violence without suffering costly losses in personnel. By the end of January, DRU leaders apparently decided to avoid direct confrontation with government forces and reverted to sporadic guerrilla terrorist tactics that would reduce the possibility of suffering heavy casualties.

III.   The Government: The Search for Order and Democracy

Central America's smallest and most densely populated country is El Salvador. Since its independence in 1838, the country has experienced chronic political instability and repression, widespread poverty, and concentration of wealth and power in the hands of a few families. Although considerable economic progress took place in the 1960s, the political system remained in the hands of a traditional economic elite backed by the military. During the 1970s, both the legitimate grievances of the poor and landless and the growing aspirations of the expanding middle classes met increasingly with repression. El Salvador has long been a violent country with political, economic, and personal disputes often resulting in murders.

The Present Government.   Aware of the need for change and alarmed by the prospect of Nicaragua-like chaos, progressive Salvadoran military officers and civilians overthrew the authoritarian regime of General Carlos Humberto Romero in October 1979 and ousted nearly 100 conservative senior officers.

After an initial period of instability, the new government stabilized around a coalition that includes military participants in the October 1979 coup, the Christian Democratic Party, and independent civilians. Since March 1980, this coalition has begun broad social changes: conversion of large estates into peasant cooperatives, distribution of land to tenant farmers, and nationalization of foreign trade and banking.

Four Marxist-Leninist guerrilla groups are using violence and terrorism against the Salvadoran Government and its reforms. Three small non-Marxist-Leninist political parties – including a Social Democratic Party – work with guerrilla organizations and their political fronts through the Democratic Revolutionary Front (FDR), most of whose activities take place outside El Salvador.

The Government of El Salvador – headed since last December by Jose Napoleon Duarte, the respected Christian Democrat denied office by the military in the Presidential elections of 1972 – faces armed opposition from the extreme right as well as from the left. Exploiting their traditional ties to the security forces and the tendency of some members of the security forces to abuse their authority, some wealthy Salvadorans affected by the Duarte government's reforms have sponsored terrorist activities against supporters of the agrarian and banking reforms and against the government itself.

A symbiotic relationship has developed between the terrorism practised by extremists of both left and right. Thousands have died without regard to class, creed, nationality, or politics. Brutal and still unexplained murders in December of four American churchwomen – and in January of two American trade unionists – added U.S. citizens to the toll of this tragic violence. The United States has made clear its interest in a complete investigation of these killings and the punishment of those responsible.

Despite bitter resistance from right and left, the Duarte government has stuck to its reform programs and has adopted emergency measures to ease the lot of the poor through public works, housing projects, and aid to marginal communities. On the political front, it has offered amnesty to its opponents, scheduled elections for a constituent assembly in 1982, and pledged to hand power over to a popularly elected government no later than mid-1983.

The government's pursuit of progress with order has been further hampered by the virtual breakdown of the law enforcement and judicial system and by the lack of an effective civil service.

The introduction of the reforms – some of which are now clearly irreversible – has reduced popular support for those who argue that change can only come about through violence. Few Salvadorans participate in antigovernment demonstrations. Repeated calls by the guerrillas for general strikes in mid- and late 1980 went unheeded. The Duarte government, moreover, has made clear its willingness to negotiate the terms of future political processes with democratic members of all opposition forces – most notably, by accepting the offer of El Salvador's Council of Bishops to mediate between the government and the Democratic Revolutionary Front.

In sum, the Duarte government is working hard and with some success to deal with the serious political, social, and economic problems that most concern the people of El Salvador.

U.S. Support.   In its commitment to reform and democracy, the Government of El Salvador has had the political support of the United States ever since the October 1979 revolution. Because we give primary emphasis to helping the people of El Salvador, most of our assistance has been economic. In 1980, the United States provided nearly $56 million in aid, aimed at easing the conditions that underlie unrest and extremism. This assistance has helped create jobs, feed the hungry, improve health and housing and education, and support the reforms that are opening and modernizing El Salvador's economy. The United States will continue to work with the Salvadoran Government toward economic betterment, social justice, and peace.

Because the solution in El Salvador should be of the Salvadorans' own making and nonviolent, the United States has carefully limited its military support. In January, mounting evidence of Communist involvement compelled President Carter to authorize a resupply of weapons and ammunition to El Salvador – the first provision of lethal items since 1977.

IV. Some Conclusions

The foregoing record leaves little doubt that the Salvadoran insurgency has become the object of a large-scale commitment by Communist states outside Latin America.

– The political direction, organization, and arming of the insurgency is coordinated and heavily influenced by Cuba – with active support of the Soviet Union, East Germany, Vietnam, and other Communist states.

– The massing and delivery of arms to the Salvadoran guerrillas by those states must be judged against the fact that from 1977 until January 1981 the United States provided no weapons or ammunition to the Salvadoran Armed Forces.

– A major effort has been made to provide "cover" for this operation by supplying arms of Western manufacture and by supporting a front organization known as the Democratic Revolutionary Front to seek non-Communist political support through propaganda.

– Although some non-Communist states have also provided material support, the organization and delivery of this assistance, like the overwhelming mass of arms, are in the hands of Communist-controlled networks.

In short, over the past year, the insurgency in El Salvador has been progressively transformed into a textbook case of indirect armed aggression by Communist powers through Cuba.

[WHITE PAPER – SHORT ANALYSIS – FIRST VERSION]

CHRONOLOGY OF FOREIGN INVOLVEMENT IN SUPPORT OF SALVADORAN INSURGENCY

INTRODUCTION

The following chronology is based on documents captured from the Salvadoran guerrillas between November 1980 and January 1981. Two particularly important documents caches were recovered from the Communist Party of El Salvador (PCS) and the Peoples' Revolutionary Army (ERP). Only a very small portion of the total documents recovered are attached. The documents have been analyzed by both the United States and Salvadoran Governments. United States Government analysts assess the documents as fully genuine. The documents are written using frequently cryptic language and abbreviations. A glossary is provided before each document to define selected relevant arms [sic].

– December 16, 1979
Representatives of the Communist Party of El Salvador (PCS), National Resistance (FARN), and Popular Liberation Forces (FPL), writing in Havana, thank Fidel Castro for his "help, and the help of (his) comrades of the Party" in establishing a unity agreement among these armed groups (see Document A).

– April, 1980
"Requests" (presumably for arms) are made in meeting with representatives of German Democratic Republic, Bulgaria, Poland, Vietnam, Hungary, Cuba, and U.S.S.R. in meeting at Hungarian Embassy in Mexico City (see Document B).

– April 28, 1980
In meeting of Political Commission of Salvadoran Communist Party, Party Leader Shafik Handal notes need to take advantage of possibilities for help by "socialist camp." Their attitude is magnificent," he says. Handal also notes desirability of involving "everyone of the area" (i.e. Central America) as suggested by "Fidel." (see Document C)

– May 19 - 31, 1980
Popular Revolutionary Army (ERP) is admitted to guerrilla coalition after negotiations in Havana. Coalition leadership which assumes name of Unified Revolutionary Directorate (DRU), meets with Fidel Castro on three occasions and with visiting German Democratic Republic Leader Eric Honecker (see Document D). One "Humberto" is also present and consulted on unity arrangements.

– May 19 - 31, 1980
Guerrilla leadership meets twice with Cuban Directorate of Special Operations (DOE – Clandestine Operations/Special Forces Unit of Cuban Ministry of Interior) to discuss guerrilla military plans. In addition, they met with Cuban "Chief of Communications." (see Document D)

– May 30, 1980
Shafik Handal departs Havana for Moscow. (see Document D)

– June 1, 1980
Guerrilla leadership, minus Salvadoran Communist Party Chief Handal, arrives in Managua. Joint Directorate of FSLN: (a) offers a headquarters for guerrilla directorate "with all measures of security;" (b) states that it is disposed to "contribute in material terms;" (c) assumes "the cause of El Salvador as its own;" and (d) offers "advice and exchange of opinions" to guerrillas. Visiting delegation dines with "Humberto" (presumably Humberto Ortego of FSLN Directorate). (see Document D)

– June 2, 1980
Handal meets in Moscow with Mikhail Kudachkin, Deputy Chief of Latin American Section of Foreign Relations Department of CPSU Central Committee. Kudachkin suggests that Handal travel to Vietnam to seek arms and offers to pay for Handal's trip. (see Document E)

– June 9 - 15, 1980
Handal visits Vietnam where he is received by Le Duan, Secretary General of Vietnamese Communist Party, Xuan Thuy, member of Communist Party Central Committee Secretariat, and Vice-Minister of National Defense Tran Van Quang. Vietnamese, as "first contribution," agrees to provide sixty tons of arms. (see Documents E & F)

– June 19 - July 3, 1980
Handal visits the German Democratic Republic, Czechoslovakia, Bulgaria, and Hungary where he is received by senior party and military officials. Both the GDR and Hungary raise the possibility of exchanging communist for western-manufactured weapons in order to supply the guerrillas. Hungary mentions possibility of such an exchange through Angola and Ethiopia. Czechoslovakia indicates that some Czech-manufactured arms available on the world market will be provided. All visited States provide military supply or training commitments.

– July 3 - 6, 1980
Handal visits Ethiopia where he is received by Leader Mengistu Haile Mariam and Berhanu Gayeh, Executive Committee Member. Mengistu indicates that Ethiopia will supply "several thousand weapons" and ammunition. (see Documents E & F)

– July 22, 1980
Handal is again received in Moscow, this time by Karen Brutents, Chief of Latin American Section of CPSU Central Committee. Brutents indicates that the Soviets agree in principle to transport the Vietnamese arms. (see Document E)

– July 23, 1980
"Comrade Bayardo" (Bayardo Arce of FSLN Directorate) meets in Managua with delegation of the Salvadoran Guerrilla Joint General Staff. Arce promises ammunition to the guerrillas and arranges a meeting for them with the FSLN "Military Commission." Arce indicates that, since the guerrillas will receive some arms manufactured by the communist countries, the Sandinista Army (EPS) will consider absorbing some of these weapons and providing in exchange to the Salvadorans western-manufactured arms held by the EPS. (see Document G)

– July 27, 1980
Guerrilla General Staff Delegation departs from Managua to Havana where Cuban "specialists" add final touches to their military plans. (see Document G)

– August 15, 1980
Ethiopian arms depart for Cuba. (see Document F)

– September 5, 1980
Vietnamese arms scheduled to arrive in Cuba. (see Document F)

– September 24, 1980
Guerrillas receive and distribute five hundred thousand dollars ($500,000) logistics donation from Iraq. Funds are distributed to Nicaraguan FSLN and within El Salvador. (see Documents H & J)

– September 26, 1980
Guerrilla Logistics Committee informs its Joint General Staff that 130 tons of arms and other military material supplied by the communist countries have arrived in Nicaragua for shipment to El Salvador. According to the report this represents one-sixth of the commitments to the guerrillas by the communist countries. (see Document I)

– End of September, 1980
Nicaraguan FSLN suspends its weapons deliveries to El Salvador for one month after United States Government protests to Nicaraguan leadership over supply activities. (see Document J)

– End of October, 1980
The Nicaraguan FSLN provides the Salvadoran guerrillas a new delivery schedule and resumes weapons deliveries. (see Document K)

– September - October, 1980
Guerrillas begin preparations for infiltrating weapons and equipment into El Salvador by land, air and sea. (see Documents J, L, M, N and O)

– November 1, 1980
The Guerrilla General Staff is informed that there are approximately 120 tons of military equipment now in Nicaragua ready for shipment to the Salvadoran Guerrillas. By mid-November, the guerrillas indicate that 300-400 tons of weapons and material will be in Cuba ready for subsequent transfer to Nicaragua and then, clandestinely, to El Salvador. (see Document K)

– October 29, 1980
Guerrillas decide to open "clandestine" radio station in Nicaragua with help of Cubans and Nicaraguans. (see Document P)

– November, 1980
Beginning in November, the FSLN sends to El Salvador more arms than the guerrillas can receive and distribute. Guerrillas note that boats are being overloaded in Nicaragua and ask that the FSLN better coordinate its delivery activities with the guerrillas. (see Documents Q & R)

– November 1, 1980
Salvadoran Guerrilla Logistics Representatives in Managua calls on armed groups in El Salvador – the "last link" in the supply "chain" – to work harder to absorb more arms shipments. The communist countries in some cases, the representative notes, have doubled their promised help. (see Document K)

– November, 1980
Due to overloading problems, guerrillas raise need for talks on delivery arrangements with FSLN. (see Document S)

[This first version of the White Paper (Short Analysis) was accompanied by the same list of Leftist Opposition Groups and the same Documents as the revised version. These begin on page A-15 below.]

[WHITE PAPER – SHORT ANALYSIS – REVISED VERSION]

DOCUMENTS DEMONSTRATING COMMUNIST SUPPORT OF THE SALVADORAN INSURGENCY

Two particularly important document caches were recovered from the Communist Party of El Salvador (PCS) in November 1980 and from the Peoples' Revolutionary Army (ERP) in January 1981. Only a very small portion of the total documents recovered are attached. Many of the documents are written using cryptic language and abbreviations. A glossary is provided before each document to define selected relevant terms.

CHRONOLOGICAL KEY TO THE DOCUMENTS

– December 16, 1979
Representatives of the Communist Party of El Salvador (PCS), National Resistance (FARN), and Popular Liberation Forces (FPL), writing in Havana, thank Fidel Castro for his "help, and the help of (his) comrades of the Party" in establishing a unity agreement among these armed groups (see Document A).

– April, 1980
"Requests" (possibly for arms) are made in a meeting at the Hungarian Embassy in Mexico City with representatives of the German Democratic Republic, Bulgaria, Poland, Vietnam, Hungary, Cuba, and U.S.S.R. (see Document B).

– April 28, 1980
In a meeting of the Political Commission of the Salvadoran Communist Party, Party leader Shafik Handal notes the need to take advantage of possibilities for help by the "socialist camp." Their attitude is "magnificent," he says. Handal also notes desirability of involving "everyone of the area" (i.e., Central America) as suggested to "Fidel." (see Document C)

– May 19 - 31, 1980
Popular Revolutionary Army (ERP) is admitted to the guerrilla coalition after negotiations in Havana. Coalition leadership, which assumes name of Unified Revolutionary Directorate (DRU), meets with Fidel Castro on three occasions and with visiting German Democratic Republic leader Eric Honecker (see Document D).

– May 19 - 31, 1980
Guerrilla leadership meets twice with Cuban Directorate of Special Operations (DOE – clandestine operations/special forces unit of Cuban Ministry of Interior) to discuss guerrilla military plans. In addition, they met with the Cuban "Chief of Communications." (see Document D)

– May 30, 1980
Shafik Handal departs from the Havana meeting for Moscow. (see Document D)

– June 1, 1980
Guerrilla leadership, minus Salvadoran Communist Party chief Handal, arrives in Managua. Joint Directorate of FSLN: (a) offers a headquarters for the guerrilla directorate "with all measures of security;" (b) states that it is disposed to "contribute in material terms;" (c) assumes "the cause of El Salvador as its own;" and (d) offers "advice and exchange of opinions" to the guerrillas. (see Document D)

– June 2 - July 22, 1980
Salvadoran Communist Party Chief Shafik Handal visits: (a) the USSR, (b) Vietnam, (c) the German Democratic Republic, (d) Czechoslovakia, (e) Bulgaria, (f) Hungary, and (g) Ethiopia.

— June 2, 1980
Handal meets in Moscow with Mikhail Kudachkin, Deputy Chief of the Latin American Section of the Foreign Relations Department of the CPSU Central Committee. Kudachkin suggests that Handal travel to Vietnam to seek arms and offers to pay for Handal's trip. (see Document E)

— June 9 - 15, 1980
Handal visits Vietnam where he is received by Le Duan, Secretary General of the Vietnamese Communist Party, Xuan Thuy, member of the Communist Party Central Committee Secretariat, and Vice Minister of National Defense Tran Van Quang. Vietnamese, as "first contribution," agree to provide sixty tons of arms. (see Documents E and F)

— June 19 - 24, 1980
Handal visits German Democratic Republic where he is received by Hermann Axen, member of the GDR Politburo. Axen states that the GDR has already dispatched 1.9 tons of supplies to Managua. (On July 21, GDR leader Honecker telegraphs GDR Embassy in Moscow, indicating that additional supplies will be sent and that the GDR will provide military training, particularly on clandestine operations. GDR telegram adds that, although Berlin possesses no Western-manufactured weapons (which the Salvadoran guerrillas are seeking), efforts will be undertaken to find "a solution to this problem.") (see Documents E and F)

— June 24 - 27, 1980
Handal visits Czechoslovakia where he is received by Vasil Bilak, Second Secretary of the Czech Communist Party. Bilak notes that some Czech arms circulating in the world market will be provided. Transportation will be coordinated with the GDR. (see Documents E and F)

— June 27 - 30, 1980
Handal visits Bulgaria where he is received by Dimitir Stanichev, member of the Central Committee Secretariat. Bulgarians agree to supply German-origin weapons and other supplies. (see Documents E and F)

— June 30 - July 3, 1980
Handal visits Hungary where he is received by Communist Party General Secretary Janos Kadar and "Guesel" (probably Central Committee Secretary for Foreign Affairs Andras Gyenes.) The latter offers radios and other supplies and indicates Hungarian willingness to trade arms with Ethiopia or Angola in order to obtain Western-origin arms for the Salvadoran guerrillas. (see Documents E and F)

— July 3 - 6, 1980
Handal visits Ethiopia where he is received by Chairman Mengistu Haile Mariam and Berhanu Bayeh, Executive Committee member. Mengistu indicates that Ethiopia will supply "several thousand weapons" and ammunition. (see Documents E and F)

— July 22, 1980
Handal is again received in Moscow, this time by Karen Brutents, Chief of the Latin American Section of the CPSU Central Committee. Brutents indicates that the Soviets agree in principle to transport the Vietnamese arms. (see Document E)

— July 23, 1980
"Comrade Bayardo" (Bayardo Arce of FSLN Directorate) meets in Managua with a delegation of the Salvadoran guerrilla Joint General Staff. Arce promises ammunition to the guerrillas and arranges a meeting for them with the FSLN "Military Commission." Arce indicates that, since the guerrillas will receive some arms manufactured by the communist countries, the Sandinista Army (EPS) will consider absorbing some of these weapons and providing to the Salvadorans Western-manufactured arms held by the EPS in exchange. (see Document G)

– July 22, 1980
Guerrilla military leadership meets in Managua, Nicaragua with PLO leader Yasir Aragat. (see Document G)

– July 27, 1980
Guerrilla General Staff delegation departs from Managua for Havana where Cuban "specialists" add final touches to their military plans. (see Document G)

– August 15, 1980
Ethiopian arms depart for Cuba. (see Document F)

– September 5, 1980
Vietnamese arms are scheduled to arrive in Cuba. (see Document F)

– September 24, 1980
Guerrillas receive and distribute five hundred thousand dollars ($500,000) logistics donation from Iraq. Funds are distributed to the Nicaraguan FSLN and within El Salvador. (see Documents H and J)

– September 26, 1980
Guerrilla logistics committee informs its Joint General Staff that 130 tons of arms and other military material supplied by the communist countries have arrived in Nicaragua for shipment to El Salvador. According to the report, this represents one-sixth of the commitments to the guerrillas by the communist countries. (see Document I)

(NOTE: To get an idea of the dimensions of this commitment, the Vietnamese offer of only 60 tons included 2 million rifle and machine gun bullets, 14,500 mortar shells, 1620 rifles, 210 machine guns, 48 mortars, 12 rocket launchers, and 192 pistols.)

– End of September, 1980
Nicaraguan FSLN suspends its weapons deliveries to El Salvador for one month after the United States Government protests to the Nicaraguan leadership over the supply activities. (see Document J)

– End of October, 1980
The Nicaraguan FSLN provides the Salvadoran guerrillas a new delivery schedule and resumes deliveries. (see Document K)

– September - October, 1980
Guerrillas begin preparations for infiltrating weapons and equipment into El Salvador by land, air and sea. (see Documents J, L, M, N and O)

– November 1, 1980
The guerrilla General Staff is informed that there are approximately 120 tons of military equipment now in Nicaragua ready for shipment to the Salvadoran guerrillas. By mid-November, the guerrillas indicate that 300-400 tons of weapons and material will be in Cuba ready for subsequent transfer to Nicaragua and then, clandestinely, to El Salvador. (see Document K)

– October 29, 1980
Guerrillas decide to open "clandestine" radio station in Nicaragua with the help of the Cubans and Nicaraguans. (see Document P)

– November, 1980
Beginning in November, the FSLN sends to El Salvador more arms than the guerrillas can receive and distribute. The guerrillas note that the boats are being overloaded in Nicaragua and ask that the FSLN better coordinate its delivery activities with the guerrillas. (see Documents Q and R)

— November 1, 1980
Salvadoran guerrilla logistics representative in Managua calls on armed groups in El Salvador — the "last link" in the supply "chain" — to work harder to absorb more arms shipments. The communist countries in some cases, the representative notes, have doubled their promised help. (see Document K)

— November, 1980
Due to overloading problems, the guerrillas raise the need for talks on delivery arrangements with the FSLN. (see Document S)

— January 10, 1981
The guerrillas launch their "general offensive" against the Salvadoran government. It failed.

Leftist Opposition Groups In El Salvador

1. A. PCS — The Communist Party of El Salvador is the oldest organization of the far left and has historically been oriented toward Moscow. It has abandoned its former attitude toward violent revolution and now espouses armed action against the Salvadoran Government.
    B. UDN — The National Democratic Union is the political front of the PCS and has a variety of component organizations such as labor unions and urban poor.

2. A. FPL — the Farabundo Marti Popular Liberation Forces is the largest terrorist/guerrilla group and professes a revolutionary Marxist creed. Its leader, Salvador Cayetano Carpio, was a member of the PCS before breaking with the orthodox party and helping form the FPL.
    B. BPR — the Popular Revolutionary Bloc, the front group of the FPL, is a large coalition of peasant, worker, student, teacher, etc., groups. It has been responsible for numerous strikes, occupations of buildings, marches, etc.

3. A. ERP — The Popular Revolutionary Army is a terrorist/guerrilla group organized in the early 1970's by dissatisfied members of the PCS. It has been particularly active in bombings and kidnappings.
    B. LP-28 — The 28 February Popular Leagues, the front group for the ERP, is a modest-sized coalition of students, teachers, and peasants.

4. A. FARN — The Armed Forces of National Resistance is a terrorist/guerrilla group which was formed in the mid-1970s by a splinter group of the ERP.
    B. FAPU — The United Popular Action Front, the front group for the FARN, consists of several student, farmworker, and urban slumdweller organizations.

5. A. PRTC — The Revolutionary Party of Central American Workers is a small terrorist/guerrilla group organized in the mid-1970's.
    B. MLP — The Movement of Popular Liberation, the front group for the PRTC, is headed by Fabio Castillo.

6. MNR — The National Revolutionary Movement is a small Social Democratic oriented party headed by former Junta member Guillermo Ungo.

7. FAL — The guerrilla arm of the PCS, formed in 1979 when the communist party decided to engage in armed subversion and terrorism.

8. MPSC — The Popular Social Christian Movement was formed in March 1980 by dissident Christian Democrats and is headed by Ruben Zamora Rivas.

9. FD — The Democratic Front is a coalition of left-of-center parties, the MNR and MPSC, as well as professional and labor groups formed in early April 1980.

10. FDR – The Revolutionary Democratic Front is a coalition of the CRM and FD formed in mid-April 1980. It is now headed by Guillermo Ungo.

11. CRM – The Revolutionary Coordinator of the Masses is the umbrella group for leftist organizations which was formed in January 1980.

12. DRU – The Unified Revolutionary Directorate is the recently formed control board for leftist organizations and comprises the leadership of the principal terrorist/guerrilla groups, the PCS, the FPL, the ERP, and the FARN. The DRU has declared that it will guide the revolution. It has superseded the CRM.

13. FMLN – The Farabundo Marti Peoples Liberation Front is the coordinating board of the guerrilla organizations comprised of the ERP, FPL, PCS, PRTC and FARN. Its orientation is radical Marxist. It is controlled by the DRU.

DOCUMENT A

Letter from representatives of the Communist Party of El Salvador (PCS), the National Resistenace (FARN), and the Farabundo Marti Peoples' Liberation Forces (FPL) to Cuban President Fidel Castro (dated Havana, December 16, 1979).

GLOSSARY A

Fidel – Fidel Castro
FPL – Peoples' Liberation Forces. A Salvadoran guerrilla group
National Resistance – Armed Forces of National Resistance. A Salvadoran guerrilla group.

TRANSLATION OF DOCUMENT A

Havana, 16 December 1979

Comrade Fidel:
    Our opening words bring to you the brotherly and revolutionary greetings of the heroic people of El Salvador. Comrade, brother and friend: the rich revolutionary practice, faithful to the proletarian internationalism of the Cuban people – headed by its Leninist vanguard, the Communist Party of Cuba, guided by your brilliant leadership as an unyielding and exemplary revolutionary – has been decisive for us, the representatives of El Salvador's revolutionary organizations, in understanding the urgent need for undertaking transcendental steps in the process of the unity of our people.
    Today we can tell you, Fidel, that thanks to your help, to the help of your party comrades and to the inspired example of the revolutionary people of Cuba, we have undertaken a transcendental step by signing an agreement which establishes very solid bases upon which we begin building the coordination and unity of our organizations: the unity and single direction so needed by our people in order to progress in its struggle to achieve popular freedom, democracy, peace and socialism.
    This letter is accompanied by a copy of this agreement. It will allow you to appreciate its magnitude and scope and will surely bring you deserved satisfaction and renewed impulse in your indefatigable labors aimed at unity among the revolutionary ranks of our peoples who are oppressed by imperialism and dominant exploitative classes.
    We shall honor the agreement we have signed just as we have proved our commitment to the heroic struggle of our people.
    As we have remained faithful to the struggle of our people, so shall we prove worthy of the exalted internationalist and revolutionary example you embody, because the patient and wise work that Cuban solidarity has contributed to our success in taking another step toward unity is leaving its imprint on the accelerated pace that characterizes our people's march toward the ultimate success of its revolution.

For the Communist Party of El Salvador:

> /s/ S. Handal
> Secretary General of the Central
> Committee of the PCS

For the National Resistance:

> /s/ D. Fuentes (?)
> First Political-Military Officer

For the "People's Liberation Forces (FPL) Farabundo Marti":

> /s/ Marcial
> First Officer of the Central Command

La Habana, 16 de diciembre de 1979

Compañero Fidel:

Nuestras primeras palabras son para manifestarte muy fraternal y revolucionariamente en nombre del heroico pueblo de El Salvador.

Compañeros, hermano y amigo: la más práctica revolucionaria, fiel al internacionalismo proletario del pueblo cubano, encabezado por su vanguardia leninista el Partido Comunista de Cuba, guiados por tu lúcida estrategia de implementable y ejemplar revolucionario, la más decidida para que nosotros como representantes de las organizaciones revolucionarias de El Salvador comprendiéramos la necesidad ineludible de avanzar pasos trascendentales en el proceso de unidad de nuestro pueblo.

Podemos decirte, hoy, Fidel, que gracias a tu ayuda, a la ayuda de tus compañeros de Partido y al noble importante del pueblo revolucionario de Cuba, hemos dado un paso trascendental, firmando un acuerdo que afecta bases muy sólidas entre los que iniciamos la coordinación y unidad de nuestras organizaciones; unidad y dirección única que tanto necesita nuestro pueblo para avanzar en su lucha hasta la conquista de la liberación popular, la democracia, la paz y el socialismo.

Acompañamos a esta carta, la copia de ese acuerdo, cuya lectura te
permitirá conocer su amplitud y alcances y, de seguro, te aportará
justa satisfacción y nuevo estímulo a tu incansable labor unificadora

.....2/

ra de las días revolucionarios de nuestros pueblos oprimidos por
el imperialismo y por las clases dominantes explotadoras.

Así como hemos venido respondiendo a la heroica lucha de nuestro
pueblo, así responderemos al acuerdo que hemos firmado.

Así como hemos respondido a la lucha de nuestro pueblo, así responderemos al ejemplo revolucionario, digno e internacionalista que tú
representas, porque la labor paciente y sabia con la que la solidaridad cubana ha contribuido a que nuestros damos este paso unitario,
está marcado el paso acelerado conque nuestro pueblo marcha a la
realización de su revolución.

Por el Partido Comunista de El Salvador:

Secretario General Comité Central PCS

Por la Resistencia Nacional:

Primer Responsable Rama Nacional RN

Por las "Fuerzas Populares de Liberación (FPL) Farabundo Martí":

Primer Responsable del Comando Central

DOCUMENT B

Excerpts of notes on trip to Mexico by member of Political Commission of Salvadoran Communist Party ("Logan") (dated April 26, 1980).

GLOSSARY B

CP – Communist Party

CRM – Revolutionary Coordinator of the Masses, Federation of political fronts of Salvadoran armed groups.

GDR – German Democratic Republic

P. – Party (Communist Party)

Perl. – Perla (Cuba)

S.I. – Socialist International

Sov. – Soviet

TRANSLATION OF DOCUMENT B

(Begin Excerpt)
   It is one thing or another –
4th The Program: I agree with it, but could we have a different one?
Memo: In the political analysis (word illegible), but the present moment requires us to move away from this into the coordination of our actions. In the international arena, not everything is favorable. We have to work on it. We have not gained everything.
Hector: Also in relation to that.
I: I took advantage of the opportunity to mention the (word illegible) in relation to the S.I. Hector said that the delay of the invitation sent to Santo Domingo was a result of administrative and not political problems. They talked about the advantage of mentioning everything to David.
Mayorga: I am at your service. If you ask me to be a street cleaner or a launderer.
Socialist Embassies
Wide-ranging: German Democratic Republic, Bulgaria, Polish, Vietnam, Hungarians, Cuba, held at the Hungarian Embassy
The meeting was a good one. A lot of questions.
He gave them the requests.
Then the bilateral meetings: One by one of (word illegible)
Vietnam: good
Bulgarians: good
Polish: We talked very much, 3 hours
Hungarian: Very interesting. Gloria started talking about the only P. (party) which they began with militarist inclinations and rejected the P.C. (Communist Party) The Hungarian replied: it is because of the P. (party) that the socialist world opens the door to you. It was a different case in Nicaragua. The last meeting was with the Soviet.
From the German Democratic Republic: small souvenirs; operation
–"Pan de Lata" – rocket/launchers
            in addition to (word illegible) with CRM
            they want to agree on a party "Perl."
   – also-files = NO

Fair (bazaar)
a) Manuel b) Diab and c) Juan Jose
   Cassettes are need with the voices of the directors of the coordinating body

(greetings or speeches) and with speeches of (word illegible) F.D. Handkerchiefs with the signatures of the directors of the Coordinating Body and Stamps Sent
5,000 key rings

Florecitas

(End Excerpt)

266

8/ - Es una misma u otra cosa.-
4º) El programa.- Yo estoy de acuerdo, pero a podría tener otro programa?

Hemo: En el análisis político coincidencia pero el momento actual exige a partir de esto a la coordinación: las acciones. Internacionalment no todo es favorable. Hay que trabajarlo. No todo está ganado.-

Víctor: También sobre lo mismo.

Yo: aproveché para mencionar las preguntas sobre la I.S.- Hubo mención q' fué debido a problemas administrativos y no político la tardanza de la invitación a Santo Domingo. Hablaron sobre la conveniencia de hablar - sobre: todo en David.

teprrga: estoy a su disposición. Si de horrendos me ponen, de Suicidas.

Embajadores Socialistas

Se cumplió: R.D.A, Bulgaria, Polaco, Vietnam, Hungría, Cuba en el local de Embaj. de Hungría
La reunión buena. Muchas preguntas. Se les tiró las políticas.

— 267

a/ Luego las bilaterales: uno por uno...
Con Vietnam: ~~Suave~~
Bulgaros : - " -
Polaco : Se habló mucho 3 horas.-
Hungaro: Muy interesante: Gloria empezó hablar.
P. único. q' ellos escogieron ē. c.- el lu
militarista y negaban 2° P.E.- El lu
contesto: es por el P. q' el mundo =
cialista los I abrí las puertas o vide
En Nicaragua fué distinto
La última reunión fué con el Sov.
   De RDA: Suministros cortos; operación
- Para de Lata" ──┬── lema colectes
              ├── además de platín con C RA.
              └── quien convenir de P. a Partí.
- además - archivo = NO

┌──── to ────┐

- Feria
a) Manuel b) Diab y c) Juan José
   Se necesitan Cassetes: con las voces de
los jefes de la coordinadora (saludos
o discursos) con discursos de 10
del F.D.-
   Pañuelos con las firmas de los
Jefes Coordin y Sellos. Enviados
     J. 200 llaveros
     F. Inscritón

DOCUMENT C

Excerpt from notes on meeting of Political Commission of Salvadoran Communist Party, April 28, 1980.

GLOSSARY C

C.P. – Communist Party

FAL – Liberation Armed Forces. Military unit of Communist Party of El Salvador.

Felipe – FPL. Peoples Liberation Forces. Salvadoran guerrilla group.

Fidel – Fidel Castro

Mex. – Mexican

P. – Party. Communist Party

Rene – Resistencia National (RN). The Armed Forces of National Resistance. Salvadoran guerrilla group

Tico – Costa Rican

TRANSLATION OF DOCUMENT C

(Begin Excerpt)
We acted accordingly. I do not look behind, rather, I look ahead with boldness.
On the basis of this panorama, we should tackle the problems, which are:
focus on the main tasks without losing sight of them.
– Main tasks: Make adjustments in the Party to carry out the struggle. We have made progress, but it's not enough. We have created the FAL, but it must act, it must go into action.
– We are reorganizing the Party, but problems persist.
– Action-related measures – to improve things – have yet to be completed – these measures affect the rest of the task.
– Such is the case of Arturo (the teacher) whom we have lost because of delays.
– With the cadres on hand we could organize several battalions within a short time.
– However, should we be at all unable to ready our people we should place them under other commands.
– We should achieve, or accelerate the creation of the "Polo" with Felipe, without attempting to place the brunt of it on Rene. Some of the problems we have could be resolved by that move.
– On my part, I have devoted a lot of attention to the FAL, but it still could be better. For that reason, I intend to recommend a reorganization in the work of the Directorate.
– Rene is justified in his replies, since the masses under attack could deteriorate, could lose confidence.
– I'm in agreement with taking advantage of the possibilities of assistance from the socialist camp. I think that their attitude is magnificent. We are not yet taking advantage of it.
– We must speed up the reorganization and put the Party on a war footing, and block whatever impediment there is.
– It is fundamental to accelerate the agreement to unify the labor movement so that it may play a unifying role in the insurrection.
– We must solidify the bases, and together infiltrate every sector of the State.
– Help the SIGES and other labor unions to shed their vacillations.
– The agreement must not be made at the union level.
– It must be at the level of the Single Labor Movement, and from that point we could

then examine the situation in the countryside.
- We could agree on a joint leadership.
- The idea of involving everyone in the area has already been suggested *to Fidel himself*. There is no opinion from the "friends" (local brothers), although they noted this as they were present at that time (when the matter was brought up).
- *Fidel* thought well of the idea.
- We should encourage the participation of the area organizations, mainly those of the *Communist Party*, which should play a role:
- For our part we have involved the Mex. and H. parties but they have not responded well.
- We have provided funds for them to help us, but it has been poor.
- The *Tico comrades* have been also indolent with regard to our needs and they contribute very little.
- We need to shake up the parties in the area, for their attitude does not rise to the occasion.
- We need to draw support from the socialist camp.
- In order not to neglect the organizational work of the FAL I should devote more time to the area of command, setting time aside from the organizational work.
- (Illegible) is proposing a general (armed) outbreak, or the beginning of a new process in which the military struggle . . .

(End Excerpt)

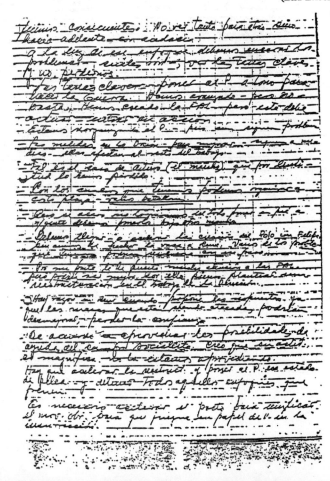

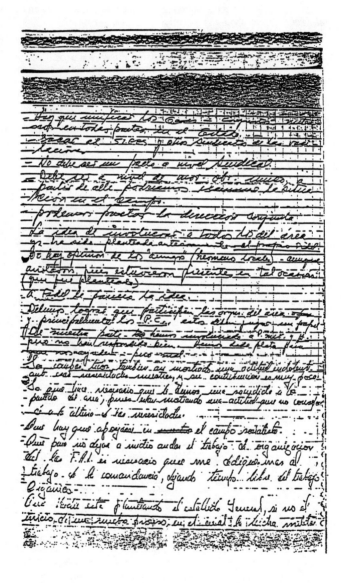

DOCUMENT D

Report on trip of "Eduardo" (member of Political Commission of Salvadoran Communist Party) from May 5 to June 8, 1980.

GLOSSARY D

CCCP – USSR

CRM – Revolutionary Coordinator of Masses. Federation of political fronts of armed groups.

D.U. – Unified Directorate of Salvadoran insurgent groups

DOE – Cuban Directorate of Special Operations. Covert operations/special forces directorate of Cuban Ministry of Interior

E.M. – General Staff

Front – Nicaraguan FSLN (Sandinistas)

Fid. – Fidel Castro

FDR – Democratic Revolutionary Front. Federation of political fronts of armed groups, their respective trade unions, and three non-Marxist groups.

ERP – Salvadoran guerrilla group

Hercules – ERP. Salvadoran guerrilla group

Humberto – Humberto Ortega, member of Nicaraguan FSLN Directorate

Joint M. Plan – Joint Military Plan

Milicos – members of the armed forces

ORPA – Revolutionary Organization of the People in Arms. Guatemalan guerrilla group.

PC – Communist Party

PCH – Communist Party of Honduras

PGT – Guatemalan Labor Party

Rene – Resistencia Nacional. Salvadoran guerrilla group

Simon – Shafik Handal. Leader of Salvadoran Communist Party.

S.J. – San Jose, Costa Rica

Teg. – Tegucigalpa, Honduras

Toys – weapons

PCS – Salvadoran Communist Party

TRANSLATION OF DOCUMENT D

THE REPORT OF EDUARDO: – TRIP OF 5 MAY TO 8 JUNE '80

1. **HONDURAS:** –
   a) Interview with former Rector (arranged through PCH)
   b) Interview with Aldana (our suggestions); still to be reported on: – (a) Internal problems of the PCH; (b) offers to supply qualified specialists and the logistical possibilities (routes, runways, market etc.), (c) they are requesting a man or a delegate to be assigned to Tegucigalpa to tend to the toy market and to give guidance in the publicity area.
   c) Bilateral (meeting) with the CP (our suggestions).
   d) Attempts to meet with Milicos – –
      J.J., without meaning to, encouraged the schismatic factions.

2. **GUATEMALA:** –
   a) Bilateral with ORPA fell through again.
   b) Bilateral with PGT (our suggestion).
      – Octavio spoke at one part of it;
      – They held a Plenary;
      – Impressions.

3. **COSTA RICA:** –
   a) Interview with Roni (our suggestion).
   b) Interview with Manuel (our suggestion):
      – His help in organizing the arrival of the FDR;
      – I listened to his advice, doubts;
      – Site for a possible meeting with area PC.
   c) Establishment of Tri to organize and plan the work:
      – Difficulties;
      – Drawing up of a program for the CRM in S.J.;
      – Drawing up of a program for the arrival of the FDR delegation;
      – Interview with J.M.A.
   d) Reorganization, redistribution of the authorities/responsibilities (atribuciones) of Manuel and J. and others.

---

4. **HAVANA (19 May):** –
   – While awaiting arrival of RN delegation, had interviews with comrade Silva of the Analysis Department.
   – (20 May) Bilateral meeting with Felipe; informed them about the Honduran situation.
   – Meeting with German and Aurelio.
   – Bilateral with the Hercules delegation.
   – Bilateral with Rolando.
   – (21 May; 9am) Agreed to begin the meeting (previously bilateral between Rene and Hercules) which lasted all morning; for this reason, it was carried over into the afternoon.
   – First, the Tri met – submitted agenda, the invitation of the host comrades.
   – Acceptance of the Hercules and the conditions: Rene reports on the new cases.
   – Incorporation of the Hercules; they are told of their acceptance and the conditions.
   – With the agenda now cleaned up, there remained (only) the matters of: enrollment of the E, Unified Leadership, and the joint Politico-Military Strategic Line.
   – Two editorial committees named: – Vladimir and Eduardo for the document

on the Unified Leadership; and Simon and Carmen for the Joint Politico-Military Strategic Line.
- Discussion begins.
- Delegations meet with Humberto.
(22 May) – Discussions continue, completing the first round discussions.
- Interview with Fidel in the palace: solemnity and fraternity. Friendly atmosphere; filming and photography. Concludes with protocol supper.
(23 May) – Interview with the DOE delegate concerning the EM, and then with the chief of Communications.
- Distribution of the documents: – amendments for the new draft.
- Courtesy visit to Fidel.
(24 May) – More amendments and new draft.
(25 May) – Visit to UPM and another meeting with Humberto: opinions concerning internal documents.
(26 May) – D.U. Manifesto
Visit by Fidel to sign documents Visit to the DOE to confirm joint M plan Interviews with UPM, Viet Nam, EGP leadership Bil(ateral?) (talks?) with Felipe: Report by Marcial
(29 May) – Interview with E. Honecker
(30 May) – Simon's trip
(31 May) – Press conference
(1 Jun) – Return

5. *MANAGUA*
Bilateral with representatives of the PSCh
Interview with PRTC
Meeting with "El Frente" ("The Front") to discuss:

The Chofer matter	I will find about Hugo there
the "Papa Lico" matter	We brought up the case of Luis Enrique

Interview with GDR
Interview with CCCP
Interview with the Joint Directorate
   - They offer the D.U. headquarters with all measures of security and they offer their (international) field of operations, which they control
   - Offer "Ready to contribute in material terms"
   Everything depends on:
      - Setting up of the Committee (?)
      - Delineation of concrete plans
   Their help will be in accordance with the plans what the enemy uses
   - The Joint Command assumes the cause of E.S. as their own
   - They are placing themselves at our disposal for the evaluation or exchange of information
   - Dinner at Humberto's house
- Composition of the Cel. and definition of its powers.
   - Cases: Ovidio and his wife and Hugo

6. *COSTA RICA*
- What Jose reported on his trip from the FDR concerning developments
   Generally good – Benito and "El Chele"
- Trip to Turrialba
   - Good impressions of the FDR trip
   - difficulties at the CRM level
   - Each of them (BPR and FAP) has their own Solid(arity) Committees
   - Good relations at the level of the TRI, especially
   - with Fel(ipe?) since teo (magic bean) and his style of work puts the others on the spot
   - He had organized bilateral that did not work out ([at] the Tri level) with V.P.

7. *HONDURAS*
   − Brief interview with Aldana who was told about the results of the "Unidad"
   − (Aggrav) detailed report (by) Dav) on internal division
   − Bilateral planned with C.P. that did not take place (?)
   − Asked for help: economic, vehicular
   − Proposed to help them organize logistical work

14 Jun 80

INFORME DE EDUARDO/ VIAJE DEL : de mayo AL 8 DE JUNIO /8C

1.- HONDURAS:

− a) Entrevista con ex-rector (previa mediación del PCH.)

− b) Entrevista con Aldana (nuestros planteamientos)
    −lo que falta que informar: a) Problemas internos del PCH,'
    b)ofrecimientos de proporcionar especialistas calif. y posibil
    ..dades logísticas :(ruta, pistas, mercado, etc])
    c) solicitan hombre o delegado destacado en Teg. para atender
    mercado de jugetes y dé orientaciones en campo publicidad.-

-c)Bilateral con CP (Nuestros planteamientos)

-d) Intentos por reun. con Milicos

− J.J. alentó sin quererlo, las tendencias escisionistas

2.- GUATEMALA:

− a) Bilateral con ORPA. fracasó nuevemente

− b) Bilateral con PGT (nuestro planteamiento)
    − En una parte.intervino Octavio.-
    − Tenían Plano
    .. impresiones

3.- COSTA RICA:

− a) Entrevista con Roni (nuestro planteamiento)

− b) Entrevista con Manuel (·
    − su ayuda para organizar llegada del FDR·
    − escuché sus consejos, dudas
    − la seda ante posible encuentro de los PC del área·

− c) Integración de Tri..para organizar y planificar trabajo
    − dificultades
    − elaboración de Programa para la CRM en S.J.
    − elaboración de Programa para llegada de la deleg. del FDR
    − entrevista con J. M A.'

− d) Reorganización, redistribución de atribuciones de Manuel y J
    y otros.·

6.- HABANA: (19-V-)

- Mientras llega delegación RN., entrevistas con C.Silva del Departamento de Análisis

- 20-V- . Bilateral con Felipe, se les informa do situación hondureñ

- Encuentro con Germán y Aurelio

- Bilateral con deleg. de Hércules

- ~~Bilateral~~ Bilateral con Rolando

- 21-V- .9 AM Acuérdase iniciar el encuentro, previa bilateral entre René y Hércules, la cual se ~~xxxxxxxxxxxxxxxxxxxxxxxxxxx~~ prolonga toda la mañana, razón por la cual la reunión se traslada por la tarde.

- Primero se reune la TRI: Somete la Agenda, la invitación de los Comp. anfitriones

- Aceptación de los Hércules y las condicionantes: René pone a conocimiento los casos nuevos

- Incorporación de los Hércules; Se le comunica su ingreso y las condiciones

- Ya depurada la Agenda, la cual quedó: Ingreso del E, Dirección Unificada y Línea Estrat. Pol-Mil. conjunta

- Nombranse dos Comisiones redactoras: Vlad. y Eduar. para el documento da Dirección Unificada, y Simón y Carmen para Línea Estrat: pol-mil conj:

22xxx Iniciase la discusión

- Encuentro de las delegaciones con Humberto

22-V- Continúese la discusión, la cual agota la primera ronda de discusiones.

- Entrevista con Fid. en Palacio: Solemnidad y fraternidad. Ambiente amistoso, filmaciones y fotogr., culmina con cena prot.

23-V- Entrevista con del. del DOE sobre E.M. y luego con Jefe de Comunicaciones

- Depuración de los documentos : enmiendas para la nueva redacción

- Visita de cortesía de Fid.

24 -V Más enmiendas y nueva redacción

- 25 - V -· Visita a UPE y nuevo encuentro con Humberto: opiniones
  sobre los documentos·internos.

- 26- V- ꭗꭗꭗꭗꭗꭗꭗꭗꭗꭗꭗꭗꭗꭗꭗꭗꭗꭗꭗꭗꭗꭗꭗꭗꭗꭗꭗꭗꭗ
  Manifiesto de la D.U.

= Visita de Fid. para firma de documentos

- Visita Él DOE para aserto. del Plan M. conjunto

- Entrevistas con dirección dd UPE, Viet Nam, ECP.
- Bil don Felaipe: inf. de Marcial.

29-V- Entrevista con C. Honecker

- 30-V- viaje se Simón

- 31-V- Conf. de Prensa -

— - 1-VI— Regreso

ꭗꭗꭗꭗꭗ

S.- MANAGUA:

- Bilateral con delegados representantes del PSCh.
= Entrevista con PRTC
- Encuentro con El Frente para:
  - Caso Chofer   - allí me enteré caso Hugo
  - " papá Lico - Plantaamos caso de Luis Enrique
- Entrevista con RDA
- Entrevista con CCCP
- Entrevista con BIR. CONJUN.
  - Ofrecen Sede de la D.U., con toda las med. de segur. y
    ofrecen su campo de acción (Internacional) que manejan
  - Ofrecto. "disp. de aportar en térm. materiales"
    todo depende de:
    - Instal. de Comisión (?)
    - definic. de los planes concretos
    su ayuda será de acuerdo a los planes y de acuerdo a lo
    el enemigo utilice
  - La D. Conj. asume como propia la causa de E.S.,

  - se ponen a nuestra disposición para el asesoramiento o in-
    tercambio de experiencias

  - Cena en casa de Humberto

- Constitución de Cel. y deficición de atribuciones.
  - Casos: Ovidio y Sra. y Hugo.

6.- COSTA RICA:

- Lo que informa José socre desarrolla jornada del FDR
  - En general bueno- Benito y el Chele
- Viaje a Turrialba
  - Impresiones buenes de la jornada del FDR
  - dificultades a nivel de CRM
  - Cada uno;BPR y FAP, tienen sus propios Comites de Solid
  - Buenas relaciones a nivel de TRI, especialmente con Fel., ya que tao :(frijol mágico) y con su estilo de trab. pone en aprietos al resto.
  - Había organizado bilateral que no fructificó (a nivel de Tri) con V.P.

7.- HONDURAS: -

- Breve entrevista con Aldana a quien se le informó de los resultados de la Unidad
- Informo Dav. de profundización (agravt,) de la división interna.
- Programan bilateral con C.P. que no se afectuó (?)
- Solicitan ayuda: Ecos., vehículo
- Se les plantea ayuda para organizar trab. logist.

14 - VII-80.

DOCUMENT E

Excerpt of report of trip to the socialist countries, Asia, and Africa by Shafik Handal, Secretary General of the Salvadoran Communist Party, June 9 - July 3, 1980.

GLOSSARY E

C – Cuba

CC – Central Committee

CP – Communist Party

CPSU – Communist Party of the Soviet Union

DRU – Unified Revolutionary Directorate.   Joint leadership of Salvadoran armed groups

GDR – German Democratic Republic

Here – Cuba

PCB – Bulgarian Communist Party

The Comrade – Shafik Handal, Secretary General of the Salvadoran Communist Party

V – Vietnam

TRANSLATION OF DOCUMENT E

Trip to the Socialist Countries, Asia, and Africa

1. Vietnam, from 9 to 15 June. Received by Le Duan, secretary general of the Vietnamese CP; Xuan Thuy, member of the secretariat of the central committee and vice president of the National Assembly; and Tran Van Quang, lieutenant general, deputy minister of National Defense. Friendly and enthusiastic reception. They agreed to provide aid in weapons, the first shipment consisting of: 192 9-mm pistols; 1,620 AR-15 rifles; 162 M-30 medium machine guns; 36 M-60 heavy machine guns; 12 M-50 heavy machine guns (caliber 12.7mm); 36 6-mm mortars; 12 81-mm mortars; 12 DKZ-57 antitank rocket launchers. Ammunition: 15,000 cartridges for M-30 and M-60 machine guns (7.62mm); 130,000 cartridges for M-50 machine gun (12.7mm); 9,000 shells for 61-mm mortars; 4,000 shells for 81-mm mortars; 1,500 shells for DKZ-57 antitank weapon. Approximate weight of the entire shipment: 60 tons.

According to a message received at the embassy here on 24 July and read to the comrade, the above-mentioned materiel will be ready for shipment during the first five days of September. If sent by ship, it will be delivered in Ho Chi Minh City. It is recommended that it be packaged as commercial goods, stowed in dry holds at the bottom of the ship, and covered with real commercial goods.

The comrade requested air transport from the CPSU, but he left Moscow on 23 July without obtaining a reply. At the embassy here on 28 July he asked that a cable be sent urging a reply. Before he left here on 6 August there had been no reply. This was communicated to the ambassador of V. along with our decision to send the materiel by ship. The ambassador of V. expects that within a short time – around 7-8 August – we will communicate to him the details of the transport operation. It was decided that if a favorable reply to the request for air transport was received in time, we would take advantage of it, in which case we would need to coordinate with the Vietnamese. The reply of the CPSU will be received by Norma, the representative here.

2. Ethiopia, from 3 to 6 July. Received by Haile-Mariam Mengistu and by Berhanu Bayih, member of the executive committee of the COPWE and secretary for international relations of the same. Extraordinarily warm reception. Mengistu informed the comrade of the decision to contribute "several thousand weapons," which was confirmed by a cable from our embassy there on 3-4 August as follows: 150 Thompson submachine guns with 300 cartridge clips; 1,500 M-1 rifles, one thousand M-14 rifles. Ammunition: 90,000 rounds, caliber 45 mm, for the Thompson submachine guns; 360,000 rounds of M-1 ammunition and 240,000 rounds of M-14 ammunition with 2,000 cartridge clips. In addition, a supply of spare parts for these weapons.

3. Bulgaria, from 27 to 30 June. Received by Stanichiev, member of the secretariat of the central committee of the BCP and secretary for international relations of the BCP, with powers of decision. He informed the comrade of the donation of the following: 300 submachine guns of German manufacture (rebuilt, from World War II), Shpagin make, with 200,000 rounds; 10 machine guns, caliber (numerals cut off at edge of page), of the same make, with 50,000 rounds. He promised that the materiel would be sent here shortly by their own means or in coordination with the Germans or Czechs. Stanichiev pointed out that it was a question of aid to the PCS. However, the comrade informed him of the agreement in effect in the DRU concerning the distribution, with which he was in agreement.

Furthermore, he promised that the bureau of the party would approve other requests consisting of 10,000 uniforms according to the pattern which would be sent to him, and 2,000 individual medical kits for combatants. In fact, on 18 July Stanchiev met with the comrade in Moscow on the occasion of his attendance at the Olympic Games, and he informed him that these requests had been approved.

The medical kits will be sent, and the uniforms will be sent, and the uniforms will be manufactured when they receive the patterns and sizes. All will be sent here. It was a very warm and fraternal reception; the conduct of the PCS was praised.

4. Czechoslovakia, from 24 to 27 June. Received by Bilak, second secretary of the central committee, member of the bureau and secretary for international relations. He informed the comrade of the decision already to send a quantity of weapons of Czech manufacture to the land and to this one, because it would take a very long time to obtain Western weapons; moreover, some of the Czech-made weapons are circulating on the world market. He promised to coordinate with the GDR to transport this materiel here in German ships. A member of the Czech delegation attending the first anniversary of the Nicaraguan revolution informed (name illegible) of the need to coordinate the shipment of this materiel. He did not specify what this materiel consisted of, because it was up to the military to select it. Warm, enthusiastic, and emotional reception by Bilak himself.

5. Hungary, from 30 June to 3 July. Received by Janos Kadar, secretary general of the Hungarian CP, and "Gueisel", secretary for international relations and member of the Political Bureau. Gueisel agreed to accept a request for two-way radios, although he did not specify the number (the comrade asked for 40 shortwave and 12 ultra-short wave radios). He asked whether the operating manuals should be in Spanish or English. The comrade replied that Spanish would be preferable, but that if that would delay the shipment, English would be acceptable. He offered medicines, field first aid kits and medical packs for soldiers. The offer was accepted. He offered to make 10 thousand uniforms according to the pattern and size sent to him. The comrades' decision about the pattern is still pending. Concerning weapons, he said that they didn't have any of Western, Chinese or Yugoslav origin and they would be willing to participate in a deal with Ethiopia or Angola. The comrade expressed his skepticism about the possibility of a trade and suggested other alternatives:
a) Ask friendly governments to purchase Western-made weapons.
b) Give money to the comrades so that they can buy the weapons.
c) Give Czech weapons of the type that are sold on the world market to the comrades.

He offered to study these possibilities and submit them to the Bureau for their decision. The welcome was fraternal and there was agreement in the points of view on the emphasis. Gueisel said that they would concern themselves with resolving the problems of weapons "since we want to be part of providing this aid". The electric current in El Salvador is 110-220 volts. This is useful information to determine the type of radio equipment. 6–GDR 19-24 June. Received by Acsen, member of the BP and secretary of international relations. He said that a 1.9 ton shipment of medicines, 50 first aid kits, 200 auxiliary kits, 2,000 combat kits, 10 megaphones with batteries, cameras and 16mm movies cameras had already been sent to Managua and he offered to respond to the other requests which were principally for weapons.

On 21 July the GDR Embassy in Moscow informed the comrade that Honeker had sent a cable which said that the BP had approved: a) authorization to the solidarity committee to provide resources, not directly military, to the DRU, valued at 2-3 million Marks in accordance with concrete requests from the Salvadoran side. For this reason, they ask us to send a comrade to Berlin with authorization to discuss these requests in detail b) contributing to the training of military cadres especially in covert operation and they expect concrete requests. c) Since they had no Western-made weapons, they decided to continue seeking a solution to this problem although no time frame was set for this. The welcome was warm and fraternal. They praised the PCS. 7–USSR. First meeting: 2 July with Mikhail Kudachkin, deputy chief of the Latin American Section of the Department of International Relations of the CC of the CPSU. He reported that for lack of an opportunity to discuss it with the leadership, a decision had not yet been reached concerning the requests presented on 19 May by the delegation from the Politico-Military Revolutionary Coordinator. He proposed the possibility of a high level meeting with Ponomariov, a member of the Central Committee and Secretary of International Relations. He suggested a trip to Vietnam since, in his opinion, the comrade is the right one to obtain the necessary assistance. He offered to finance the trip and did so. The comrade presented a request that 30 communist youths, who were studying in the USSR and had asked to become part of the struggle, receive military training; he supported the requests presented by the Politico-Military Coordinator for weapons, explosives, ammunition, materials for making explosives, and money for the purchase of arms. And he drafted a written request for the meeting with Ponomariov which was to be held upon his return from Hanoi. The meeting could not be held then, and was changed to the return trip to the socialist countries of Europe and Ethiopia, which was not possible then either due to the jobs and commitments assumed by Ponomariov. On the eve of the departure from Moscow to here, that is to say on 22 July, the meeting was held with Brutents, head of the CC Latin American Section, and not with Ponomariov as was anticipated. Meanwhile, the comrade had presented a request to the CP to transport the weapons that the Vietnamese comrades provided. Brutents expressed CPSU solidarity and agreement with the ideas expressed by the comrade concerning the unity of the revolutionary forces and the struggle in the country, in view of the danger of foreign intervention and other aspects. And he responded to the requests in the following fashion:

a) In principle, there is opinion in favor of transporting the Vietnamese weapons but there has been no approval on the part of the leadership organs.

b) They do not have Western weapons and, closed as the possibilities of a trade with friendly governments appears, they do not see how to resolve this problem.

c) There is approval in principle for training the group of communist youths, though perhaps for lack of quotas, they would receive less than the 30.

The comrade again requested weapons and transportation of those that Vietnam provided, expressing the conviction that the CPSU is capable of resolving these problems, as well as insisting upon the training of the group of 30 comrades. After this meeting, the comrade made known through other channels his disagreement with the absence of the meeting at the proper level and lack of decision concerning the requests for assistance. On 29 July, he was notified by the Soviet Embassy here of a cable that had been received for him from Moscow, the content of which is as follows:

a) The CC of the CPSU wishes to receive the comrade for discussions in September or October.

b) And they agreed to train the group of 30. The Comrade asked to send a cable expressing appreciation for the message and requesting that the CPSU resolve within a short time the matter of the transportation of the Vietnam weapons and the decision to give them assistance in weapons.

He had not yet received any reply as of August 5. It was agreed that when the reply arrives, Comrade Norma is to be notified so that she can inform me. The comrade is expressing concern as to the effects that the lack of decision by the Soviets may have, not only regarding the assistance that they themselves can offer but also upon the inclination of the other parties of the European socialist camp to cooperate, and he requests that from the highest level. End Excerpt

Gira por los países socialistas, Asia y África.

1- Viet-Nam. Del 9 al 15 de junio. Recibido Le Duan, secretario gene
del PCV, y por Xuan Thuy, miembro del Secretariado del CC y Vice-
sidente de la Asamblea Nacional, y por Tran Van Quang, Tte. Gral
Vice-ministro de Defensa Nacional.

Recibimiento solidario y entusiasta. Acordaron dar ayuda en armas
cuyo primer aporte consiste en:

— 192 pistolas 9 mm; 1620 fusiles AR-15; 162 ametralladoras media
M-30; 36 amet. pesadas M-60; 12 amet. pesadas M-50 (cal. 12.7 =
36 morteros de 61 mm; 12 morteros 81 mm; 12 lanza-cohetes antit
ques EM-57; parque: 15 mil cartuchos para pistolas 9 mm; 1 mil
y medio AR-15 (5.56 mm); 420 mil para amet. M-30 y M-60 (7.62 =
130 mil para amet. M-50 (12.7 mm); 9 mil obuses para morteros d
61 mm; 4 mil obuses para morteros 81 mm; y 1500 obuses para ant
tanques DKU-57. Peso aproximado de todo el envío: 60 ton.

Según mensaje recibido en la embajada aquí, 24 de julio, y leíd
al compañero, aparte de detallar el anterior material, se infor
que estará listo para su despacho en los primeros 5 días de sep
tiembre próximo. Si por barco serán entregado en Ciudad Ho Chi:
y recomiendan empacar como mercancía económica, colocar en bode;
que deben ser secas y en el fondo del barco, cubriéndolo con ot
mercancías realmente económicas; esto para que se tenga en cuen:
por ambas partes.

Están listos también para empacar de manera conveniente para tr
porte aéreo, siempre como mercancía económica.

El transporte aéreo fue solicitado por el compañero al PCUS, pe:
salió de Moscú sin obtener respuesta el 23 de julio. En la emba;
aquí, el 25 de julio, pidió enviar cable urgiendo respuesta, y e
5 de agosto, antes de salir de aquí, no la había, lo cual le fue
comunicado al embajador de V., junto con la decisión de nosotro
de traerlo por barco. El embajador de V. espera en plazo breve,
 rededor del 7-8 agosto, le comuniquemos nosotros pormenores de 1
operación de transportación. Quedó establecido que de haber respuesta favorable oportuna para el transporte aéreo solicitado, s
aprovecharía el mismo, para lo cual se necesita siempre una coor
dinación de nosotros con las V. La respuesta del PCUS la recibir
Norma, la Representante aquí.

2- Etiopía. Del 3 al 6 de julio. Recibido por Jaime Mengistu Marian y
por Berhanu Bayih, miembro del Comité Ejecutivo del COFME y Secret
rio de Relaciones Internacionales del mismo.

Recibimiento extraordinariamente caluroso.

Mengistú le informó al compañero la decisión de aportar "varios mi
les de armas", lo cual quedó concretado por medio de cable de nues
embajada allá, aproximadamente 3-4 de agosto, de la siguiente maner:

— 150 Thompson (sub-amet.), con 300 cargadores; 1500 fusiles M-1:
 mil fusiles M-14. Parque: 90 mil tiros cal 45 mm para los 2, y
 360 mil M-1 y 240 mil tiros M-14 con 2 mil cargadores. Además, u
 lote de piezas de repuesto para estas armas.

Hoja 2.

El mismo cable dice que este cargamento saldría en barco nuest:
el 5 de agosto.

3- Bulgaria. Del 27 de junio al 30 del mismo mes. Recibido por Stani
ev, miembro del Secretariado del CC del PCB, y Secretario de Rela
nes Internacionales del PCB, quien con facultades de decisión con
có al compañero la donación de:

— 300 sub-amet. de fabricación alemana (de la segunda guerra mund
reconstruida) marca Schpagen, con 200 mil tiros, y 30 amet. cal
de la misma marca con 50 mil tiros. Prometido enviarlo en pla
breve aquí por sus propios medios, o coordinando con los aleman
o checos.

Stanichiev hizo constar que se trata de una ayuda al PCB, pero e:
compañero le informó sobre el acuerdo que rige en la DRI para l
distribución, con lo cual estuvo de acuerdo.

Además, ofreció que el Buró del Partido aprobaría otras peticio:
consistente en 10 mil uniformes conforme al modelo que lo sea: e:
ado; 2 mil botiquines individuales para combatientes. En efecto,
18 de julio, el mismo Stanichier se encontró con el compañero en
Moscú en ocasión de su concurrencia los Juegos Olímpicos, y le c
municó que estas peticiones habían sido aprobadas.

Los botiquines serán enviados, y los uniformes se fabricarán cua
do reciban modelos y tallas, todo lo cual será enviado aquí.
Fue un recibimiento muy caluroso y fraternal, siendo elogioso para
con la conducta del⸺⸺ PCS.

4- **Checoslovaquia.** Del 24 al 27 de junio. Recibido por Bilak, Segundo
Secretario del CC, miembro del Buró y Secretario de Relaciones Int
nacionales.

Comunicó al compañero la decisión tomada ya de enviar a la tierra
a ésta, una cantidad de armas de fabricación checa, teniendo en cu
ta que sería muy demorado conseguir armas occidentales y que por c:
parte algunas de las armas de su fabricación circulan en el merced:
mundial. Ofreció coordinar con la RDA para transportar en barcos al
manes hasta aquí este material. Un miembro de la delegación checa
asistente al ler aniversario de la Rev. nicaraguense, comunicó a I
⸺⸺ la necesidad de coordinar el envío del material.

No precisó en que consiste este material, porque estaba en manos de
los militares seleccionarlo.

Recibimiento caluroso y entusiasta y emotivo por parte del propio
Bilak.

5- **Hungría.** Del 30 de junio al 3 de julio. Recibido por Janos Kadar, -
Secretario General del PSL, y Gueisel, Secretario de Relaciones Internacionales y miembro del Buró Political.

Ofreció,Gueisel, aceptar petición de radios comunicadores, aunque n
fijó número (pidió el compañero aparatos de comones de ondas corta
y ultras cortas; 40 y 12 respectivamente). Preguntó si los manuales
de operación desea venir en español o inglés, respondiendo el compa
ñero preferib.emente en español: pero si ello demora el envío, se -
acepta en español inglés.

·Hoja 3.

Ofreció medicinas, botiquines de campaña y paquetes médicos para
soldado. Aceptándose el ofrecimiento.

Ofreció fabricar 10 mil uniformes, conforme el modelo y talla qu
se envíen.

Está pendiente por parte de los compañeros resolver sobre el mod
lo.

Sobre armas, dijo no tienen de procedencia occidentales, chinas
yugoslavas, y estarían dispuestos a participar en un canje con B
pía o Angola. El compañero expres ó su excepticismo acerca de la
sibilidad del canje y sugirió otras alternativas:

a) Encargar a gobiernos amigos comprar armas occidentales.
b) Dar dinero a los compañeros para que ellos compren las armas.
c) Dar armas checas a los compañeros de los tipos que circulan en
el mercado mundial.
Ofreció estudiar estas posibilidades; someterlas al Buró para sus
resoluciones.

La acogida fue fraternal y coincidente los puntos de vista en el
foque. Gueisel dijo que se preocuparían por resolver la cuestión
las armas "ya que no queremos-quedarnos al margen de prestar esta
ayuda".

La corriente eléctrica en El Salvador es de 110-127·voltios en ca
todo el país, excepcionalmente de 220 voltios. Dato de utilidad p
ra determinar el tipo de aparatos de radios.

6- **RDA.** Del·19 al 24 de junio. Recibido por Acsen, miembro del EP y :
cretario de Relaciones Internacionales.

Dijo haber enviado ya a Managua una carga de 1.9 ton., consistent:
en medicina, 50 botiquines médicos, 200 botiquines auxiliares y -
2 mil botiquines de-combatiente, 10 megáfonos con baterías, cámar
fotográficas, cámaras cinematográficas de 16 mm, y ofreció respond
sobre las demás peticiones-principalmente las armas.

El 21 de julio la embajada de la RDA en Moscú informó al compañero
que mister Honeker envió cable para hacerle informar en el que se
decía que el SP aprobó: a) autorizar al Comité de solidaridad pro-
porcionarles medios a la DRU, no directamente militares, por valor
de 2-3 millones de marcos, conforme a los pedidos concretos de la
parte salvadoreña, para lo cual piden enviar a un compañero a Berlín autorizado para definir estas solicitudes. b) Contribuir a la
formación de cuadros militares especialmente en trabajo conspirati
vo y esperan solicitudes concretas. c) Como no tienen armas occide
tales, decidieron seguir buscando una solución a este problema, au
que no se fijó plazo para ello.

La acogida fue calurosa y fraternal. Elogiaron la conducta del PCS.

7— URSS. Primer encuentro: 2 de junio, con Miguel Kudashkin, vice-jefe
de la Sección de América Latina del Dpto. Relaciones Internacionale
del CC del PCUS. Informó que aún no había decisión, por falta de —
oportunidad para discutirlo en la Dirección, sobre las solicitudes
presentadas por la conjunta delegación de la Coordinadora Revoluci
naria Político-Militar, presentada el 19 de mayo. Propuso la posibi
lidad de encuentro a alto nivel)con Ponomariov, miembro del Secretariado del CC y Secretario de Rel. Int.) Sugirió viajar a Viet-Nam
ya que a su juicio el compañero es el indicado para obtener allí la

Hoja 4.

ayuda necesaria. Ofreció financiar el viaje, y así se hizo.

El compañero presentó solicitud para que 30 jóvenes comunistas que
estudian en la URSS y que pidieran incorporarse a la lucha, re-
cibieran adiestramiento militar; respaldó las solicitudes de armas
explosivos, municiones, materiales para fabricación de explosivo, (
nario para la compra de armas, presentadas por la delegación de la
Coordinadora R. Pol.-Militar. Y formuló por escrito petición para e
encuentro con Ponomariov, que debería realizarse al regreso de Econ
El encuentro no pudo realizarse entonces, y se transfirió para el re
greso de la gira a los países socialistas de Europa y Etiopía, lo —
cual tampoco pudo ser, por las ocupaciones y compromisos adquiridos
por Ponomariov. En la víspera de la salida de Moscú hacia ésta, es
decir el 22 de julio, tuvo lugar el encuentro con Brutento, jefe de
la Sección de América Latina del CC, y no con Ponomariov como se
esperaba. Entretanto, el compañero había presentado solicitud al PC
para transportar las armas que dieron los cros. vietnamitas. Bruten
expresó la solidaridad del PCUS y la concordancia con las ideas ex-
presadas por el compañero acerca de la unidad de las fuerzas revolucionarias y la lucha en el país, frente al peligro de intervención
extranjera y otros aspectos. Y respondió a las solicitudes de la siguiente manera:

a) En principio hay opinión favorable a transportar las armas de Vie
Nam pero falta que lo apruebe los organismos dirigentes.
b) No poseen armas occidentales y cerradas como parece las posibili
dades de canje con gobiernos amigos, no ven como poder resolver e
te problema.
c) Hay aceptación en principio para entrenar al grupo de jóvenes comunistas, aunque quizás por falta de cupos, recibirían menos de —
los 30.

El compañero replanteó la solicitud de las armas y del —
transporte de las que aportó Viet-Nam, expresando la convicción de
que el PCUS estaría capacidad de resolver estos problemas, insis-
tiendo igualmente en el entrenamiento del grupo de 30 compañeros.

Después de este encuentro, el compañero hizo conocer por otros canales, su inconformidad por la falta del encuentro al nivel debido y la
no resolución de las solicitudes de ayuda. El 29 de julio, fue noti-
ficado por la embajada sov. aquí de un cable recibido de Moscú, para
él, cuyo contenido es el siguiente:

a) El CC del PCUS desea recibir al compañero para conversaciones en —
septiembre u octubre. Y
b) Han acordado entrenar al grupo de los 30.

El compañero pidió remitir cable agradeciendo la comunicación y pi-
diendo resolver a plazo breve el transporte de las armas vietnamitas
y la decisión de entregarles ayuda en armas de parte del PCUS.

El 5 de agosto aún no se había recibido respuesta. Se convino que al
llegar ésta se comunique a la compañera Norma para que ella informe
a nosotros.

El compañero expresa preocupación por lo que pueda afectar la falta
de decisión de los sov., no sólo a xx la ayuda que ellos mismos pue-
san ofrecer, sino también a la disposición de cooperar de los demás
partidos del campo socialista europeo, y solicita que del más alto ni

FIN DC FRAGMENTO

DOCUMENT F

Report on the meeting of the Unified Revolutionary Directorate (DRU), September 30,
1980 (Excerpt on the trip of the Secretary General of the Communist Party of El
Salvador — list of weapons commitments).

GLOSSARY F

Ana Maria — Ana Guadalupe Martinez of the ERP guerrilla group

COCEN — Central Committee

Esmeralda — Cuba

TRANSLATION OF DOCUMENT F

IX. The PC secretary general's trip
    Offer from Vietnam (they will be in Esmeralda on 5 September)
192 9-mm pistols
1,620 AR 15
162 M30 machineguns
36 M60 heavy machineguns
12 12.7 caliber M50 machineguns
36 62-mm mortars
12 81-mm mortars
12 DKZ-57 antitank rocket launchers
15,000 9-mm cartridges
1,500,000 AR 15 cartridges
240,000 M30 machinegun cartridges
240,000 M60 (7.62) machinegun cartridges
130,000 M50 (12.7) machinegun cartridges
9,000 rounds for 61-mm mortars
1,000 rounds for 81-mm mortars
1,500 rounds for DKZ-57 antitank rocket launchers
Ethiopia   60 tons
150 Tompson submachineguns with 300 loaders
1,500 M1 rifles
1,000 M14 rifles
90,000 45-caliber rounds for the Tompson
300,000 M1
240,000 M14 with 200 loaders
Spare Parts
This shipment was leaving on 15 August for Havana
Bulgaria
300 German-made submachineguns with 200,000 cartridges
10 30-caliber "comet." (not further identified) with 50,000 cartridges
10,000 uniforms
2,000 individual first-aid kits for the soldiers
These last two items will be sent when they have received the specifications.
Czechoslovakia
They will send Czechoslovak weapons. They cannot exchange for Western weapons.

They did not specify the quantity of weapons.
Hungary
HF and UHF radios
40 HF and 12 UHF
10,000 uniforms according to specifications and sizes which will be sent.
GDR
1.9 tons of medicines
50 medical first-aid kits
200 auxiliary first-aid kits
2,000 soldiers' first-aid kits
10 megaphones, movie cameras

A DRU representative shall be sent to Berlin with specific proposals totaling
$1,000,000.00 for nonmilitary equipment.
Political matter with regard to Sombrero.
The viewpoints expressed to the secretary general of the PC by high officials of Sombrero   were   read.
REVOLUTION OR DEATH! THE ARMED PEOPLE SHALL WIN!
THE POLITICAL COMMISSION OF THE COCEN
(CENTRAL COMMITTEE)

ANA MARIA
Second In Command

1 September 1980

-7-

IX - ~~Informe del secretario general del PC~~

~~Ofrecimiento de Viet~~ Nam (5 de septiembre estarán en Esmeralda)

192 pistolas 9 mm.
420 AR 15
162 ametralladoras M 30
86   "   pesadas M60
12   "   M50. calibre 12.7
86 morteros de 62 mm.
12 morteros de 81 mm.
12 lanzacohetes an ti-tnaque DKZ-57
500,000 cartuchos de 9 mm.
500,000   "   de AR 15
240,000   "   para ametralladora M 30
10,000   "   "   "   M 60 (7.62)
95,000 Obuses para morteros de 61mm.
5,000   "   "   "   81 mm.
1,500   "   "   anti-tanques DKZ-57

Etiopía   60 Toneladas

150 subametralladoras Tompson con 300 cargadores.
1,500 fusiles M1
1,000   "   M14
50,000 tiros calibre 45 para las Tompson
300,000 M1
240,000 M14 con 200 cargadores.

Piezas de repuesto

El 15 de agosto salía este cargamento para Habana.

Bulgaria

200 subametralladoras de fabricación alemana con 200.000
tiros.
10 comet. calibre 30 con 50.000 tiros
10.000 uniformes
2.000 botiquines individuales para combatiéntes

Estos dos últimos rubros serán enviados cuando se le propor-
cione modelos.

~~Checoeslovaquia~~)

Enviarán armas checas. No pueden cambiar en.occidentales.
No precisaron cantidad en armas.

~~Hungría~~

Radio-comunicadores de ondas cortas y ultra corta.

40 cortas y 12 ultracortas
10,000 uniformes. conforme modelos y talla que se envíen

-8-

~~RDA.~~

9 toneladas en medicinas
50 botiquines médicos
200 botiquines auxiliares
4000 botiquines de combatientes
10 megáfonos, cámaras, cinematografía y de cine.

~~Enviar un representante de la RDA a Berlín con propuestas concretas por valor de $5,000,000 no para medicos no militares~~

Asunto político con respecto a. Sombrero.

Se leyeron los puntos de vista dados al Srio. General del PC.
por altos personeros de Sombrero.

REVOLUCION O MUERTE!   EL PUEBLO ARMADO VENCERA!

~~LA COMISION POLITICA DEL COCEN~~

~~NATMARIA~~
~~Seguridad Responsable~~

1o. septiembre/80

DOCUMENT G

Trip Report (undated).

GLOSSARY G

Arafat — Yasir Arafat, leader of the Palestine Liberation Organization (PLO)

Bayardo (Ballardo) — Bayardo Arce, member of Nicaraguan FSLN (Sandinista) Directorate

EMGC — Salvadoran guerrilla Joint General Staff

Fidel — Fidel Castro

Front – Nicaraguan (Sandinista) FSLN

H – Havana

Humberto – Humberto Ortega of Nicaraguan FSLN Directorate

M – Managua

ORPA – Guatemalan guerrilla group

RN – National Resistance. Salvadoran guerrilla group.

TRANSCRIPT OF DOCUMENT G

TRIP REPORT

We, all the representatives, arrive at M. on 13 July. We gathered in one house because Bayardo's assistant told us that it was possible that they would telephone us at any moment since they were very busy with the celebration and it was very difficult to hold (a meeting) since the best time was after the 19th.

We manage to get a meeting with the assistant by insisting, since they did not plan to do even that. In the meeting with the comrades we discovered the following situation:

1. That they had stopped all the shipments until they knew the plan.

2. The matter of the 2050 was not very clear; everything was old, used material.

3. That they did not have time to take care of us (since) our date of arrival had been delayed.

In view of this we stated the following:

1. That we were not in agreement with the fact that they had made the aid which they gave conditional upon their approval of the plan. That the problems for which they specifically had not sent the material were operational problems of coordination with those receiving it in the country, and that these problems could be solved; but that what they were asserting was a political condition.

2. That the DRU had received the information that the 2050 and other types of material were already ready and that in the country they were operating under the assumption that this material was about to enter.

3. That we understood the special situation they were in, but that we were in a war situation and for this reason we had delayed and because of this same situation we needed to carry out our work immediately. That we proposed the following:

a) A speedy meeting with the military commission of the Front to give them a general report on the plan so that they would be brought up to date, and when they had an opportunity they would communicate what they had learned to the representatives of the National Directorate.

b) That after this meeting we would leave for H. to hold discussions with the "specialists" in charge to finish touching up the plan.

c) That after returning from H. we would meet with the representatives of the Directorate of the Front.

CONCLUSIONS:

1. G. (assistant to Ballardo) withdrew the condition of the approval of the plan for giving aid and insisted that the problems were operational and on our part.

2. As for the meeting with the military commission, it was difficult since everyone was involved in preparing the celebration. But he said that we should stay together in one place because if any opportunity arose at any hour of the day or night they would call us.

3. As for the trip to H., he did not think so because all the people from there were coming to the celebration and it was possible to wait. He said that the possibility even existed of holding a joint meeting here after the 19th.

4. We submitted a formal written request concerning the meeting with Bayardo and the military commission.

14 Jul 80: We spent it together working on the plan the EMGC (Meeting with the Cuban; he insisted that we wait.)

15 July 80: ditto

16 July 80: ditto

17 July 80: ditto

18 July 80: Abren visited us; he asked for our understanding for the Front and said that their opinion was that we should meet first with the Front and that one could not go to H. to do anything at this time.

19 July 80: We were told to keep ourselves locked up and not to go out to see the ceremony.

20 July 80: ditto

21 and 22 July: On the 21st G. arrived; we have been talking to him constantly and we restated all the points already explained and also the following:

a)   That if they did not attend to us either we would go to H. or return to the country, since we were wasting time.

b)   In mutual agreement with the rest of the EMGC I made a request for a little (very little) ammunition for the zone of Morazan.

G. showed his disagreement with our departure and said that we should wait until he went to report it: that this attitude was absurd. He said he would also report the request for ammunition.

Also on the 21st the comrades who operate there as the "Representation of the DRU" in M. asked for a meeting with us in which they stated the following:

a)   The Front undervalued them and ignored them.

b)   The Front made decisions which they had to respect without any possibility of discussing them.

c)   There was not a relationship of mutual respect, but rather one of imposition.

d)   The Front was very conservative and it had a tendency to look down on the situation in the country and to protect the Nicaraguan revolution.

e)   There were standard regulations for all representatives which eliminated any possibility of political work; even for visits to other embassies one had to work through the Front, which wanted to know the agenda and afterwards the conclusions which had been drawn.

f)   That the message which they, as the representation of the DRU, had worked out for the 19th was cut back in 14 of the 16 slogans which they had made for it without any possibility of discussing the matter.

g)   The comrades of the RN (National Resistance) insisted vigorously that the sovereignty and interests of the DRU were being harmed, and that all the representatives there were like ambassadors and should be treated as such. In this meeting, and everywhere else, they made much mention of the fact that there was communication with them and they said the following to the Front on how it should be: "Gentlemen, all right, we understand that Nicaragua must be protected, but for that there is an art and a science which is called 'CONSPIRACY.' Let us conspire together."

h)   They requested that they and the EMGC work on the problem together, since the Front attached more importance to the latter since it felt the latter was a body of higher level and, they said, the Front did not pay any attention to them.

CONCLUSIONS:

1.   We believed that there would be a more positive attitude on the part of the Front, but that we could not ignore the fact that they have always attached little importance to the international situation (particularly Comrade Bayardo) and that they had a greater tendency to attach importance to their own revolution; this had already been made manifest before their triumph and it was being manifested now. We believed that in this sense it was necessary to stress more the positive attitudes which were being taken, committing themselves to these attitudes so that the aggressive attitudes toward nationalism do not become stronger.

2.   As for the meeting, we felt it was inappropriate because this body (EMGC) had a specific mission to fulfill and it was unable to dilute its activity, and on the other hand it was necessary for the DRU representatives to gain respect and personal status and for the EMGC to intervene would be to accept the Front's idea that the EMGC is

higher up in the political hierarchy.

3.   In view of the fact that the members of the directorate of the Front have different attitudes, such as that of Bayardo and that of Humberto, it would be preferable for the DRU representatives to send their statements in writing with a copy to each member of the National Directorate to guarantee that all of them would know these statements just as we have done.

COMMENT:

My evaluation was that by means of a concrete problem the RN was putting forward its conception of "independence" and that it was necessary to attach more importance to "other allies" such as Panama, Mexico, and so on, and I there showed my concern that there were approaches which did not correspond to that agreed on for the DRU, that there were delicate points which had to be discussed with more seriousness and responsibility and to be communicated to within the DRU, and that I did not share the view that they were "ambassadors" the RN recanted.

As for the conclusions, I saw in them the intention of the FPL not to mix up matters to avoid getting us into political contradictions with the Front which would prevent us from getting logistical aid on the part of the EMGC and I accepted the proposed resolution. On the other hand, it appeared to me that as to its method of relating with us, the Front reflected two things: 1) that it had an incorrect notion, tending to make unilateral decisions without our participation and 2) that the Front did not have confidence in the maturity of the Salvadoran left and in the degree of true unity (I did not state this, on the 22nd there was a meeting with Arafat.)

23 July 80: Bayardo and G. arrived. The most important of the things they stated were as follows:

1.   They doubted the number of military forces which we gave; they wondered if it was possible that we were exaggerating the numbers we gave one another (they mentioned their experience with different factions).

2.   That our propaganda was bad and that we did not have an international audience, that the image of our country was that of a massacred people. Even they themselves, who are our neighbors, sometimes felt confused.

3.   That someone had said that the 2,000 rifles were for us, that they had said that this is what they had available, that part of it had to be given to the Guatemalans, because we cannot neglect what is going on there. That there were enough hunting weapons which they could give us.

4.   That the Guatemalans (ORPA — Revolutionary Organization of the People in Arms) had an arms deal and that they requested a loan of $200,000 paid in 2 months if we could lend it.

5.   Since we were going to receive aid which all would pass through Nicaragua, they had thought of a "triangular deal;" that is, they would give us arms from the EPS (Sandinist Peoples Army) and then replace them with those which are coming, and also they would exchange those which are only used in the socialist world (particularly for the EPS) with others from the capitalist world.

6.   That the request for ammunition was approved.

7.   That they had agreed upon the meeting with the military commission for the following day before we would leave for Cuba.

For our part we objected to the criticisms to what we had said. We stated all the points which had already been given to G. on 14 July 1980, we stated that the representation wanted to meet with them, and that we did not favor the business with the money but that we would communicate it to the DRU, and finally that we wanted to have a working program as well-defined as the matter of the rifles and that they should approve the shipments without political conditions such as the approval of the general plan.

CONCLUSIONS:

a)   (word illegible) hold the meeting and we would leave for Cuba by the 27th because before then nothing could be done there and also Fidel would still be here.

INFORME SOBRE VIAJE.-   — 3v3 (57)

~~Llegamos a~~, ~~el día 13 de julio~~ todos los representantes. Nos concen-
mos en una casa a raíz de que el ~~asistente de~~ Bayardo, nos dijo que era posible que nos llamarían en cualquier momento, porque estaban muy ocupados
en la celebración y eso era bien difícil de realizar que lo más seguro es
hasta después del 19.

La reunión con el asistente la logramos sobre la base de la insistenci
ya que ni siquiera eso pensaban hacer. En la reunión con el compañeronos
encontramos con la siguiente situación:

1- ~~.....~~
2- ~~que los 2050 no estaba muy claro y todos eran materiales viejos~~ ~~de repetición.~~
3- ~~.....~~

Ante ello nosotros planteamos:

1- Que no estábamos de acuerdo en que se condicionara la ayuda a que e
llos dieran su aprovación al plan. Que los problemas por los que no había
sido enviado el material en concreto era por razones operativas de coordi
nación con la recepción interna, que esos problemas se podían resolver; p
ro que lo que ellos planteaban era una condición de decisión política.

2- Que la DRU había llegado al informe de que los 2050 y otro tipo de
material ya estaba listo y que en el país se estaba trabajando sobre la b
se de que ese material iva a empezar a entrar.

3- Qu e entendiamos lo de la situación especial en que ellos se encon
traban, pero que nosotros estábamos en situación de guerra y por ello -
nos habíamos atrasado y que por esa misma situación necesitábamos desarro
llar nuestro trabajo en lo inmediato..Que nosotros proponíamos lo siguien
te:

a) Una reunión rápida con la comisión Militar del Frente para darles u
informe general del plan para que ellos estuvieran altanto y en cuanto tu
vieran oportunidad lo comunicaran a los encargados de la Dirección Nacio
nal.

b) Que luego de esa reunión nosotros partiríamos a la H. a discutir co
los encargados "especialistas" para terminar de pulir el proyecto.

c) Que al regreso de la H. nos reuniríamos con los encargados de la Di
rección del Frente

Conclusiones:

1- G. (asistente de Ballardo) se retractó de la condición de aprovació
del plan para dar ayuda e hizo incapié en que los problemas eran operativ
y de parte nuestra.

2- Que en cuanto a la reunión con la Comisión Militar era difícil, po
que todos estaban metidos en la preparación de la celebración. Pero que n
mantuvieramos concentrados por si surgía alguna posibilidad a cualquier h
ra del día o de noche ellos nos llamarían.

3- Que en cuanto al viaje a la H. no le parecía porque toda la gente d
allá venía a la celebración y que era posible esperar. Que incluso existi
la posibilidad que después del 19 hubiera una reunión conjunta aquí.

4- Nosotros entregamos una solicitud formal y escrita sobre la reunión
con Bayardo y la Comisión Militar.

14/VII/80: ~~Estabamos concentrados y trabajando en el plan, el RMGC(Xanni
por si cubano ministro en que esperaramos)~~

15/VII/80: IDEM

— 2 —   3v4

16/VII/80: IDEM
17/VII/80: IDEM
18/VII/80: Nos visitó Abren, nos pidió comprensión para el Frente y q
la opinión de ellos era que nos reuniéramos primero con el Frente y que
la H. no se podía ir a hacer nada en estos días.
19/VII/80: Se nos dijo que nos mantuviéramos encerrados y no saliéram
a ver el acto.
20/VII/80: IDEM
21 y 22/VII/80: El 21 llegó el G. al cual habíamos estado llamando co
tantemente y le replanteamos todos los puntos ya expuestos y otro más:
a) Que si no nos atendían que ó no ivamos a la H. o regresábamos
al país, pues estábamos perdiendo el tiempo.

b) De común acuerdo con el resto del EMGC hize una solicitud de un po(
(muy poco) de munición para la zona de Morazán.

G manifestó desacuerdo con nuestro regreso y dijo que esperaráramos q:
él iva a comunicarlo, que esa actitud era absurda. Que también iva a com:
nicar la solicitud de parque.

El mismo 21 los compañeros que allá se maneja como la "Representación
de la DRU" en M. nos pidieron una reunión a nosotros en la cual plantear(

a) Que el Frente los subvaloraba y ni les prestaba atención.
b) Que el Frente tomaba desiciones que había que acatar sin posibilid:
   de discusión.
c) Que no había una relación de mutuo respeto sino de imposición.
d) Que el Frente era muy conservador y que tenía tendencia a desprecis
   la situación en el país y proteger la revolución Nica.
e) Que había un reglamento normativo para todos los representantes, e:
   cual anulaba toda posibilidad de trabajo político, que incluso para
   visitar a otras embajadas u organizaciones había que hacerlo a través del
   Frente, el cual quería conocer la agenda y despúes las conclusiones que s
   habían sacado.
f) Que el mensaje que como "representación" de la DRU habían elaborado
   para el 19 había sido recortado en 14 de 16 consignas que se habían plan
   teadoen él sin posibilidad de discutirlo.
g) Los compañeros de la RN hacían mucha insistencia en que se estaba l
   sionando la soberanía y los intereses de la DRU y que todos los representantes ahí eran como embajadores y así debía tratárseles. Mensionaron muc
   en esta reunión y siempre que hubo comunicación con ellos que al Frente s
   le había dicho, y, así tenía que ser "~~S̶e̶ñ̶o̶r̶e̶s̶,̶ ̶e̶s̶t̶a̶ ̶b̶i̶e̶n̶,̶ ̶n̶o̶s̶o̶t̶r̶o̶s̶ ̶e̶n̶t̶e̶n̶d̶e̶~~
   ~~m̶o̶s̶ ̶q̶u̶e̶ ̶h̶a̶y̶ ̶q̶u̶e̶ ̶p̶r̶o̶t̶e̶g̶e̶r̶ ̶a̶ ̶N̶i̶c̶a̶r̶a̶g̶u̶a̶,̶ ̶p̶e̶r̶o̶ ̶p̶a̶r̶a̶ ̶e̶l̶l̶o̶ ̶h̶a̶y̶ ̶u̶n̶ ̶a̶r̶t̶e̶ ̶y̶ ̶u̶n̶a̶~~, —
   ~~c̶i̶e̶n̶c̶i̶a̶ ̶q̶u̶e̶ ̶s̶e̶ ̶l̶l̶a̶m̶a̶:̶ ̶C̶O̶N̶S̶P̶I̶R̶A̶C̶I̶O̶N̶,̶ ̶c̶o̶n̶s̶p̶i̶r̶e̶m̶o̶s̶ ̶j̶u̶n̶t̶o̶s̶~~".

H) Solicitaban que ellos y el EMGC plantearan juntos el problema, pues
el Frente le daba más importancia porque consideraba que era un organismo
de mayor nivel y que a ellos no les harían caso.

Conclusiones:·

1- Que nosotros creíamos que de parte del Frente había una actitud pos
tiva, pero que no podíamos ignorar que ellos siempre le habían dado poca :
importancia a la situación internacional (particularmente el compañero Ba·
yardo) y que tenían más tendencia a dar importancia a su revolución, que
ya se había manifestado antes del triunfo y que se manifestaba ahora, que
en ese sentido había que hacer más incapié en las actitudes positivas que
estaban tomando comprometiendolos en ellas para impedir que tomen fuerza ·
las actitudes regresivas al nacionalismo.

2- Que en cuanto a la reunión veíamos inconveniente porque este organi:
no (EMGC) tenía una misión concreta que cumplir y no podía diluir su acti·
vidad y que por otro lado había que ganar respeto y personalidad a la rep

lel Frente sobre cual organismo era políticamente más gerárquico.

3- Que ante el hecho de que en los miembros de dirección del Frente había diferentes actitudes , tales como la de Bay. y la de Humberto, que lo
preferible era que la representación de la DRU mandara sus planteamientos
por escrito con copias a cada uno de los miembros de la Dirección Nacional
para garantizar que los planteamientos los conocieran todos tal como los t
ciamos nosotros.

Comentario:
~~L̶a̶ ̶R̶N̶ ̶m̶a̶n̶i̶f̶e̶s̶t̶ó̶ ̶q̶u̶e̶ ̶d̶e̶p̶e̶n̶d̶e̶ ̶l̶a̶ ̶R̶N̶ ̶e̶s̶t̶a̶b̶a̶ ̶m̶e̶t̶i̶e̶n̶d̶o̶ ̶e̶n̶ ̶g̶r̶a̶v̶e̶ ̶d̶e̶ ̶u̶n̶ ̶p̶r̶o̶b̶l̶e̶m̶a̶~~
~~c̶o̶m̶o̶ ̶e̶s̶ ̶l̶a̶ ̶c̶o̶n̶c̶e̶p̶c̶i̶ó̶n̶ ̶d̶e̶ ̶"̶I̶n̶d̶e̶p̶e̶n̶d̶e̶n̶c̶i̶a̶"̶ ̶y̶ ̶q̶u̶e̶ ̶n̶o̶ ̶s̶e̶ ̶h̶a̶b̶í̶a̶ ̶q̶u̶e̶ ̶d̶a̶r̶l̶e̶s̶ ̶m̶á̶s̶ ̶i̶:̶~~
~~p̶o̶r̶t̶a̶n̶c̶i̶a̶ ̶a̶ ̶o̶t̶r̶o̶s̶ ̶a̶l̶i̶a̶d̶o̶s̶"̶ ̶c̶o̶m̶o̶ ̶P̶a̶n̶a̶m̶á̶,̶ ̶M̶é̶x̶i̶c̶o̶~~, etc. y manifesté ahí mi ·
preocupación de que había enfoques que no correspondían a lo acordado por
la DRU, que eran puntos delicados que había que discutir con más seriedad :
responsabilidad y comunicárselo a la DRU adentro, que no compartía el cri·
terio de que eran "Embajadores". La RN se retractó.

En cuanto a las conclusiones yo ví en ella la intención de las FPL de
no mesclar las cosas para evitar que nos metiéramos en contradicciones po
líticas con el Frente que impidieran lograr la ayuda logística por parte
del EMGC y acepté la propuesta de resolución. Por otro lado me parecía qu
el Frente en cuanto a método de relación con nosotros reflejaba dos cosas
1) que había una concepción no correcta tendiente a tomar desiciones unil
terales sin nuestra participación .
2)Que el Frente tenía desconfianza de la madurez de la izquierda salvador
ña y del grado de verdadera unidad (esto no lo manifesté, el 22 hubo reun
con Arafat.)

23/VII/80: Llegó Bayardo y G. lo esencial de lo que plantearon fue lo siguiente:

🔹 Que ellos dudaban de la cifra de fuerzas militares que dábamos, que si no existía la posibilidad de que nos estubieramos abultando las cifras unos a otros (mencionó su experiencia entre tendencias).

🔹 Que la propaganda nuestra era mala que no teníamos espacio Internacnal, que la imagen del país era la de un pueblo masacrado. Que incluso el que estaban cercanos a nosotros a veces se sentían confusos.

🔹 Que quien había dicho que los 2000 fusiles eran para nosotros, que llos habían dicho que eso es lo que tenían en disposición, que parte de e llo había que darle a los Guatemaltecos, porque nosotros no podíamos des dar el proceso guatemalteco. Que había bastantes armas de cacería que no podían dar.

🔹 Que los chapines (ORPA) tenían un negocio de armas y que solicitab un préstamo de $200,000 pagados en dos meses que si los podiamos prestar

🔹 Que como nosotros ivamos a recibir ayuda que todo iva a pasar por caragua ellos habían pensado en "triangualar", es decir, darnos ellos ar las del EPS y luego reponerlas con las que vengan y también cambiar las solo se usaban en el mundo socialista (particularmente por el EPS) por o del mundo capitalista.

🔹 Que la solicitud de parque estaba aprobada,

🔹 Que ya se había acordado la reunión con la Comisión Militar para e día siguiente antes que salieramos para Cuba.

De parte nuestra objetamos las críticas a que nos mentíamos. Plantean todos los puntos que ya se le habían expuesto al G. el día 14/VII/80, co nicamos que la representación quería reunirse con ellos, que lo del din no lo veíamos bien pero que comunicaríamos a la DRU , y al final que que amos tener un programa de trabajo bien definido asía como lo de los fus - que se aprovaran los envíos sin condiciones políticas tales como la a;

Conclusiones:
a)

DOCUMENT H

Report on the meeting of the Unified Revolutionary Directorate (DRU), September 24, 1980.

GLOSSARY H

Ana Maria – Ana Guadalupe Martinez of ERP guerrilla group

DRU – Unified Revolutionary Directorate. Joint leadership of Salvadoran guerrilla groups

EMGC – Guerrilla Joint General Staff

Esmeralda – Cuba

Front – Nicaraguan FSLN (Sandinistas)

I – Iraq

Lagos – Nicaragua

Marcial – Cayetano Carpio of FPL guerrilla group

RN – National Resistance, Salvadoran guerrilla group

TRANSCRIPTION OF DOCUMENT H

MINUTES OF THE MEETING:
UNIFIED REVOLUTIONARY DIRECTORATE
POLITICOMILITARY–DRU–/. 24 September 1980.

Attending:
Hugo-Rene
Ana Maria – Marcial
Jonas – Eduardo
Agenda:
1. Reports
2. Evaluation
3. Assignments
I.   Ana Maria:
Report of the letter of Comrade Mauricio, which gives details of the death of Comrade Neto, first official in charge of the RN (National Resistance), in an airplane accident. Comrades Hugo and Rene elaborate with the reports sent by Comrades Esteban and Maria.
Agreements:
   a)   To send a note of sympathy and solidarity to the RN National Directorate.
   b)   Issue a public communique on the same subject.
II.   Comrade Hugo reports that Comrade Eduardo has been going every day (except Saturdays) to the point of contact which was agreed upon with Comrade Neto to coordinate the meetings with the RN directorate to deal with its petition to reenter the DRU. It is reported that no one from the RN has arrived (to make) contact; the conclusion reached is that possibly Comrade Neto was not able to inform his Directorate.
Agreement:
Search for a contact with the RN Directorate through all existing channels to join with it as soon as possible.
III.   Report on the mission abroad of the DRU members: Comrade Jonas, Eduardo and Marcial.
Comrades Jonas and Eduardo elaborate on the reports of Comrade Marcial in the following order:
i - Report on activities in Sombrero, Palmera, Arena and Pinares in the following fields: official contacts and results, agreements: with sister organizations and progressive persons; meetings and measures taken with the representatives of the DRU organization and with those of the FDR.
ii - Report on the meetings, agreements and measures in Lagos:
   —With the Front's National Directorate.
   —With the logistic commission of the DRU.
   —With the PRTC (Revolutionary Party of Central American Workers)
   —On the meeting with Comrade Neto of the RN and the request by his organization to reenter the DRU.
iii - On the meetings with the Comrades of Esmeralda.
   — With the C. M and Abr in Lagos
   — With the C. Br.
   — With the C. in F.
Agreements on urgent matters:
   a.   Concerning consolidation.
It is agreed to prepare and send the report to Comrades of the Front and of Esmeralda. This task is entrusted to Comrade Marcial.
   b.   The same (task) to the DRU representatives abroad.
   c.   It is decided to distribute the solidarity aid received from I. in the following manner:
   — 250 for logistical and communications expenses in Lagos. Of this, 50 for the reserve fund requested by the comrades of the Front and 250 for reception, logistics and communications expenses in the country. Out of this 50 for the reserve fund of the DRU.

   d.   It is decided to name the DRU member aboard at the next meeting and the DRU representatives in Palmera and Pinares.
   e.   It is decided to determine the duties of the DRU members when they are outside the country while studying its operation.
   IV.   It is decided to keep minutes of every DRU meeting and issue bulletins for the knowledge of the DRU representatives abroad. Temporary authority to do so has been given to Comrade Marcial.
   g.   It is decided to approve the arrangement, measures and agreements as well as the performance of the mission carried out by the DRU members, Comrades Jovel, Eduardo and Marcial during the tour they have just completed.
"UNITED IN STRUGGLE UNTIL FINAL VICTORY"
Unified Revolutionary Directorate — Politicomilitary
El Salvador, Central America
Wednesday, 24 September 1980

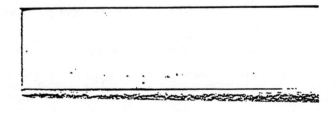

ACTA DE REUNION: DIRECCION REVOLUCIONARIA UNIFICADA POLITICO
MILITAR - C R U - /. 24 de Septiembre de 1980.

Asistencia:
. Hugo - René
. Ana María - Marcial.
. Jonés   - Eduardo.

Agenda:
1- Informes
2- Evaluación.
3- Nombramientos.

I.- Ana María:
Informes de carta de C. Mauricio, donde dá datos sobre la muerte del C. Neto, Primer
Responsable de la R. N., en accidente de aviación. El Compañero Hugo y René, amplían
con los informes enviados por los compas Lateben y María.
Acuerdos:
a)- enviar una nota de pesar y solidaridad a la Dirección Nacional de la R N.
b- Emitir un comunicado público en el mismo sentido.

II. El C. Hugo informa que el C. Eduardo ha estado yendo todos los días (excepto el
sábado) alpunto de contacto que se convino con el C. Neto para concertar las reunio
nes con la Dirección de la R N., para tratar sobre la petición de reingreso a la-
DRU. Se informa que de parte de la RN nadie ha llegado a los contactos; llegandose-
a la conclusión de que posiblemente al C. Neto no pudo informar a su Dirección.
Acuerdo:
Buscar el contacto con la Dirección de la RN por todos los canales que haya, para -
unirse con la misma a la mayor brevedad posible.

III. Informe de la Misión en el exterior de los miembros de la DRU: Ca. Jonás, Eduardo y Marcial.
Los Compas Honás y Eduardo informan ampliando los informes de el Compañero Marcial en
el orden siguiente:
i- Informe de las tareas en sombrero, Palmera, Arena y Pinares , en los siguientes -
terrenos: contactos oficiales y resultados, acuerdos: Con organizaciones hermanas --
y personalidades progresistas; reuniones y medidas tomadas con los representantes -
de las Or ganizaciones de la DRU y con los del FDR .

ii- Informe de las reuniones , acuerdos y medidas en Lagos. :
- Con la Dirección Nacional del Frente.
- Con la Comisión de logística de la DRU.
- Con el PRTC.
- Sobre la reunión con el C. Neto de la RN y la petición de reingreso a la DRU de su
Organización.

iii- Sobre las reuniones con los Compas de Esmeralda. :
- Con el C. M y Abr en Lagos.
- Con el C. Br.
- Con el C. en F.

[the following page appears to have been inserted erroneously; no translation appears among any of the White Paper documents]

2.

Todavía no puede nombrarse pués, y que al integrarse deberán nombrarse coordinadores durante una fase inicial.

En el Estado Mayor General también debe de haber coordinadores, lo mismo en las secciones y en las comisiones conjuntas. En la DRU debe de haber un coordinador General político Militar y coordinadores en las areas concretas .

Fundamenta su argumentación en distintos aspectos del trabajo conjunto que muestran de bilidades; por Ej. En la operatividad conjunta, en los partes de guerra, en la necesidad de revisar los cálculos cuantitativos de combatientes, en los cálculos de bajas del enemigo que considere inexáctos, en diversos enfoques que considera que todavía no son del todo coincidentes; por Ej. el concepto de vanguardia etc.

C. Marcial: Expone que considera que deben hacerse los nombramie tos y asignaciones de las responsabilidades individuales de inmediato, porque es una necesidad urgente para que la DRUp pueda cumplir más ágilmente su papel de dirección y que su trabajo adopte correctos métodos y ritmo de trabajo que le permitan entrar a la solución de sus deficilidades y desajustes que se han ido acumulando precisamente por las postergaciones en dar los saltos de calidad primero, para que la DRU tuviera los mecanismos necesarios para tomar decisiones y luego, para que la DRUpueda tener; dirección colectiva con responsabilidad individual. Que por este salto de calidad en el funcionamiento de la DRU le permitirá ejercer en forma dialectica una influencia directa positiva no sólo sobre los organismos de la misma, sino sobre las organizaciones que lo componen; que por eso no puede aplazarse más la satisfacción de esa necesidad histórica.

C. Hugo. Considera que es necesario dar responsabilidades individuales de dirección, - pués de lo contrario la DRU irá desmejorando su funcionamiento. Que es necesario reforzar los grados del trabajo unitario, porque eso permitirá tener una verdadera capacidad de dirección ; por Ej. si en el CMCC, los asuntos van lentos, no es por falta de capacidad de los compañeros sino porque nadie está de lleno en ese trabajo. Que lo que corresponde es que los miembros de la DRU se dediquen a tiempo concreto y que agilicen sus lazos con otras organizaciones. Es necesario las diversas instancias paralelas y agilizar los lazos de la DRU con otras Organizaciones y ampliando las instancias de la DRU.

Recalca que el proceso de unidad ha dado pasos continuos y muy importantes, basados en la gran identidad de la síntesis estratégica, táctica, teórica y práctica que tiene su expresión en el documento del 22 de mayo.

Que sobre los Estados Mayores de Frente al cres conveniente que se nombran coordinadores y en cuanto al CMCC, es necesario que se nombre al jefe; y en la DRU, debe nombrarse el comandante en jefe y asignar responsabilidades individuales. Que en este momento no es posible que no puedan ejercer un mando efectivo por las actuales condiciones de desarrollo del trabajo conjunto, pero tomarían verdadera efectividad al iniciarse la aplicación del plan de guerra conjunto.

En nuevas intervenciones los Crs. argumentan las posiciones expuestas.

RESOLUCIONES:

1- Sobre las ideas de establecer reuniones plenarias de la DRU y el funcionamiento de una Comisión ejecutiva de la DRU y otros aspectos para el desarrollo de las formas de su funcionamiento, se acuerda elaborar un proyecto para estudiarla en próxima reunión.

2- Que se nombren responsabilidades en el interior de la DRU, tomando en cuenta el grado que se ha alcanzado en el proceso unitario.

3- Que se asignen responsabilidades a nivel de coordinación en el CMCC.

4- Que se nombren coordinadores en los estados mayores generales de Frentes.

5- Que se nombren responsabilidades de coordinadoras en las comisiones de la DRU.

[end of erroneously inserted page]

2

Acuerdos de asuntos urgentes:

a- Sobre coyuntura.
Se acuerda preparar y enviar la información a los Cs. del Frente y de Esmeralda. Se encomienda esta tarea al C. Marcial.
b- Lo mismo que a los representantes de la DRU en el exterior.
c- Se acuerda distribuir la ayuda solidaria recibida de I. de la siguiente manera.

- 250 para los gastos de logística y comunicación en Lagos. De esto, 50 para el fondo de la reserva solicitado por los Ca. del Frente y 250 para los gastos de recepción logística, y comunicaciones en el país.
De estos , 50 para fondo de reserva de la DRU.
o- Se acuerda nombrar en la siguiente reunión al miembro de la DRU en el exterior, y los representantes de la DRU en Palmera y Lineros.
e- Se acuerda determinar las atribuciones de los miembros de la DRU cuando están fuera del País al estudiar el funcionamiento de la misma.
IV. Se acuerda llevar actas de cada reunión de la DRU, y emitir boletines para conocimiento de los representantes de la DRU, en el exterior, provisionalmente se autoriza hacerlo al c. Marcial.
g- Se acuerda aprobar las disposiciones, medidas y acuerdos , así como la actuación r la misión realizada por los miembros de la DRU, Cs. Joval, Educaroo y Marcial en l para que acaben de terminar "

" UNICOS PARA COMB-TIR HASTA LA VICTORIA FINAL "

Dirección Revolucionaria Unificada Política Militar.

El Salvador, Centro América, Miércoles 24 de septiembre de 1980.

DOCUMENT I

Excerpt of report on meeting of guerrilla Joint General Staff (EMGC) of September 26, 1980.

GLOSSARY I

EMGC – Guerrilla Joint General Staff

DRU – Unified Revolutionary Directorate.   Joint Leadership of guerrilla group

Lagos – Nicaragua

TRANSLATION OF DOCUMENT I

E.M.G.C. MEETING
26 September 1980

Those Present: Ramon
Vladimir
Jonas

Agenda: (1) Reports
(2) Analysis of the Military Situation
(3) Operation and Structure of the EMGC
(4) Campaign Number 1

1.   The General Staff did not have infrastructure (facilities) for this meeting and we began by looking into the possibilities while seated in a small coffee shop. Finally Comrade Ramon, confronted with the impossibility of finding meeting places that offered the necessary security requisites, decided to take us to a house where he said the meeting would not be expected.

The meeting lasted from 0840 to 1239 hours for two reasons: One being that the house was not set up for a meeting and the second that Comrade Vladimir had a meeting at 1300 hours.

I am including these facts in the report because this has been more or less the operating situation of the Joint General Staff since it came from Cuba. It has had five noon-time meetings. It has no assigned or defined working infrastructure. Its work has been limited to the following tasks: Brief the DRU on the overall war plan, and decide on an operational campaign called "Independence." It brought up the need for logistical distribution by percentages and upon not reaching any agreement, dropped the problem in the lap of the DRU. It brought up the need to form intelligence and communications sections and name the Joint General Staff leaders and officers for its various sections. It brought up the need to create Zone staffs to prepare the military forces to implement the general war plan. And, because in the latter two aspects, it cannot make decisions, it passed them on to the DRU so that it would decide and approve them. Up to now, it has drawn up four meeting memoranda and has sent them on to the DRU.

2. In accordance with the operational report of the EMGC, I questioned the fact that this body has not worked out a tactical military plan in accordance with the general war plan and with the actual military situation on a national level that takes into account the logistical, structural, instructional and operational aspects as well as those aspects that are strictly operational (that had been used for the general strike of 13-15 August and for campaign "Independence"); that the EMGC has followed a policy of dealing with organizational structure questions, of naming leaders, and distributing arms based on percentages, and has neglected or has not performed its advisory role to the DRU in terms of military policy; that it contradicts military reality to discuss percentages of arms when hardly some 4 tons of the 130 warehoused in Lagos have been brought into the country. These 4 tons have been in intermittent supply and the material now in Lagos is only equivalent to one-sixth of all the material obtained that the DRU will have (eventually) concentrated in Lagos.

END OF EXCERPT

política militar; que es contradictorio con la realidad militar discutir
porcentajes de armas cuando de 130 toneladas embodegadas en Lagos a penas se han logrado meter al país unas cuatro toneladas, siendo este aprovisionamiento inconstante y el material ahora existente en la oz solo equivalente a una sexta parte de todo el material ~~~~~~~~~~~~~~~ conseguido con que contará la DRU concentrado en lagos.

También es contradictorio con la realidad hablar de estructurar secciones del E.M.G.C. si este no tiene resuelto el problema de su infraestructura para su propio funcionamiento como tal y sin un análisis de nuestras fuerzas militares, su naturaleza y las necesidades de la guerra y el nivel de guerra que vivimos; que prueba de este mal funcionamiento es el hecho de que en un mes y diez días solo haya habido cinco reuniones de mediosdías; que no ha habido reunión con la Comisión Logística por lo cual dicho organismo no tiene criterios definidos sobre las necesidades de cada frente de guerra y para esta etapa del plan para sobre la que se de esos criterios elaborar un plan de prioridades en el trabajo logístico; y dicha comisión trabaja según lo que cree más conveniente y sin tener siquiera opinión del Estado Mayor. Que el Plan Militar escrito no corresponde al plan militar elaborado por el Estado Mayor; y tampoco se le a expuesto a la sección de operaciones. Por último y lo más delicado es que la DRU está conduciendo la situación política a un ritmo tal que las contradicciones sociales y políticas se van precipitando y cobrando

DOCUMENT J

Excerpt of letter from "Fernando" to "Federico" (dated September 30, 1980)

GLOSSARY J

DRU – Unified Revolutionary Directorate.   Joint leadership of Salvadoran guerrilla groups.
Front – Nicaraguan FSLN.
GDR – German Democratic Republic.
RN – National Resistance. Salvadoran guerrilla group.
Simon – Shafik Handal, Secretary General of Salvadoran Communist Party

TRANSLATION OF DOCUMENT J

BEGIN EXCERPT
      In a previous note I reported to you that Lalo had returned from studying where Lucho is. He requested information from Hugo (text unclear) he is very enthusiastic and has drawn up the following work plan:
          Construction of 120mm guns (gun, shell and casing)
          Hand grenades (offensive and defensive)
          Anti-tank grenade (launcher, detonator and shell)
          Contact mine (detonator, fuse and casing)
          Anti-personnel mine (detonator, fuse and casing)
          Automatic activation for contact and anti-personnel mines.
He expressed that he is also ready to help economically and he thinks he can work here in making the pieces for which materials are difficult to acquire there and that they would be completed there. But for this it is necessary to have a meeting with those who are going to work there in order to come to an agreement on which pieces will be made there and which here. He also has the idea that he could get everything together there and he would be willing to transfer here. In order to make this decision (if he would work here I need authorization from inside as well as from Augusto). I find it difficult that one can do it here because I have already sounded out Augusto's opinion and he expressed that what we already have is sufficient. That means only that we would work without his consent, although that is not advisable. Also Simon thinks that we should not do it that way. In any event it is necessary and it must be resolved.
      We have spoken with Angel at length about the work in Honduras; we have (words illegible) detail about the needs there. The tasks which must be accomplished

there are the following: a) look for another house, since the current one was taken away from the; b) to set up an infrastructure for large vehicles (trailer trucks), which must be a shed with a roof in order to unload or a farm in adequate locations. It is necessary to resolve the issue of depositing the equipment, since as of today nothing has been done; I do not know the reason for this, inasmuch as we had talked at length with you. This is basic, because we must maximize the security of the work activity; c) a detailed study of the landing strips as it is known that we are going to use them; d) a study of the Honduran-Nicaraguan customs (Honduro-nicas); e) we have also spoken about adequate personnel, especially with regard to drivers; today we are interested in those who have heavy equipment licenses. In this regard I am arranging the arrival of a few comrades of Canadian nationality, but it is not assured and they should be sought out elsewhere; f) if it is necessary to continue with the study of the blind paths on the Honduran-El Salvador border, which is basic; one does not have to resign oneself to a few; here one can take advantage of what the Morazanic front could offer, but the principal support we can provide ourselves.

I have spoken at length with Rodolfo and Angel. The above mentioned topic has been clarified, since it is they who have the responsibility of carrying out those tasks. I have recommended to them that they operate like a cell organization where they discuss and agree upon the work. It seems to me that Angel is too often discouraged and this does not allow him to make the time to take adequate security measures. He gets nervous and thus does not get along well with Rodolfo. They have had altercations beyond what is normal and have had disagreements. On his part, Rodolfo is very slow and lacks initiative. We have had a meeting together and I have made clear to both of them the necessity of overcoming these situations. It concerns me especially that they do not work well on security measures. I hope to have a weekly meeting with them in order to quickly remedy this problem.

A situation which I want to remind you of is that concerning the springtime. It is basic that we resolve it in order to (?) the work methods and means, something fundamental in the covert operations. It is assumed that we were clear on this when I visited them there. I do not know what happened.

Regarding the economic problem I wish to inform you that we are more or less alright, since we have made a decision to use some centavos that were obtained in solidarity. This week we authorized the joint purchase of a van at a cost of $25,000.00. We did this because we have been using only small vehicles. I would like you to inform Hugo that a solidarity of the GDR has been made effective which reaches $100,000.00. Also comrade Guillermo arrived from the Commission of Internal Logistics, who brought instructions on that given by Iraq, from which they left $200,000 for logistics. We are drawing up a plan for acquiring new methods of transport.

Angel also asked me the question about the course for him and another friend, which I am going to carry through on immediately. Regarding this I understand that it has to do with what we discussed when I visited you, about the qualified technicians and professionals. This is already taken care of, but in general in such a way that when someone arrives his trip is handled again. In my opinion we could send a good number of personnel from this class and not send them one by one; there are favorable conditions; I would only need the list of specialties and the number of personnel in order to handle it in time so that they would not be here losing time. If you wish, they could tell me what profession each of them has, since this would help me with the processing. Luis is already where Lucho is.

I wish to inform you also that a comrade pilot is here who made Simon come at the beginning of the month and I have arranged a training period for him where Jose is since there are good conditions for it.

Regarding the next shipments, there are problems. Last 27 September a meeting with Gustavo was held in which he informed us of the Front's decision to suspend shipments during a period of approximately one month. They brought up a security problem beginning with a meeting which they say they had with one James Cheek, a representative of the North American Department of State. They say that he manifested knowledge about shipments via land through Nicaragua; in small vehicles and that we carried out attempts by sea. They raise the question of possible bad management of the information on the part of personnel working on this and that they are going to carry out an investigation. We have made an evaluation of the previous question and it seems very strange to us that a gringo official would come to them to practically warn about a case such as this. If it were true that they have detected something concrete, it is logical that they would hit us and they would arm the great propaganda machine and not that they would warn us (we are not friends); we believe that this could be a means of pressure while the problem of the RN is solved. This is on one side and on the other is that it has to do with a political decision related to the U.S. elections, that is a possible understanding in order not to cause problems to Carter before November. Regarding this one must remember — also Lucho pressed in the sense that a breather in the fighting must be considered in order to see how the Carter-Reagan problem is solved. Beginning with the previous issue, we have carried out steps for the immediate revocation of that decision and have taken as a basis the report on the situation in the interior which comrade Guillermo brought from the Reception Committee on the military problems in the interior. As of right now we still do not have an answer. Make Hugo aware of this and tell him to raise this at the level of the DRU. We would like to have suggestions on this, although it would be going too far to say that this decision by the Front affects us in a negative way.

Well my brother, I hope that the problems which we have in this strategic work are soon resolved, since if it is otherwise I fear that they could hit us very hard.

Best wishes to everyone.

(signature)
Fernando

En nota anterior te informaba de que Lalo había regresado de estudiar de donde Bruno /pide información a su ... está muy entusiasmado y la elabora ... siguiente plan de trabajo:

- Construcción de cañones de 120 m (cañón, granada, dispositivo de de activación
- Granadas de mano (ofensiva y defensiva)
- Granada anti-tanque (fusil de lanzamiento, dispositivo eléctrico y granada)
- Minas de concreto (dispositivo eléctrico, espoleta y recipiente)
- Minas antipersonales (dispositivo eléctrico, espoleta y recipiente)
- Activación automática para las minas de concreto y antipersonales

El manifiesta estar dispuesto incluso a ayudar económicamente y piensa que puede trabajarse aquí en la fabricación de las piezas que allí ofrecieran dificultarse en la adquisición de los materiales y que allí se completarán. pero para esto es necesario que se tuviera una entrevista con los que van a trabajar allí para ponerse de acuerdo en qué piezas se fabrican allí y cuales aquí. También tiene la idea de que puede trabarse - allí todo y estaría dispuesto a trasladarse allí. para tomar esta decisión (si se trabajara aquí yo necesito autorización de adentro así como de su gusto). Yo encuentro difícil que aquí se pueda porque ya se sondeaío la opinión del adentro y esto manifiesta que es suficiente con lo que ya tenemos; sólo que trabajáramos sin su consentimiento, aunque no es recomendable, e incluso siendo propia que así no debemos hacerlo. De todas maneras esto es necesario que resolverlo.

Con Angel hemos conversado ampliamente sobre el trabajo en Honduras; hemos en detalle sobre las necesidades allí. Las tareas vas allí deben cumplirse son las siguientes: A) buscar otra casa, ya que la actual se las quitarán; b) infraestructura para vehículos grandes (furgones), la cual debe ser una galera con techo para esconder los ... res adecuados. Es necesario resolver lo de los depósito del equipo, ya que hasta hoy nada se ha hecho; desconozco las razones de esto, pues lo habíamos hablado ampliamente contigo. Esto es fundamental, pues tenemos que asegurar al máximo la actividad del trabajo; c) estudio detallado de las ... es conocido que vemos a ... ; c) estudio de las aduanas hondureño-nicas; e) hemos hablado asimismo del personal ... que tengan licencia de oficio pesado; sobre esto estoy gestionando la medida de unos compañeros de nacionalidad canadiense, pero no está seguro y debe buscarse por otro lado; f) es necesario continuar con el estudio de los pasos ciegos de la frontera Honduras-El Salvador, lo cual es fundamental; no hay que conformarse con poder, pues puede aprovecharse lo que pudiera ofrecer el frente norteñico, pero lo principal lo ponemos nosotros.

Be hablado ampliamente con Rodolfo _____ lo arriba mencionado ha
quedado claro. que son ellos quienes tienen la responsabilidad de impulsar
esas tareas. Yo les X he recomendado que funcionen como un organismo calcu-
lar donde discutan y se pongan de acuerdo en el trabajo. Me parece que
____ es desespera demasiado ; esto no se permite hacer tiempo para tomar
las medidas de seguridad adecuadas, se pone nervioso y esta hace que no
se lleven bien con Rodolfo, incluso han llegado a tener alterados fuera

lo normal y entrar en desacuerdos; por su parte, Rodolfo es muy lento y
falto de iniciativa. Hemos tenido una reunión conjunta, los he puesto X
claros a ambos, sobre la necesidad de superar estas situaciones. Me preo-
cupa, especialmente que no trabajen bien en las medidas de seguridad: es-
por _____ tener una entrevista semanal con ellos para mejorar pronto este problema.

Una situación que quiero recordarte es lo referente a lo de la prima
____ esto es imposible el que lo resolvemos para _____ los medios y métodos de trabajo, algo fundamental en la conspiración. Sobre esto se su-
pone que ya estábamos claros cuando los visité allí, desconozco que pasó.

Sobre el problema económico quiero informarte que estamos más o menos
bien pues hemos tomado una decisión de utilizar algunos centavos que han
sido obtenidos en solidaridad. permite esta semana. Hemos autorizado la
compra conjunta de un _____ con un costo de $_____; esto porque só-
lo hemos estado utilizando vehículos pequeños. También quisiera que
se informes _____ que ya se hizo efectiva una solidaridad de la RDA que
asciende a $_____ así mismo llegó el compañero Guillermo de la co-
misión de los _____ informa quien traía instrucciones de _____ lo donado
por _____, de lo cual dejo para logística $_____ hemos elabora-
do un plan de adquisición de medios de transporte.

_____ plantea también la cuestión de un curso para él y otro socio,
lo cual es inmediato voy a tramitarlo; sobre esto entiendo que se trata
de lo que hablamos contigo cuando te visité, de los técnicos, profesio-
nales calificados. Esto ya está tramitado, pero en general de tal manera
que cuando alguien llega se tramita de marzo su viaje. Yo opino que nosotros podríamos enviar un buen número de personal de esta clase, no estar
enviando uno por uno; hay condiciones favorables; sólo necesitaría el lis-
tado de especialidades y la cantidad de personal para tramitarlo con tiempo para que no estén aquí perdiéndolo. Si quisiera que me digan que profe-
sión tiene cada uno, pues esto me facilita el trámite. Ya Luis está donde
Lucho.

_____ informarte también que se encuentra aquí un cierto un piloto que
hizo venir Simón desde _____ de _____ para él un período de estancia _____ desea José que hay buenas condiciones para ello.

Sobre los próximos envíos de problema; el pasado 27 de Sept. se rea-
lizó una reunión con _____ en la que se nos informó de la decisión del
frente de suspender los envíos durante un período aproximado de un mes;
ellos plantearon un problema de seguridad a partir de una reunión que dicen haber tenido con un tal _____ Speck, delegado del departamento de estado norteamericano; dicen que _____
_____ terrestre a través de Nicaragua, en vehículos pequeños
y que realizábamos intentos por la vía _____; plantean posible mal manejo de la información por parte del personal que trabaja en esto, que
ven a realizar una investigación. Nosotros hemos realizado una evaluación
de lo anterior y nos da parecido muy extraño o que un funcionario gringo les
_____ prácticamente a prevenir sobre un caso como este. Si fuera cierto
que algo concreto han detectado lo lógico es que nos golpeen y aún el
gran propaganda y no que nos prevengan (ni amigos somos); nosotros cree-
mos que esto puede ser un medio de presión para mientras se resuelve el
problema de la PX; esto por un lado, por otro, que se trata de una decisión política relacionada con las elecciones norteamericanas, es decir
que se trata de un socio _____ para no causarle problemas a Carter antes de noviembre; sobre esto debe recordarse que incluso Lucho y _____
_____ en el sentido de que debiera considerarse un respiro en la lucha

para ver como se resuelve el problema Carter-Reagan. Nosotros a partir
de lo anterior hemos realizado gestiones para la inmediata revocación
de esa decisión y se ha tomado como base el informe de la situación en e
el interior que traía el compañero Guillermo de la comisión de recepción, sobre los problemas militares en el interior; al momento de escri-
birte esto no tenemos respuesta aún. Dale a conocer esto a _____ dile
que lo plantee a nivel de la RDA; nos gustaría tener indicaciones sobre
esto, aun que está demás insistir en que esta decisión del frente nos a-
fecta en forma negativa.

Bueno mi hermano, deseo que los problemas que tenemos en este trabajo
estratégico se resuelvan pronto, pues de lo contrario temo que nos puedan golpear fuertemente.

Saludos fraternales a toda la familia.

Fernando

DOCUMENT K

Letter from "Vladimir" to "Joaquin", "Jacobo", and "Marcial" (dated November 1, 1980)

GLOSSARY K

DRU – Unified Revolutionary Directorate. Joint leadership of guerrilla groups.

Esmeralda – Cuba

FMLN – Farabundo Marti Liberation Front. Salvadoran guerrilla federation.

Lago – Nicaragua

Marcial – Cayetano Carpio. Leader of FPL guerrilla group

Vladimir – DRU logistics representative in Nicaragua

TRANSLATION OF DOCUMENT K

Report No. 4
Lago, 1 November 1980

Comrades Joaquin, Jacobo, Marcial
DRU of the FMLN
Received a fraternal and combative greeting:
On the 29th Comrade Rodrigo of logistics was here on a visit. He brought us several notes (from Esteban, Marcial and a report from the DRU). Along with the comrade we saw the condition of the shipment. We have tied up the maritime and land shipments; as for the air shipment we are awaiting your decision as to what can be received.

Here, as regard the shipments, they have been packing the bundles day and night. In fact, these people from Lago have stepped things up. It is such a hot potato for them that they are now pushing us, as this cannot be endured much longer. On the other hand, the warehouses in Esmeralda are filled to the brim with the shipment that arrived last week, over 150 tons. Also, they will have a backlog because more shipments will be arriving this week in Esmeralda reaching between 300 and 400 tons. So, this has become a sort of chain, of which we are the last and most important link. This is causing us concern regarding the entire operational plan for the domestic reception, because if we fail to tighten our own link, it will lead to political and operational repercussions that will reach far away lands where they are seriously adhering to their commitment to us. Comrade Simon will be arriving in the country and will elaborate on this. We discussed all of this with Rodrigo and he too will be able to explain further if necessary.

On 19 October we forwarded an enclosed plan subject to the confirmation of the points dealing with the reception submitted by the comrades from domestic logistics; this plan was approved by the Front, but dates were changed on the 25th thereby scheduling the first shipments to begin on the fourth. They also said we would be getting the shipping schedule this week. Yesterday, 30 October, they handed me a schedule that practically doubles the previously projected amount, with a plan to smuggle into the country 109 tons this month alone, which represents 90% of the total stored here. They appear to be in a hurry and determined. We received the schedule you sent and discussed it with Rodrigo; we tried to tie up as many bundles as possible.

On this regard, and according to how the situation is viewed here, the consensus is that we could handle a plan such as the shipment of 109 tons with the resources on hand, but the fundamental problem yet to be resolved concerns the reception. The problem we are now confronting is different from the previous situation, but we are going to take steps to face up to it. However, there is an important factor which we must bear in mind, and that is that aside from the external problems this might create, in addition to arguments it might generate, it is nonetheless decisively and strategically important to arm the revolutionary combatants, for this is a crucial phase in the revolution. For our part, we are aware of the operational problems this situation creates internally, and the fact that if we continue prolonging the shipment of arms we jeopardize the future of the revolution. Consequently, we must be just as determined to risk everything in resolving the problem concerning the reception of firearms as we are in combating the enemy. I believe it is almost impossible to smuggle 109 tons this month, but we must make every effort to bring in as much as we can. From Rodrigo's report we can immediately grasp the situation, which Marcelo had already described during his recent visit here. It reflects the deep contrast that exists between the need to arm the people, a critical and serious fact, with the practical and real efforts being made in the area of internal reception. The comrades explained here the tasks already in motion, but greater and more intensified efforts are necessary; they should form a cadre from within the DRU or jointly with the EMGC to be in charge of this superhuman and heroic endeavor. That must be undertaken, for on this depends not only the future of the war but of the revolution as well.

This is a decisive phase due to the different domestic and foreign factors which you probably have analyzed in depth. On the one hand, the U.S. elections no longer pose any problems (the results do not matter). The comrades in the Front are ready to take a firm step in an irreversible manner. Also, they are pressured by the next stronger wave already in sight, and that is the shipment that is being delayed in Esmeralda.

It is impressive how all countries in the socialist bloc fully committed themselves to meet our every request and some have even doubled their promised aid. This is the first revolution in Latin America to which they have unconditionally turned to assist, before the taking of power. For their part, they are continuously observing our every move, not just where we are concerned, but some are beginning to wonder why we haven't brought the arms into the country.

On the other hand, regarding the problem of domestic war supplies, it has been predetermined that in this first stage it is imperative to smuggle the greatest number of firearms, because although the war is entering a crucial and complex political and military stage, both for us and for the enemy, it can still support (in spite of all the difficulties that might arise) relatively simple operational plans compared to what is yet to come. Once there is open war, supply operations take on a more complex character, are made on a larger scale and combat operations are bigger than anything we can mount today. All this leads to the great significance a major effort has today to ensure a strategic phase in the revolution. We had a meeting of minds with Rodrigo regarding all channels of communication (mail and telephone), so as to achieve good coordination. He's carrying the latest schedule; we have secured almost every land and sea route; we still have to work on how to resolve the air route. We'll be laying out the last details on how best to pack the merchandise and will be aligning the points of departure to begin this important mission.

As regard communications, we are taking steps to purchase all equipment for the DRU, the EMGC and for various fronts. The technical equipment is costly, but we're going ahead. Nothing had been done in this regard. The code and method for DRU-Lago have been established. Comrade Sonia requested one day travel to Esmeralda for consultations. She left on the 29th and still has not returned; we have heard nothing about her delay.

I made arrangements with the Front for 12 comrades to begin a communications course. I selected the best suited from a group of scholarship holders who are here doing nothing (from within the three organizations). The course begins 3 November. These comrades will be ready to handle communications in all fronts. It's possible that by the time they complete the course and are back in the country you may have received all the equipment. With regard to the request for the radio mentioned in your note, the people in the front had informed me the day before they had decided to modify the commercial radio equipment. I will continue to make arrangements for the shortwave. I hope for a reply on Sunday, the 3rd.

Simon will travel there on the 3rd. He's carrying a broad political report regarding everything here.

The chapines (Guatemalans) are all here signing the unity (document). This is a transcendental event because it took place here in Lago. They wanted to have at least a high-ranking comrade from the DRU present during the signing. Simon will not be able to stay. We have, however, formed a delegation made up of Miguel S., Maria and myself to attend the event. Broj and AB might come here for the event.

Revolutionary Greetings!

> UNITED IN STRUGGLE UNTIL THE
> FINAL VICTORY!
> REVOLUTION OR DEATH, WE WILL WIN!

NOTE:

Whenever you send official notes from the DRU it would be best if these were signed by one of the three. The only information I've received has been the note via Joaquin and minutes from the DRU; the most recent I have is dated 12 October 1980. There have been no official military reports.

2 a.m. – 1 November 80

/s/ Vladimir

El 19 de Oct. mandamos un plan adentro sujeto a la confirmación de los puntos de recepción de parte de los compas de logística interna; este plan fue aprobado por el frente y el 25 ellos lo hicieron ajustar a las fechas dejado los primeros envíos a partir del 4. Esta semana, también ellos nos dijeron que nos iban a dar el calendario de envíos. Ayer 30 Oct. me dieron un calendario en el que prácticamente doblan la cantidad anteriormente programada, y nos proponen meter sólo en este mes, 109 tons. al país; lo que equivale a enviar un 90% de la cantidad embodegada aquí. Se notan bastante apurados y decididos. Por parte nuestra recibimos el calendario, lo discutimos con Rodrigo y tratamos de amarrar la mayor cantidad de envíos posibles.

Sobre esto, la valoración según se ve aquí la situación, es que nosotros podríamos absorber un plan como el de mandar las 109 tons. con los sectores que hay; pero el problema fundamental a resolver es el de la recepción. Ahora el problema que se nos viene encima es diferente a la situación anterior y vamos a tomar medidas para enfrentarla; sin embargo, hay un aspecto importante que es necesario tomar en cuenta; y es que independientemente de los problemas externos que esto provoque_

-2-

y las discusiones que aquí genere, es importante, decisivo y estratégico armar los combatientes revolucionarios y que esta etapa es en definitiva para la revolución. Por parte nuestra, estamos conscientes de los problemas operativos que esto crea internamente y que de seguir prolongando el envío de las armas ponemos en juego el futuro de la revolución. Por tanto, debemos estar decididos, de la misma forma con que combatimos al enemigo a jugárnosla toda en el problema de la recepción de fierros. Yo creo, que va a ser casi imposible que metamos este mes las 109 tons. pero debemos hacer todos los esfuerzos por meter lo que más podemos. Del informe que dio Rodrigo aquí se palpa inmediatamente una situación que ya había adelantado Marcelo cuando estuvo aquí recientemente. Y es de que contrasta profundamente la necesidad de armar al pueblo y lo crítico y grave que es esto, con los esfuerzos reales prácticos que se hace en el terreno de la recepción interna. Aquí informaron los compañeros los trabajos que se tienen adelantados; pero es necesario meterle más y de fondo; deberían poner un cuadro de dirección de la DRU ó del E.M.C. conjunto al frente a este esfuerzo sobrehumano y heroico que hay que hacer; porque de esto depende no sólo el futuro de la guerra sino el de la Revolución.

Esta etapa es decisiva por distintos factores internos y externos que ustedes de seguro ya habrán valorado profundamente. ~~Por ejemplo aquí se sabrá por comicios por las elecciones de EEUU (los resultados son importantes).~~ Los compas e frente, ya están decididos a dar el paso en firme de manera irreversible. Están también presionados por la otra ala más fuerte que está a la vista y es el cargamento que ya se está atorando por Sonora de. Es impresionante, como todos los países del campo Soc. se metieron a ayudarnos a todas las solicitudes que hicimos y algunos doblaron la ayuda que prometida. En la primera revolución de S.L. a la que se han volcado incondicionalmente en su ayuda, antes de la toma del poder. De parte de ellos, están en una observación constante sobre todos los pasos que damos y no sólo sobre nosotros sino que comienza a preocuparles a algunos porqué no hemos metido las armas al país.

Por otro lado, en los problemas del abastecimiento interno de la guerra se prevé que en esta primera etapa es urgente meter la mayor cantidad fierros posibles, porque la guerra, aunque está entrando en fases más complejas políticas y militares para nosotros y el enemigo, todavía p. atañecer (con todo y los problemas que se vengan encima) con algunos aspectos operativos relativamente sencillos, comparados a todo lo que se viene después en ..... en guerra abierta, los operativos de abastecimiento son mucho

i t.i ... periores a los que hay para

- 3 -

montar. De lo cual se desprende, la gran importancia que tiene, hoy y gran esfuerzo que hay que hacer y así asegurar una parte estratégica de la revolución.

Con Rodrigo quedamos en todos los canales de comunicación (correos y teléfono que se tenga una buena coordinación. Él lleva el último calendario; como afianzado casi todo lo terrestre y marítimo; lo aéreo hay que ver como lo resolvemos. Estaremos preparando los últimos detalles para embarcar la mercadería de la mejor forma posible y poniendo en los puntos de partida los recursos que aquí se tienen para iniciar esta gran tarea.

En lo que se refiere a las comunicaciones estamos gestionando la compra todo el equipo para DRU, EMGC, y para los distintos frentes. El equipo iónico es caro pero lo vamos a comprar. En esto no había nada hecho. Ya las claves y formas DRU-Lago quedaron establecidos. La compa Sonia dió ir a Esmeralda 1 día a hacer unas consultas. Se fué el 29 y no ha regresado todavía, no sabemos nada de su atraso.

Por otro lado, gestioné ante el frente un curso de comones para 12 compañeros el curso duraba 10 días. La gente la agarró de los secarios más ideales se están aquí sin hacer nada (de las tres organizaciones). El curso comienza el 3 Nov. Estos compas irían listos para las comunicaciones de todos los frentes y posible que cuando ellos terminen el curso y entren al país ustedes ya hayan recibido todos los aparatos.

Sobre la solicitud de radio, que se planteó en la nota que me mandaron, a los del frente un día antes me informaron que habían decidido reforzar los aparatos de una radio comercial. Seguiré gestionando la de onda corta, pero la respuesta el Domingo 3 de esto.

Simón saldrá el 3 hacia allá. Él lleva un informe político amplio de todo de aquí.

Los chapines todos están aquí firmando la unidad. Es un acto trascendental que se ha hecho en Lago. Querían que a la firma similicion por lo menos un mpa primer responsable de los de la DRU. Simón no se va a poder quedar. Se ve hemos hecho una delegación compuesta por Miguel S., María y yo para así. Y al acto, probablemente para acá se desplace BROJ y AB. al acto.

Saludos Revolucionarios. ¡ UNIDOS PARA COMBATIR HASTA LA VICTORIA FINAL !

¡ REVOLUCION O MUERTE VENCEREMOS !

NOTA:
cuando se manden notas oficiales de la DRU sería bueno que las firmara alguien de los tres. La única información que he recibido fue la nota mía Joaquín y actas de la DRU la más reciente que tengo es del 12 de Octubre 80. Informes militares oficiales no a habido ninguno.

2 am. — 1 NOVIEMBRE - 80

Vladimir.

DOCUMENT L

Notes on arms deliveries (undated)

GLOSSARY L

Note: Numbers and letters refer to different types of weapons.

TRANSLATION OF DOCUMENT L

FIRST SHIPMENT

21 − M79 (40 mm grenade launcher, U.S. manufacture) − 72 per box
1512 − 12 grenades M79
336 − FAL (rifle)
168 − M1 and M2
117,600 7.62 (mm) rounds
64,480 .30 (in) M1 rounds
672 − FAL cartridges
336 − M1 cartridges
672 − FAL magazines
504 − bandoliers
15 − RPG2
225 − rockets for the RPG2
2 − M60 (rifles) − Do not lose the clips
210 packages weighing 80 lbs each
16,800 lbs. in total

336	$1512 \div 21 = 72$	$117,600 \div 336 = 350$
168		
504	$336 \times 50 = 16,800$	8,400

Garand Rifle = 14 27 rounds each 27 maximum
 287 rounds
 14 rounds each 14 minimum

M1 Carbines 40 25 rounds each   total = 1,000 rounds

G3 Rifle 22
 7.62 (mm) = 8,000 to 9,000 (rounds)
FAL = 10

FAL 7.62 rifle = 32 with 250 rounds each
86 weapons
(number indistinct) Galil (rifles)
 8 rifles 2.23 (5.56 mm) 170 rounds each
(number indistinct) M16 (rifles)
Total 94 weapons
200 pistols
.45 pistols = with 8 rounds each
9 mm pistols = with 25 rounds each
.22 revolver = − −
.38 revolver − scarce
Submachineguns
6 Madsens
2 Thompsons
1 .45 rifle
1 9mm machinegun

1 .30-06 Browning machinegun Scarce?
2 RPG2s with 5 grenades each
1,120 (mm) = 1 Sn. Simon. 1 "reten"
181 = 1 Sn. Simon 1 "reten" 7 (word indistinct)
       Trucks have been seen with cargo. (Words indistinct)
1 – Ramon does not have (word indistinct) men; but rather *a safe storage area.*
2 storages for 150 (word indistinct)
                1 meter wide
                120 long
Personnel at 1 house. Go up to the dock of the house
3 in each boat
1 hangar and Lagos workshop, house for pilots, 2 mechanics,
(word indistinct) (Salado) 2 pilots (word indistinct) for the big plane.
       1 small reserve plane
       2 large reserve planes
       1 pilot for small plane   Jim.
(Writing in upper right hand corner)
With boat
7 – M79 (grenade launchers)
504 M79 grenades
112 FAL (rifles)
.56 M1 and M2 (rifles or carbines)
39,200 7.62 (mm) (presumably rounds)
20,160 rounds (of) .30 (in)
224 cartridges
114 M1 cartridges
224 magazines
198 bandoliers
70 trips

```
  336        1512   121      117,600 336
  168        0.42   72        1680  350
  504        00.              0600
            336×50
            16800  ⟶  8,400
```

```
1. Comando = 14  27   c/u    = 7 máximo  }  28 = Tiros
                 14/4        14 mínimo   }
Carabinas M₁ 40      25/c    Total = 1000 Tiros

Fusil G₃ 22

FAL = 10    ⟶  7.62 = 8000 = 10.00

Tal fusil 7.62 = 32 c/u  256 tiros c/u

            86 armas

Galil } 8 fusiles 2.23 (5.56) 170 tiros c/u
M16 }
Total  94 armas

        200 pistolas
pistolas 45 = con 6 tiros c/u
pistolas 9mm = con 25 tiros c/u
Revólver 22 =
Revólver 38 = 6 cargo
Sub ametralladoras
  6 Madzan
  02 Thompson
1 fusil 45.
1 fusil ametralladora 9 mm
1 fusil ametralladora browning 30.06 ¿? Es?
2 RPG2 con 5 granadas c/u
```

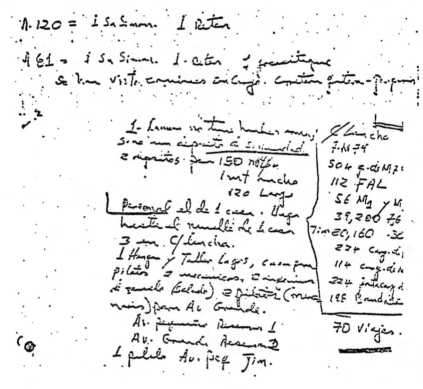

DOCUMENT M

Report on logistics plans (undated)

GLOSSARY M

EMGC — Salvadoran guerrilla Joint General Staff

TRANSLATION OF DOCUMENT M

LOGISTICAL CONCEPTS

The logistical plan must go hand-in-hand with a military plan, i.e., an assessment of exactly what are our strategic points and how to guarantee their maintenance and strengthening.

The military plan must be in full accord with the political plan and guarantee political objectives in terms of global and current strategy.

Situational objectives require tactical combat training for our forces to prepare them as effectively as possible to respond to operational needs set by the leadership.

From the point of view of the logistical plan, two aspects have to be solved: the tactical and the strategic.

On the basis of these fundamental criteria, the following plan is proposed:

a — Insure that we maintain our strategic rearguard zones.

b — Increase the operational capacity of the urban zones.

c — Guarantee our logistical receipt capability and supply-line capabilities and also strengthen them.

d — Insure our distribution capability.

e — Creation of strategic arsenals under the control of the EMGC.

Specifically, this plan translates into:

1.   Primarily supplying the war fronts and not organizations. and within the fronts, based on a military plan that posits concrete military action that permits a qualitative change in the military situation. This qualitative change must be predicated on the premise that with the least effort, the rearguard zone and operations in the entire front are assured so as to keep the military forces of the enemy in the area dispersed and "nailed-down."

On the basis of this military plan, the Joint General Staff may approve the apportionment of arms requests.

2.   Provide for adequate means of supply by dividing up its distribution to a specific front of fronts in accordance with what might be operationally most reasonable.

Also provide for adequate supply routes to each front in accordance with available means.

Resources supplied by sea arrive in the southeast, the Southern Zone of the Mid-Central Zone.

Supplies by land arrive either in Honduras or El Salvador

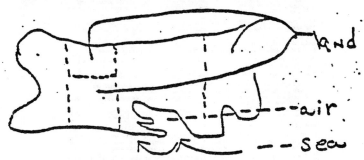

Supplies by air, at this time, have not worked. In this first phase, it is most likely that they begin to operate in the eastern part of the country.

The proposed division is as follows:

By sea: First supply the receipt zone consisting of the Intipuca-Bucaran mountain range, secondly the Mid-Central Zone, and thirdly Morazan and the eastern part in general.

By land: Supplies arrive at any point and should go first to Chalatenango, secondly, to San Salvador and La Libertad, and thirdly, to the western region (Santa Ana, Ahuachapan, and Sonsonate).

By air: On all fronts Morazan, southern Oriente, San Vicente, Cabanas, and Chalatenango have priority.

The essential criterion in providing supplies is to concentrate on strategic points and not disperse supplies. As for the urban and suburban areas, the criterion is to increase operational capacity rather than skirmishes. The Western Zone is also tasked with the need to increase its operational capacity.

The other criterion for concentrating supplies is based on the fact that weapons arrive at certain places points because route, means, and necessity all coincide. (Therefore all supplies from Honduras should supply the northern part of the country.)

The effectiveness of this plan is limited to the fact that it must accomplish the logistical objectives set forth by the military planning of each front as approved by the EMGC.

4.   The planning of military maneuvers by each front should be geared to providing answers to the following questions:

a — How many men are we going to arm in this first phase.

b — Make an evaluative assessment of how many men we are going to arm during the second phase and in the final offensive based on the objectives set forth in the general overall war plan, and the feasibility of setting up supply routes and means as well as the quantity contained in the arsenal.

5.   The qualitative change of the military situation implies that the military plan for each front must consist of:

a – Beginning to control highways.

b – Controlling access roads to the rearguard.

c – Keeping the area of movement of the enemy military force in the rearguard areas restricted.

d – Guaranteeing the capacity to maintain operational campaigns in urban areas and in areas on the peripheries of the cities.

NOTE: This plan is based on there being an excellent supply source in Lagos.

IDEAS SOBRE LOGISTICA.

El plan logístico tiene que ir en función de un plan militar, es decir ne una e-
valuación,de cuales son nuestros puntos estratégicos y como garantizar su soste-
nimiento y fortalecimiento.

El plan militar debe ir en concordancia plena con el plan político. Garantizar -
los objetivos políticos, tanto los globales estratégicos como los coyunturales.

Los objetivos coyunturales requieren una adecuación táctica en la forma de com -
batir de nuestras fuerzas para estar preparados con la mayor efectividad posible
para responder a las necesidades operativas que la comandancia plantea.

Desde el punto de vista del plan logístico , tiene que solucionarse los dos aspec
tos: el táctico y el estratégico.

A partir de estos criterios básicos de plantea el siguiente plan:

a- Garantizar que sostenemos nuestras zonas de retaguardia estratégicas.
b- Aumentar la capacidad operativa de las zonas urbanas.
c- Garantizar nuestra capacidad de recepción logística y de nuestras líneas de a-
bastecimiento, así como fortalecerlas.
d- Garantizar nuestra capacidad de distribución.
e- ir creado los arsenales estratégicos bajo el control del CMCC.

Este plan se traduce a lo concreto en:

1- Aprovisionamiento en base a frentes de guerra y no de organizaciones y dentro
de los frentes en base a un plan militar que plantee la maniobra militar concreta que permita un cambio cualitativo en la situación militar.

Ese cambio cualitativo tiene que plantear que con el menor esfuerzo, se logre
asegurar la zona de retaguardia y la operatividad en todo el frente para mantener
dispersas y " fijadas " a las fuerzas militares enemigas de la zona.

Sobre la base de dicho plan militar el CMCC puede aprobar las proporciones de
armas solicitadas.

2- Adecuar los medios de abastecimiento dividiendo su servicio a determinado fren
te o frentes de acuerdo a lo que operativamente sea más razonable.

Adecuar así mismo las rutas de aprovisionamiento a cada frente , en concordancia con los medios de que se dispone.

Los medios marítimos llegan al sur de oriente y la zona sur de la zona parecen
tral.

Los medios terrestres llegan unos a Honduras y otros a El Salvador.

terrestre

– aéreo,
– marítimo

Los medios aéreos, por ahora, no han funcionado. Lo más probable, en esta pri
mera fase, es que empiecen a funcionar en el oriente del país.

La división propuesta es:
Marítima: aprovisionar primera zona de recepción, constituida por sierra Inti
pucá- Bueserán;

·..· r·

2. · ─ ·· ─ ·

2ª Zona Paracentral, 3ª Morazán y oriente, en general.

Terrestre: Llega a cualquier punto, cabe aprovisionar: 1ª Chalatenango, 2ª San Salv. La Libertad, 3ª Occ. (Sta. Ana, Ahuachapan, Sonsonate).

Aéreo: Aprovisionamiento de zona de oriente y zona paracentral.

3— En todos los frentes, tienen prioridad: Morazán, sur de Oriente, Sn. Vicente, y Caba ñas, Chalatenango.

El criterio esencial del aprovisionamiento es concentrar en los puntos estratégicos y no dispersar. En cuanto a los núcleos urbanos y sub-urbanos el criterio es aumentar la capacidad operativa, más que de choque, la zona occidental, también es aprovisionade con criterio de aumentar su operatividad.

El otro criterio de concentrar se basa en el hecho de que las armas llegan a esos puntos porque coinciden la ruta, al medio y además, la necesidad (así todo envío por Hon duras caso abastecer la zona norte del país.)

Este plan tiene limitada su vigencia a que se cumplen los objetivos logísticos plantea dos por la planificación militar de cada frente y aprobados por el DRU.

4— La planificación de la asesoría militar de parte de cada frente va solucionando las respuestas a:

a— Cuantos hombres vamos a armar en esta primera fase.

b— Hacer una evaluación-tesis de cuantos hombres vamos a armar en la 2ª fase y en la ofensiva final a partir de los objetivos que plantea el plan general de guerra y la factibilidad de contar cados y rutas de abastecimiento así como de la cantidad con que se cuenta en el arsenal.

5— El cambio cualitativo de la situación militar implica que al plan militar de cada frente cabe comprender:

a— Comenzar el control de carreteras.

b— Control de vías de acceso a la retaguardia.

c— mantener reducida el área de movimientos de la fuerza militar enemiga establecida en las zonas de retaguardia.

d— Garantizar la capacidad de mantener las campañas operativas en las zonas urbanas y de las áreas periféricas de las ciudades.

Nota: Este plan partiría de que exista una real fuente de abastecimiento en Lagos.

DOCUMENT N

Notes on delivery arrangements (undated)

GLOSSARY N

ERP – Peoples' Revolutionary Army. Salvadoran guerrilla group.

FAL – Liberation Armed Forces. Guerrilla group of Salvadoran Communist Party

FPL – Popular Liberation Forces Salvadoran guerrilla group

ISTA – Salvadoran Government Agrarian Reform Institute

Lagos – Nicaragua

PRTC – Revolutionary Party of Central American Workers Guerrilla group.

TRANSLATION OF DOCUMENT N

| 2 Trailer trucks: 1 in Costa Rica with driver as far as the volcano | FPL | 400 |
| | | 100 |

1 in construction until 15 Nov.	FAL=60
up to Honduras (Choluteca)	ERP=60
1 to add to the 15 Nov. one up	
to Honduras	520
1 extra which will be bought	

R.N. It has 3 trailer trucks that have entered recently.

AIRSTRIPS: ISTA Saturday and Sunday: Workers: The personnel of the airstrips are ours. It is not possible to use the airstrips during weekdays since there are workers in the area. Two are for small aircraft.

FPL: 100 men on reserve for
        FAL contact = (blotted out) hours
        FPL contact = 48 hours

12 Nov.: 9 tons - 9 tons - 1 ton - 2 tons
21 total tons West West - Central p. West

	Sea Sea	Air	Land
Totals	18	1	2 = 21 tons
		6 tons	
		——	
		7 tons	

80/4000
(numbers illegible = 120 weapons

Criteria to move out of
Los Lagos. But you can
(center cut off)

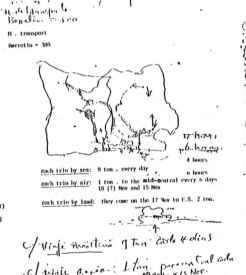

reception (?)

(blotted out) transport

defense

operations for annihilation

    units of diversion

strategic units (?)   (two words blotted out)

points of attack   (one word blotted out)

M . transport
Barretin = 300

each trip by sea: 9 ton . every day
each trip by air: 1 ton . to the mid-central every 6 days
                  10 (?) Nov and 15 Nov
each trip by land: they come on the 17 Nov to E.S. 2 ton.

Huéspedes: 1 ... con ... ...
S.   (Tlaquepaque);
          1 en construcción el 15 Abv. hasta

Trabajadores: (Chalatec..)
          1 ampliando al 15 Nov. hasta

RN: 1 mes que → se va recuperar.
     los 3 ... han vuelto. ya un
     ta días.

$$FAL = 60$$
$$EPP = 60$$
$$\overline{} \atop 520$$
100

→ 48

FPL: 100 hombres de reserva ƒ

Contacto FAL = 00 hor
Contacto FPL = 48 h

Distancias: Tlajomulco y Dom. Tlajomulco. El pue
l de la Pista es Nuestra. Día de Semana no se
cible utilizarlas por frecuencia de lo trabajado
es. Son 2 para aviones pequeños.

12 de Nov.: 9 Ton — 9 Ton — 2 Ton — 2 Ton
          en total   osta   osta   P. central   occite
          Mar   Mar   Aéreo   Terrestre
Totales   18   7   6 Ton   2 = 21 Ton.
                              7 Ton.

Mínimo 180

210
170

Criterios de descalojar lo
(Para su franelic..)

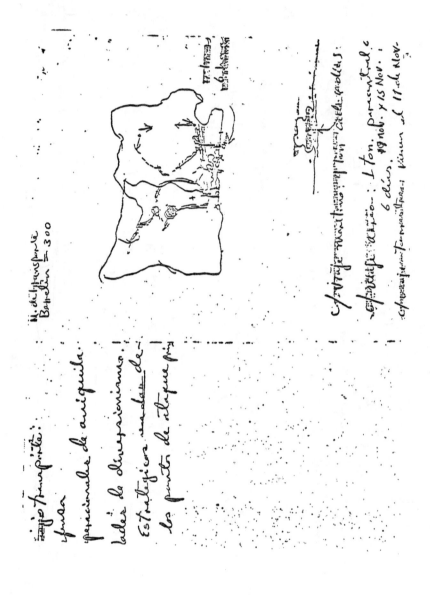

B ERP.
5 FAL
7 FPL.

120 ... 30 ...
10
4
4

124 FPL
1.2 ERP
10 FAL
4 PRTC.
100,000 | 2100
                 → 300
                   500

100.   30,000

4000 ~ 5000
3000 ~ 3300 ERP
700   ~ 1200 ~ 1500 FAL
700   ~ 800 ~ 1000 FPL
                    9,000

463 +
50
513 Total

1.25 FAL
3.37 ERP   30
1.20 FPL.   80 ← chorra
                10 FAL = cha

ci ... ellegan 10
ci... ... ellegan 10
melcan. (20 caballos a i

En los casas
12 ERP
10 FAL
4 PRTC.
4 FPL

130   20 FAL
       12 ERP
total   4 prtc
        114 FPL

II A Actinidad de t
en San Miguel 15 N
   1 B - Galope en Buy

DOCUMENT O

Report of Comrade Jonas Montalvo (undated).

GLOSSARY O

DC – Christian Democrats

DRU – Unified Revolutionary Directorate. Joint leadership of guerrilla groups.

Lagos – Nicaragua

PCS – Salvadoran Communist Party

RN – National Resistance. Salvadoran guerrilla group.

TRANSLATION OF DOCUMENT O

BRIEF REPORT SENT BY COMRADE JONAS MONTALVO (ERP)

While in Panama, the DRU delegation received word from the U.S., through its (the DRU's) ambassador in that country, in which they proposed a discussion regarding elections and the formation of a new government as a transition formula if Carter wins the election. They can offer no more than that, which is also what Majano is offering (the GN, the PN, etc).

The Panamanians have also stated that a proposal for discussion has been made by the U.S. They stated that there is an internal problem in the U.S. election situation and that Carter cannot permit the revolutionary victory in El Salvador. The crux of the problem appears to be fear of Reagan's victory. In that regard, the Central American DC harbors that same fear, as do the Panamanians, Venezuelans, Nicaraguans, and Cubans. They are of the opinion that there are two glaring problems for Carter, one being the hostages in Iran and the second being that of El Salvador.

The Nicaraguan and Cuban comrades have expressed great annoyance with regard to the crisis in the Army because they feel that the DRU did not know how to take advantage of the situation. They feel that the situation was profitable and that at least the DRU should have taken a stand.

With regard to the problem of the RN comrades, even though they have understood that the DRU is right, they pose two problems: One is that they do not agree with those contradictions being handled publicly and thus have been very annoyed; in addition, the Cuban comrades assumed the responsibility for denying a report that the DRU sent from the interior making it official in writing that the RN had withdrawn from the DRU.

With regard to the measures adopted and the justice of the decision concerning the RN, the Cuban and Nicaraguan comrades affirmed that the DRU is right and that what it should do is to discipline the comrades of the Resistance. They stated that they support the DRU and that they are going to continue to support it, but that they are also going to continue supporting the RN bilaterally.

The comrade chief of the PCS expressed displeasure with the public handling of the problem. Copies of the letter which the DRU sent were given to him so that he could have them delivered to a number of friends of the DRU, which the comrade opposed.

With regard to the logistical problem, Comrade Jonas believes that the problem will not be resolved abroad. He says that abroad the basic problem is one of financing and that the most serious problems for resolving the logistical aspect lie here within. He says that domestically there are problems of organization, particularly in communications, in defining priorities in planning for the reception. He says that abroad, the matter is practically resolved since the fundamental problem is one of financing and personnel and not of lack of means.

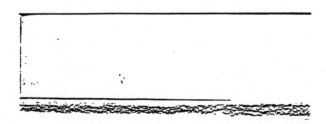

BREVE INFORME ENVIADO POR EL COMPAÑERO JONAS MONTALVO (ERP)

- Estando en Panamá, la delegación de la DRU recibió una notificación de —
los Estados Unidos a través de su embajador en ese país, en la cual pro—
ponían una discusión sobre las elecciones y la formación de un nuevo go—
bierno como una fórmula de transición mientras Carter Gana las elecciones
Que no pueden ofrecer más que eso, que es lo mismo que Majano ofrece (la
GN, la PN etc).
Los panameños manifestaron también que existe una propuesta de parte de—
E.E.U.U. que consiste en la discusión. Que hay un problema interno en la—
coyuntura electoral norteamericana y que Carter no puede permitir el —
triunfo revolucionario en El Salvador. La base del problema parece ser —
que es el temor al triunfo de Reagan. Al respecto, la DC centroamericana,
tiene ese mismo temor, al igual que los panameños, venezolanos , nicara—
guenses, cubanos. Consideran que hay dos problemas candentes para Carter—
Uno es el de los rehenes de Irán y el otro es el de El Salvador.

- Respecto a la crisis en el Ejército, los Compañeros Nicaraguenses y Cuba—
nos manifestaron mucho enojo porque consideran que la DRU no supo—
aprovechar la coyuntura. Ellos son de la opinión de que esa coyuntura era
aprovechable y que al menos la DRU debía haberse pronunciado.

- En relación al problema de los compañeros de la RN, no obstante que han—
entendido que la DRU tiene razón, se plantean dos problemas: Uno es que—
no están de acuerdo en que se haga un manejo público de esas contradic —
ciones y por ello se han molestado mucho, incluso, los compañeros cubanos
se encargaron de x desmentir una noticia que la DRU envió del interior -
oficializando que la RN se había retirado de la DRU.

- Con respecto a las medidas adoptadas y la justeza de la decisión respecto
a la RN los compañeros cubanos y nicaraguenses manifestaron que la DRU—
tiene razón y que lo que debe hacer es disciplinar a los compañeros de —
la Resistencia. Que ellos apoyen a la DRU y le ven a seguir ayudando pero
que también le van a seguir ayudando bilateralmente a la RN.

- El Compañero Primer Responsable del PCS manifestó descontento con la cues
tión del manejo público sobre el problema de la RN. A él le fueron entre
gadas copias de la carta que envió la DRU para que las hiciera llegar a—
una serie de amigos de la DRU, a lo cual el compañero se opuso.

- En cuanto al problema logístico, la opinión del compañero Jonas es que el
problema no se resuelve afuera. Dice él que afuera el problema fundamen—
tal es de financiamiento y que el problema más serio para resolver el as—
pecto logístico está aquí adentro. Que en el interior hay problemas de —
organización, pero sobr a todo de comunicaciones, de definir prioridades
de planificación para la recepción. Que afuera la cuestión está lista —
practicamente, ya que el problema fundamental es de financiamiento y per—
sonal y no de falta de medios.

2ª Zona Paracentral, 3ª Morazán y oriente, en general.

Terrestre: Llega a cualquier punto, debe aprovisionar: 1ª Chalatenango, 2ª San Salv. La Libertad, 3ª Occ. (Sta. Ana, Ahuachapán, Sonsonate).

Aéreo: Aprovisionamiento de zona de oriente y zona paracentral.

3- En todos los frentes, tienen prioridad: Morazán, sur de Oriente, Sn. Vicente, y Cabañas, Chalatenango.

El criterio esencial del aprovisionamiento es concentrar en los puntos estratégicos y no dispersar. En cuanto a los núcleos urbanos y sub-urbanos el criterio es aumentar la capacidad operativa, más que de choque, la zona occidental, también es aprovisionarse con criterio de aumentar su operatividad.

El otro criterio de concentrar se basa en el hecho de que las armas llegan a esos puntos porque coinciden la ruta, el medio y además, la necesidad (así todo envío por Honduras debe abastecer la zona norte del país.)

Este plan tiene limitada su vigencia a que se cumplen los objetivos logísticos planteados por la planificación militar de cada frente y aprobados por el DRU.

4- La planificación de la maniobra militar de parte de cada frente va solucionando las respuestas a:

a- Cuantos hombres vamos a armar en esta primera fase.

b- Hacer una evaluación-tesis de cuantos hombres vamos a armar en la 2ª fase y en la ofensiva final a partir de los objetivos que plantea el plan general de guerra y la factibilidad de montar dedios y rutas de abastecimiento así como de la cantidad con que se cuenta en el arsenal.

5- El cambio cualitativo de la situación militar implica que el plan militar de cada frente debe comprender:

a- Comenzar el control de carreteras.
b- Control de vías de acceso a la retaguardia.
c- Mantener reducida el área de movimientos de la fuerza militar enemiga establecida en las zonas de retaguardia.
d- Garantizar la capacidad de mantener las campañas operativas en las zonas urbanas y de las áreas periféricas de las ciudades.

Nota: Este plan partiría de que exista una real fuente de abastecimiento en Lagos.

DOCUMENT P

Letter from DRU to DRU representatives in Nicaragua (undated October 29, 1980).

GLOSSARY P

DRU – Unified Revolutionary Directorate. Joint leadership of guerrilla groups.

ERP – Peoples' Revolutionary Army. Salvadoran guerrilla group.

FMLN – Farabundo Marti National Liberation Front. Guerrilla federation

Island – Cuba

Lagos – Nicaragua

TRANSLATION OF DOCUMENT P

San Salvador, 29 October 1980

(OFFICIAL NOTE)

DRU Comrades in Lago:

Receive a warm and fraternal greeting on behalf of the DRU. This note is to inform you of some of the agreements reached at the DRU meeting of 27 October. Following this note you will receive Bulletin No. 1 of the DRU, which will be approved during the meeting of 30 October. The analysis plan contained in Bulletin No. 1 has already been forwarded to comrade Vladimir along with the summarized document of the General Meeting of the DRU on 19 October. A series of directives related to our work will complement that analysis. Below I have transcribed part of the document on the directives, which say:

1st Major Line of Action

CUT THROUGH THE INFORMATION CIRCLE AND TAKE OUR MESSAGE TO THE PEOPLE ON A PERMANENT BASIS.

We all know that one of the enemy's principal lines of action at the outset of its offensive against the people, was precisely to eliminate all possible means of expression (such as El Independiente, La Cronica, YSAX, the assassination of newspapermen, death threats to others and eight months of martial law). Whether we like it or not, this situation is little known and as a result the popular sectors are becoming progressively confused and are being affected by the defeatist attitude Duarte and his lackeys are trying to instill among the people.

How can it be that while in the interior of the country our military forces are engaged in heroic combat in the midst of what has become an undeniable state of war, can there be vast sectors of the population unaware of this situation which can be dangerously influenced by a defeatist attitude? Based on the above, it is extremely urgent that we cut through the informative circle and take our message to the people if we wish to take the utmost advantage of the political-military activity.

In virtue of this endeavor, all the respective organizations should put every effort on the various and creative methods of propaganda and should inform the people as to the real status of the struggle and the progress made by the FMLN.

This mission will become an extremely urgent and strategic goal, since other means of propaganda alone will not be sufficient to meet the needs of the struggle.

This fundamental task is carried out by: the Propaganda Commission of the DRU, the Joint General Staff and its Operations Unit, the Foreign Relations Commission of the DRU and leadership abroad, in the areas where this is possible.

On the same level as the main goal, the Propaganda Commission must refine, coordinate and multiply our propaganda ability by adequately utilizing and organizing all potential and present means within our organizations, adhering to the criteria of not weakening our efforts and placing the FMLN at the center of attention among the people.

To the extent possible, broadcasting programs should be maintained whether or not previously coordinated.

Regarding the radio project every possibility should be studied and a concentration of efforts on one or several projects defined according to the possibilities. Our goal should be to begin broadcasting operations in less than 30 days. For its initial operations, the Propaganda Commission should first prepare and utilize every possible means.

The Propaganda Commission should simplify and avoid to the utmost the weakening of efforts and should accelerate the propaganda support for our military activity. To this end the information activity intended for abroad should be organized.

In virtue of the above, the DRU adopts as firm agreements in this area: to develop as early as possible a plan to begin FMLN radio operations. It should be pointed out that the need to achieve this does not lie on the support of information provided by commercial radio or press agencies; it rests on the needs of our own radio, since this will raise the people's morale and will allow us to strengthen the existence of a dual power. The radio station will permit us to take advantage of our military activity and to defeat the enemy's demoralization campaign directed at our people (THIS MUST BE URGENTLY CARRIED OUT).

Bearing in mind all of this and stemming from the fact that at this stage other propaganda means have proven insufficient, it was agreed to develop three similar projects to give impetus to the establishment of the FMLN radio.

A) *THE LAGOS PROJECT* – This would be the most strategic plan and would consist in the establishment of a clandestine radio in Lagos. To carry out this project the cooperation and assistance of the Island and the Laguenos must be requested. It must be remembered that the Comrade Commander offered the equipment and assistance to this plan. It is up to you in Lagos to take all the necessary action to begin broadcasting operations as early as possible. The three organizations have already enlisted the personnel, or are about to, to form part of this operation, composed of at least six or more persons.

During this process arrangements should be made to authorize the operation on a short term and to be provided with the necessary technical and material support. The radio station will come under the responsibility of the Propaganda Commission, but at this time you are in charge of its installation. Obviously, and as a special feature, this radio station would continue broadcasting after the U.S. elections. It should be a shortwave radio capable of reaching all of our territory and Central America.

B) The second project should be worked out in Francisco's place and will entail a mobile radio unit capable of covering the national territory, always operating in shortwave. This project will function independently of Lagos and its development would avoid any variations in the attitude of Lagos from leaving us without a radio; also, keeping it compartmentalized if necessary. Support and utilization of the appropriate means should be sought during the evolution of this project. (There is a shortwave radio of the ERP in Mexico which can be readily incorporated into this project.)

C) The third project will cover a provisional stage and will be a joint effort with the ERP radio, which is already here to broadcast to the central region. This project is in the hands of Propaganda and the General Staff to accelerate its operation.

Prior to the broadcasting operations, a propaganda campaign will begin to make known the broadcasting schedule to the public.

We remain awaiting a report on your initial steps concerning this mission which, as with the work of logistics, it also requires our attention. Wishing you success in your endeavor, receive our fraternal greetings.

UNITED TO STRUGGLE UNTIL THE FINAL VICTORY!
REVOLUTION OR DEATH!   WE WILL WIN!

United Revolutionary Directorate
Political-Military (RU-PM) of the FRONT
Farabundo Marti National Liberation Front (FMLN)

(NOTA OFICIAL) · · · ·San Salvador, 29 de Octubre de 1980.

Compañeros:
Reciben un caluroso y fraternal saludo a nombre de la DRU. La presente es para comunicarles parte de los acuerdos de la reunión de la DRU del día 27. de Octubre.
Posterior a esta nota les será enviado el Boletín No. 1 de la DRU que será grabado en la reunión del día 30 de Octubre. El proyecto de análisis que integrará el Boletín No.1, le fué ya enviado al compañero Vladimir en el documento síntesis de la Reunión del Pleno de la DRU del día 19 de Octubre. Dicho análisis será complementado con una serie de directrices relativas a todo nuestro trabajo. A continuación les transcribo parte del documento sobre estas directrices que dice:
"1a. Gran Línea de acción.-
KOPPELS SEGUROS EN FUERTE TOMAR VAR NERSCROLMENSAJES LA PUERTA DO MANERA PERSONAL...
Todos sabemos que una de las líneas de acción principales del enemigo al iniciar su ofensiva contra el pueblo, fue precisamente la de eliminar toda posibilidad de expresión, (casos del Independiente, La Crónica, YSAX, asesinato de periodistas, amenazas a nuerte a otros y estado de sitio durante 8 meses)...

Querramos o no, esta situación a ido repercutiendo en que-los avances dados - por nuestra lucha son poco conocidos y tenemos como efecto de que sectores -- del pueblo se encuentran cada vez más confundidos y afectados por la moral de derrota que Duarte y su camarilla tratan de infundir en el pueblo.

Como es posible que en tanto en el interior del país nuestras fuerzas milita- res libran heróicos combates en medio de un estado de guerra que ya se vuelve innegable, hayan también grandes sectores del pueblo que desconozcan esta si- tuación y puedan ser peligrosamente influenciados por una moral derrotista.

En virtud de lo anterior, es tarea urgentísima para el máximo aprovechamiento de la actividad político-militar que estamos realizando, romper el cerco in- formativo y llevar nuestro mensaje al pueblo.

En virtud de esta tarea, todos los organismos que corresponda deberán poner - todo su empeño en las variadas y creativas formas de propagandizar y dar a co nocer al pueblo el estado actual de la lucha y los avances del FMLN.

En esta tarea se convertirá en una nota urgentísima y estratégica la puesta - en el aire de la radio del FMLN, ya que solo los otros medios de propaganda - no son suficientes ya para las necesidades de la lucha.

En esta tarea fundamental trabajan: La Comisión de Propaganda do la DRU, El - Estado Mayor General Conjunto y su sección de Operaciones, la Comisión de Re- laciones Internacionales de la DRU y la Dirección en el exterior, en los pun- tos en que esto sea posible.

Paralelo a esta meta central de la radio, la Comisión de Propaganda deberá a- finas, coordinar y multiplicar nuestra capacidad de propagandización utilizan do y organizando adecuadamente todos los medios actuales y potenciales de --- nuestras organizaciones, aplicando el criterio de no desgastar esfuerzos y - poner al FMLN en el centro de la atención del pueblo.

En tanto sea posible, deberán mantenerse operativos parlantes, coordinados o - no.

En el plan de radio, deberán estudiarse todas las posibilidades y definir una concentración de esfuerzos en uno o varios proyectos de acuerdo a las probabi lidades.

Nuestra meta debe ser que antes que venzan 30 días, deberá nuestra radio ha-- ber empezado a dar sus primeras salidas.

Para su salida, la Comisión de Propaganda deberá preparar toda una campaña -- previa, apoyándose en todos los medios posibles.

La Comisión de Propaganda deberá simplificar y evitar al máximo el desgaste - de esfuerzos y agilizar el apoyo propagandístico a nuestra actividad militar.

Para esto debe organizarse la actividad de información hacia el exterior.

En base a lo anterior, la DRU adopta como acuerdos concretos sobre este pun- to:

Desarrollar al más breve plazo un plan para poner al aire la radio del FMLN.

Cabe señalar que para esto la necesidad no es de apoyos en la información co:

... con radios comerciales o agencias de Prensa; es- ta de la necesidad de nuestra propia radio, ya que esto elevará la moral pueblo y permitirá ir cimentando la existencia de un doble poder. La Rad nos permitirá aprovechar más nuestra actividad militar y derrotar la cam de desmoralización del enemigo sobre nuestro pueblo (Y ESTO ES URGENTE Q - SE IMPULSE).

-Tomando en cuenta todo esto y partiendo de que a estas alturas son insu- tes los otros medios propagandísticos, se acordó desarrollar tres proyect paralelos para el impulso de la Radio del FMLN.

1) PROYECTO LAGOS. Este sería el plan más estratégico y consistiría en el tablecimiento de la radio internacional en Lagos. Para el impulso de esta rea deberá solicitarse la colaboración y ayuda de la Isla y los lagueños. Corresponde a Ud. en Lagos hacer todos los movimientos necesarios para q la mayor brevedad posible, ésta salga al aire, nuestras organizaciones tie nen listo el personal para designar personal para atender esta tarea por lo q en número de 6 o más.

En el manejo de esto, deberán hacerse las gestiones para que se autorice s peración a corto plazo y se nos brinde el apoyo técnico y material necesar La Radio será responsabilidad de la Comisión de Propaganda, pero en este n mento es responsabilidad de Ud. el montaje de este proyecto. Obviamente y no cosa especial, la Radio transmitiría hasta después de las elecciones U.S La Radio deberá ser de onda corta y tener un alcance que cubra todo nuestro territorio y Centro América.

B) [ilegible] Este proyecto será independiente do Lagos y su d sarrollo será para evitar que la variaciones en el comportamiento de Lagos no nos vaya a dejar sin la Radio; e incluso mantener lo compartimentado si fu ra necesario. En el desarrollo de este proyecto deberá buscarse apoyo util zar medios propios. (Existe un aparato de Radio de onda corta del RIP en Méj po que puede incorporarse de inmediato a este proyecto).

> 5) El tercer plan..es..para cubrir..una..fase..provisional y se trabajará con la..
> radio del..ER?, que..está..ya aquí..para..transmisiones en la Zona central. Este
> proyecto..pasó..ya..a..manos..de..Propaganda..y..el Estado Mayor..para..acelerar su..fun
> cionamiento.
> Previo a la..salida..al exterior de la radio, se iniciará una campaña de propaganda
> para..que..se..conozca..en..detalle..su..horario de transmisión.
> os..quedamos entonces..en espera..de un informe de..sus..primeras gestiones para
> sta tarea, que al igual..que la..logística..necesita..de..nuestra atención.
> eseándoles éxitos en..su trabajo, los saludamos fraternalmente.
>
> 11.UNIDOS.PARA COMBATIR HASTA LA VICTORIA FINAL!!
> !! REVOLUCION O MUERTE !! !! VENCEREMOS !!
>
> Dirección Revolucionaria Unificada.
> Político Militar (DRU-PM) del FRENTE
> FARABUNDO MARTI PARA LA LIBERACION
> NACIONAL (FMLN)

DOCUMENT Q

Excerpt from report on work in Nicaragua, November 1-3, 1980.

GLOSSARY Q

DRU – Unified Revolutionary Directorate.   Joint leadership of Salvadoran guerrilla groups.

Front – Nicaraguan FSLN (Sandinistas)

Lagos – Nicaragua

Vladimir – DRU logistics representative in Nicaragua

TRANSLATION OF DOCUMENT Q

With all due respects to the comrades of the DRU
Report on the work completed at Lagos during 1 and 3 November.

The objective of this trip organized by the Internal Reception Committee was to put together a schedule of shipments related to all available alternatives. In relation to the work done by myself, I must report that it was quite limited. Two separate meetings were held with Comrade Vladimir for a total of four hours. The comrades who work with external logistics and myself were present at this meeting.

These meetings were restricted to a report presented by comrade Vladimir dealing with the prospect of sending materials to our country and to the presentation of a shipment schedule put together by our comrades of the Front. I personally made sure that comrade Vladimir understood the impossibility of receiving these materials if we followed the schedule presented by him. I insisted that the schedule had been prepared without previous consultation of the reception commission. This consultation was necessary so that the schedule would fit all the alternatives available to us.

My arguments were not taken into account. Comrade Vladimir restricted himself to saying that we should take the schedule with us, that we should do all we could, and that if something could not be done, we should let it be known through the instituted means in order to carry out the necessary suspensions.

I believe that the participation by a member of the Reception Commission in the program planning and preparation of the schedule must be a full one since this person has complete knowledge of the internal situation.
(four lines blotted out)
27 M-79
(blotted out) M-79 grenades

336 FAL
1685(?) M-1 and M-2
(blotted out) cartridges 7.6g
62,480 cartridges 0.30 N-1
(blotted out) FAL loaders
230 M-1 loaders
(??4) FAL crates
98 bandoleers
(?5) (RPG) Tubes
225 RPG rockets
(blotted out) M-60 machine guns
(four lines blotted out)
355 (?) Fal with an extra loader
79 (?) M-2 rifles
58 (?) M-1 rifles
(blotted out) M-79 grenades
(blotted out) RPG-2
(blotted out) RPG rockets
88460 cartridges for each rifle
(blotted out) M-60 machine guns

Considerations on this shipment. I had previously discussed with the comrades of the Front the capacity of these means [of transport]. They indicated to me that they had a 4-ton capacity but for safety reasons they would operate with a 2-ton capacity. There was a verbal agreement on this issue.

On this trip comrade Vladimir told me that they would no longer go with 2 tons but with 3 tons and that the comrades of the Front had already conducted tests and that there were no problems.

I will say that on various occasions I asked the comrades of the Front to check the resources available and supervise them personally. This, according to them, was never allowed since they had their own technicians who did the supervising.

On the day the shipment left, the comrade in charge of the operation indicated to the comrades of the Front that they were overloaded and that these could have problems. This recommendation was not taken into account.

I write this letter so that my arguments will be studied by our directorate.

Respectfully, Rodrigo

Con todo respeto a los compañeros de la DRU.
Informe sobre trabajo realizado en Lagos durante días 1-2 de Noviembre.

El objeto del viaje encomendado por la Recepción interna consistió en la elaboración de un calendario de envíos apegado a las posibilidades de la Recepción.

Con respecto a la labor realizada personalmente debo informar que fue sumamente limitada.

Se realizaron dos reuniones con el compañero Vladimir que en total sumaron 4 horas con participación de mi persona y los compañeros de logística externa

Estas reuniones se limitaron a un informe del compañero Vladimir
con respecto a las perspectivas de envio de materiales a nuestro pa
y a la presentación de un calendario de envios elaborado por
los compañeros del Frente.

Personalmente hice ver al compañero Vladimir de la imposibilidad
de cumplir con la recepción si el envio se hacia de acuerdo a
ese calendario y que además ese calendario se habia elabora
do sin la participación de la comisión de recepción, lo cual
era indispensable para que el calendario se apegara a las pos
bilidades existentes.

Esta consideración no fué tomada en cuenta, limitándose el compa
ñero Vladimir a decir que nos trajeramos el calendario, que cum
pliéramos en lo que pudieramos y que con lo que no pudieramos
cumplir que lo manifestaramos por los medios establecidos
para efectuar las suspensiones que fueran necesarias.

Considero que para efectos de programación y calendarización
la participación de cualquier miembro de la recepción interna debe

ser
de ~~posibilidad~~ plenamente, ya que son estos los que tienen total
conocimiento de la situación interna.

[líneas tachadas/ilegibles]

siguiente

[líneas tachadas/ilegibles]

M-29
Granadas de M-79
FAL.
M-1 y M-2
Cartuchos 7.62
Cartuchos 0.30 M-1.
Cargadores de FAL.
Cargadores M-1
Portacargadores de FAL
Bandolera por Tro
RPG (TUBOS)
Cohetes RPG.
Ametralladoras M-60

~~[illegible struck-through text]~~

~~[illegible struck-through text]~~

: ~~[illegible]~~ FAL con un cargador extra c/u.

~~[illegible]~~ Fusil. M-?

~~[illegible]~~ Granadas de M-79

~~[illegible]~~ RPG-2

~~[illegible]~~ Cohetes de RPG.

~~[illegible]~~ Cartuchos por cada fusil = 88,960 Cartuchos

~~[illegible]~~ metralladoras M-60.

Consideraciones sobre este envío.

Con anterioridad había discutido personalmente con compañeros del Frente sobre la capacidad des estos medios. Ellos manifestaron que tenían capacidad para 4 toneladas pero para mayor seguridad serían operadas con 2 ton c/u. Sobre esto había un acuerdo de palabra.

En este viaje el compañero Vladimir me informa que no irían con ~~[illegible]~~ sino que con ~~[illegible]~~, que los compañeros del frente ya habían hecho pruebas y que no bía problemas.

He de manifestar que en varias ocasiones solicité al compañeros del Frente ir a ver los medios y supervisarlos personalmente, lo cual nunca fue permitido, aduciendo que ellos tenían técnicos que supervisarían.

El día que salía el envío, el compañero jefe de l. operación hizo ver a los compañeros del Frente que los medios iban sobrecargados y que podrían tener problemas. Esta consideración no fue tomada en cuenta.

~~[illegible bottom line]~~

DOCUMENT R

Letter from "Marcial" to "Vladimir" dated November 10, 1980.

GLOSSARY R

DRU – Unified Revolutionary Directorate. Joint leadership of guerrilla groups.

EMGC – Guerrilla Joint General Staff

Front – Nicaraguan FSLN (Sandinistas)

Marcial – Cayetano Carpio of Salvadoran FPL guerrilla group

Vladimir – DRU logistics representative in Nicaragua

TRANSLATION OF DOCUMENT R

El Salvador, C. A., 10 November 1980
Comrade Vladimir (official note no. 4)
We wish you good health and all.
We have received your notes including the last one which has been sent to me with Comrade Gladis.
1.   We received the first 50 Comrade Gladis brought. They have been already distributed to the EMGC primarily for the use of logistical reception.
2.   The comrade from Communications arrived. She brought the reports you sent. And the results of your work.
3.   The RN has already rejoined the DRU this week. It has fully assumed its rights and responsibilities in the first meeting. We have already undertaken the task of their integration into all commission sections and general staffs. Their admission was approved in the plenary meeting on Monday, the 3rd of this month. Comrade Ferman was already present at DE meeting of Friday the 7th. I am attaching a copy of the communique about the admission of the RN prepared at the plenary session of the DRU.
4.   For your information (not to be used publicly but only within the membership of the DRU and which is to be entirely integrated in the work progress and by the agreements taken in the sessions, I am including the actions taken in both these meetings): the one from the second plenum and the last one of the DE.
5.   I am also including a communique about the attempt on Colonel Majano.
6.   The only DRU delegation to the Second Congress of the Cuban Communist Party will be composed of the Executive Directorate (DE) of the DRU, that is, by the first four officials in charge of the organizations: Marcial, Rene, Simon and Ferman. They will also carry, naturally, credentials of their respective organizations but will be included in one joint delegation.
7.   In my position as general coordinator I received reports from the bodies of the DRU and I try to have contacts and meetings with the comrade coordinators of each body. Both in the EMGC and the logistical reception [committee] they have shared with me some of their concerns about logistical shipments and deliveries.
8.   That in Lagos (the reference is primarily the Front comrades, but in part also you) it would be necessary that they take more into consideration the opinions and plans prepared here by the committee of logistical reception; and that they feel that the plans are not so much taken into consideration specifically concerning the location, capacities, etc., but that they do it "at random." They gave examples. a) The first military shipment was excessively overloaded and one of them foundered in Lagos territorial waters and the entire cargo was lost. They were successful in saving their shipmates. The other two were overloaded. b) In view of the fact that they were overloaded more than had been expected, the comrades decided to send 100 more men and because of this they had a collision on the coastal highway. (An accident which

neither eliminates nor invalidates the route or the location; but it is an example of the measures which they suddenly have to take, when over there, measures are not coordinated with the plans and capacities given by the domestic reception). This has been pointed out to the comrades – not that measures should be taken to reduce the shipments but that there be more coordination with those within. c) It has been decided there not to send to the maritime reception of the Mid Central (Estero de Jaltepeque). The information on which this based is correct but it has to be taken into consideration there that the enemy maneuver is not permanent and that we have the better means to control the said maneuver. For example, Comrade Mauricio informed me that to control this aspect of security we send Comrade Marcello y Sebastian to make a probe and that Wednesday they make "a live" reconnaissance leaving by boat from (words illegible). (where El Espino is located). At the entrance to the Bay of Jiquilisco that they made a crossing of 8 hours, passing through the San Juan de Gozo peninsula, the mouth of the Rio Lempa up to the mouth of the Estero de Jaltepeque and there disembarked and went to the Herradura without having made contacts or [encountering] any security problems. One example of the same, the boats was lost (of those that carried the first load). It was up to the Bay of Jiquilisco without having the slightest problems. From there it was necessary to return up to [words illegible]. This shows that with a good job of reconnaissance such as they are doing now a good job can be done as long as it is continued in a good plan of coordination with you and that you take in consideration the plans which [logistic] reception has made here. In summary, they consider that there are conditions for receiving here in Mid-Central and they should not discontinue it. d) As to the reasons of security and remoteness which is adduced, this is easily correctable and together measures are being taken to provide the comrades with security and rest so that they can return on time and in conditions more favorable for security. e) Another subject which the comrades explained to me is that they are considering that when one of the comrades of the reception committee arrives you should not only listen to the information (for example in the last instance on the trip of Comrade Rodrigo) as he is doing it today, but that you should take him (bring him to the Reception) to the meeting which he has with the Front. so that he can participate in the planning work and thus the problems would be better coordinated.

9.   I understood that Comrade Ramon will leave for there next week and following day Comrade Rodrigo will follow. Shortly thereafter Comrade Mauricio will go.

10.   What has been received as a result of the successful arrival are 472 F. : 4RP-2-M.30 and other types.

11.   The comrade whom you sent to study "Rastr" has already departed.

12.   Finally I wish to report that the plenary meeting agreed to take a firm step ahead of all areas taking advantage of the reintegration of the RN. 1 – Carry out an intensive ideological campaign within the organizations run by the DRU in order to make the unity more cohesive and raise the level of unitary consciousness of leadership and rank and file. 2 – One plan of measures which have been taken in logistics in other areas: propaganda, relations, communications. But in such a way that it is organized and not spontaneous and disorganized, a set of guidelines for such steps will be made. And other measures will be taken in other areas. I will send you these documents in the next official note.

13.   Also this week a report of the analysis of the national situation will be issued on the measures approved by the DRU in all areas concerning said analysis.

14.   The measures taken for training of the comrades are good. I hope you are well.

We expect a detailed explanation of these problems much as the decision of Panama to ask for OAS intervertion which is worrying us very much. UNITED IN STRUGGLE UNTIL FINAL VICTORY.

Revolution or death. We shall win.

Marcial: – First politico military leader of the DRU acting as General Coordinator.

El Salvador, C.A. ,10 de Noviembre de 1980.-
C. Vladimir.- (Nota oficial # 4)
Deseamos esté bien de salud y de todo.-
Hemos recibido sus notas, incluyendo la última que me e
vió la c. Gladis.-
1- Recibimos los primeros 50 que trajo la c. Gladis.-
Ya se pasaron al EMGC para sus gastos de recepción l
gística principalmente.-
2-Vino la c. de Comunicaciones. Me trajo los informes
usted envió. Y los resultados de su trabajo.-
3- Esta semana ya se reintegró la RN a la DRU, . Ya estu
en plenitud de derechos y responsabilidades en la p imera reunión. Y ya
mos en la tarea de que se reintegren a todas las comisiones, seccion y
tados Mayores.- En la reunión del Pleno del lunes 3 del presente se apr
su ingreso. Y en la reunión del viernes 7 de la DE ya estuvo presente el
Fermán.- Le adjunto una copia del Comunicado que sobre el reingreso de
RN emitió el Pleno de la DRU.-
4- Para su conocimiento (no para utilizarlos en publicidad,- sino como mi
bro que es de la DRU y que necesita estar completamente enterado de la m
de los a untos y de los acuerdos que se toman en las sesiones le adjunto
actas de a bas reuniones: la del Segundo Pleno y la última de la DE.-
5-Ta bién le adjunto un comunicado sobre el atentado contra el cor. Enje
6- Ia Delegación unica de la DRU al II Congreso del Partido Comunista de
estará integrada por la Dirección Ejecutiva de la DRU, o sea por los cu
primeros responsables de las organizaciones: Marcial, René, Simón y Fer
llevarán también ,naturalmente, credencial de su respectiva organizació
ro integrarán una delegación unitaria,-
7.-Por razones de mis funciones como Coordinador General, recibo inform
los organismos de la DRU y trato de tener contactos y reuniones con los
pañeros coordinadores de cada organismo.- Tanto en el EMGC como en Rec
logística me han p rticipado algunas de sus inquietudes en relación con
envío y recepción Logística:
lo)- ▓▓
▓▓
▓▓▓ lo hacer a la
▓▓▓
▓▓▓▓▓▓▓▓▓▓▓▓▓ a)▓▓▓▓▓▓▓▓▓▓▓▓▓▓▓▓▓▓▓▓▓▓▓▓▓▓▓▓▓▓▓▓▓▓▓
carga.- Sé▓▓▓
b)▓▓▓▓▓▓▓▓▓ venía sobrecargada con ▓▓▓▓▓▓▓▓▓▓▓▓▓ los co
▓▓▓▓▓▓▓▓▓▓ 100 hombres más, que▓▓▓▓▓▓▓▓▓▓▓▓▓▓▓▓▓▓▓▓▓
▓▓▓▓▓▓▓▓▓▓ del rtu al (choque que no anula ni invalida para nada la
lugar; pero que es un ejemplo de medidas que repentinamente tienen que
cuando allá se toman medidas no armonizadas con los planes y capacidad
sadas por recep ión Interna.-Q.- S to lo indican los cs. no para que s
tomar medidas de disminución de envío, sino para que se haga más a rmo
con lo de adentro.- b)-Se ha▓▓▓▓▓▓▓▓▓▓▓ enviar para la recep
▓▓▓▓▓▓▓▓▓ para central (Esterovde▓▓▓ peque).- El Info4me que motivó
correcto; pero debe tomars e en cuenta allá que la maniobra del enemig
permanente, y que aquí se está en mayor capacidad de estar controlando
maniobra. Por ejemplo, el c. Mauricio me informó que para controlar es
to de seguridad se envió al c. Marcelo y Sebastián a hacer una prueba
▓▓▓▓▓▓▓▓▓▓▓▓▓▓▓ una explosación ▓▓▓▓▓▓▓▓▓▓▓▓▓▓▓▓▓▓▓▓▓
▓▓▓▓▓▓▓▓▓▓ donde puede▓▓▓▓▓▓▓▓▓▓▓▓▓▓▓▓▓▓▓▓▓▓▓▓▓▓▓▓▓▓
▓▓▓, lu▓▓▓▓▓▓▓▓▓ ha
▓▓▓▓▓▓▓▓▓▓▓▓▓▓ y f▓▓▓▓▓▓▓▓▓▓▓▓▓▓▓▓▓▓▓▓▓▓▓▓▓▓▓▓▓▓ anoh

mo el que ahora están haciendo, se puede trabajar bien, toda vez que se si
tableciendo un buen a viso para ustedes, y que ustedes tomen en cuenta los
anes que aquí ha ga recepción.- En res umen, consideran que hay condicio
ra recepcionar en ese luga r de la para-centr. y que no debe ser elimin
sde allí.- c)-En cuanto a las razones de seguridad y de lejanía que se ad
fácilmente remediable, y conjuntamente se están tomando medidas para dar
guri ad v descanso a los cs. para que puedan regresar en las horas y ocasi
ones más propicias para seguridad.- d)-Otro asunto que los compañeros me
usieron es que consideran que cuando llega allí un c. de la Comisión de R
pción , usted debería no sólo oírles los informes (por ejemplo en el últi
aso del vije del c.Rodrigo) como lo está haciendo hasta hoy, sino que si d
ría de llevarlo (al como de recepción) a la reunión que tiene con los fre
ara que él participe en la labor de planeamiento y que de esa manera qued
as cuestiones más a rmonizadas.-

-Ten.;o entendido que a principios de semana sale para allá,el c. Ramón y ¡
la siguiente al como. Rodrigo.- Proximamente irá el c. Mauricio.-

~~~~~~
0-~~~~~~
1-Finalmente quiero comunicarle que en la 1- reunión del Pleno se acordó
n firme paso adelante en todos los terrenos aprovechando el reingreso de
./Ñ. 1- levar a cabo una intensa campaña ideálogica en lo interior de 1
rganizaciones, dirigida por la DRU, para cohesionar la unidad y elevar el
ivel ue conciencia unitaria en direcciones y bases.- 2- Un plan de medida
ue profundicen el es tado de unidad, del tipo de las medidas que se han t
.o en logísitica en otros terrenos: propaganda, relaciones, comunicaciones
'ero que para-que sea organizado y no espo_táneo o desordenedo se haré una
:s pecie de reglamento de tales pasos .- I otras medidas en otros terreno:
:sos documentos sse los enviaré,en la proxima nota oficial.-
l2- También esta semana saldré el documento de análisis sobre la situació:
nacional y lasmedidas aprobadas por la DRU en tedos los terrenos en relac
:cn dicho análisis.- 13-Las medidas que ha tomado para entrenamiento de
Es pero se encuentrebien .-   están buenas.-

Esperamos mayoresilustraciones sobre problemas tales como la decisión
Panamá de pedir la intervención de la OEA, que nos está preocupando muchc
UNIDOS PARA COMBAT R HASTA LA VICTORIA FINAL.- Revolución o Muerte,Vencer

Parméli- Primer Res p . Político-militar de la DRU, en funciones de Coo:
           dor General.-

DOCUMENT S

Letter from "Rene" to "Vladimir" (dated November 19, 1980).

GLOSSARY S

DRU — Unified Revolutionary Directorate.   Joint leadership of Salvadoran guerrilla
groups

EMGC — Guerrilla Joint General Staff

Islanders — Cubans

Lagos — Nicaragua

TRANSCRIPTION OF DOCUMENT S

El Salvador, Wednesday, 19 November 1980

Comrade Vladimir:

Fraternal and revolutionary greetings:

Following is a summary of the resolutions concerning the logistical problems approved at the meeting of the DRU and of the EMGC on 18 November:

1. Immediate departure of Comrade Rodrigo to Lagos.
2. Comrade Rodrigo will be able to provide detailed information on the logistical and military situation of our forces and also on the plans approved by the DRU for the immediate implementation of the logistical plan.
3. A meeting of the people of Lagos with Comrade Rodrigo personally so that he may explain the situation and participate in the discussion of new plans proposed by the Domestic Logistical Commission and which have the approval of the DRU and EMGC.
4. Ask the comrades in Lagos to participate directly in the supervision of the shipments to assure that operational details are followed. In this regard seek the participation of the comrades of the Foreign Logistical Commission as well as the Internal Logistics Committee. We also take note of the negative posture toward Comrade Rodrigo concerning the supervision of the plan which encountered failures of which we are well aware.

5. See that the foundation of plans is realistic and objective, cover all domestic and foreign possibilities and make proper use of the coordination and collective decision which are part of the military tasks at present.

6. Discuss in depth, with the comrades in Lagos, the difficulties which would result from abrupt suspension of the shipments now when time can make a crucial difference either in our favor or against us. In relation to the security problems, Comrade Rodrigo will provide information so that it can be seen that the suspension of all shipments is neither necessary nor advisable despite the problems that have occurred.

7. Explain to the comrades in Lagos that our logistical plan is closely linked to our War Plans, therefore our criteria for operations and security are of *great importance and determine* the decisions to be taken. Unilateral decisions will only harm our cause.

8. See that the shipments in Lagos are immediately approved and sent – which Comrade Rodrigo has planned, pointing out the danger of an excessively long interruption of these shipments.

9. Should there be any difficulties in the approval of the plans and continuation of the flow of material, come to the country immediately (Vladimir) – to provide information and take necessary measures.

10. Ask Lagos or the islanders that they approve for us urgent shipment of 500 meters of slow burning fuses, 5,000 percussion caps for the fuses (non-electric), and some 2,000 meters of detonation cord.

This is basic since the campaign of economic sabotage has been completely suspended owing to the lack of the materials, although we do have explosive reserves available.

UNITED IN STRUGGLE UNTIL FINAL VICTORY!
!! REVOLUTION OR DEATH !! WE SHALL WIN !!

For the DRU:

Rene

_ .El Salvador, Miércoles 19 de Noviembre de 19

Compañero Vladimir:

Recibe un fraternal y revolucionario saludo.
A continuación comunico sintetizadas resoluciones en-relación al problema logístico, tomadas en reunión de la DRU y el EMGC - el día 18 de Noviembre:

1o. Salida inmediata del Compañero Rodrigo a Lagos.
2o. El Compañero Rodrigo podrá dar informe detallado de situación logís-tica y militar de nuestras fuerzas y también sobre planes aprobados-por la DRU para la continuación inmediata del plan logístico.
3o. Reunión con la gente de Lagos con la presencia directa del Compañero Rodrigo, para que explique situación y participe en discusión de nue vos planes que propone Comisión de Logística Interna y que tienen a-provación de la DRU y el EMGC.
4o. Solicitar a los compañeros de Lagos participación directa en supervi sión de envíos, para asegurarnos de los detalles operativos. En esto solicitar se permita la participación tanto de compañeros de la Comi sión Logística Exterior, como de la Comisión Logística Interna. Re-cordemos en esto la negativa dada al Compañero Rodrigo para la supe visión del plan que tuvo fallas que ya conocemos.
5o. Buscar que la elaboración de planes sea realista y objetiva, sopesa do todos los aspectos, tanto internos como externos y haciendo cor-rrecto uso de las atribusiones de coordinación y desición colectiva que existen en las tareas militares en este momento.
6o. Discutir a fondo con los compañeros de Lagos, la inconveniencia de · la suspensión abrupta de los envíos en este momento en el que el tien po cuenta desicivamente a favor o en contra nuestra. En relación al problema de seguridad , el Compañero Rodrigo dará informe para que · se vea que no es necesaria ni conveniente la suspensión. de todos – los envíos, muy a pesar de los problemas ocurridos.

7o. Planear a los Compañeros de Lagos que nuestro plan logístico está
     ligado estrechamente a nuestro Plan de Guerra y que por lo tanto --
     nuestros criterios para lo operativo y de seguridad, pesan y so.. de
     terminantes en las desiciones que haya que tomar. Las desiciones un
     laterales no harán más que perjudicarnos a todos.
8o. Lograr que de inmediato se aprueben y marchen en Lagos los envíos -
     que lleva programados el Compañero Rodrigo, señalando el peligro de
     corte demasiado prolongado de éstos.
9o. De presentarse alguna dificultad en la aprobación de planes y conti
     nuación de flujo de material, venir de inmediato al país (Vladimir)
     a dar informe y tomar medidas.
10. Solicitar a Lagos o Isleños; se nos apruebe envío urgentísimo de 5C
     metros de mecha lenta, 5.000 fulminantes para mecha (que no sean e-
     léctricos) y unos 2.000 metros de cordón detonante.
     Esto es fundamental ya que la campaña de sabotaje económico está su
     pendida totalmente debido a la falta de estos materiales a pesar de
     que contamos con algunas reservas de explosivos.

           ¡ UNIDOS PARA COMBATIR HASTA LA VICTORIA FINAL ¡

             ¡¡ REVOLUCION O MUERTE ¡¡ ¡¡ VENCEREMOS ¡¡

                              Por la DRU:
                              René

Arms flow into El Salvador

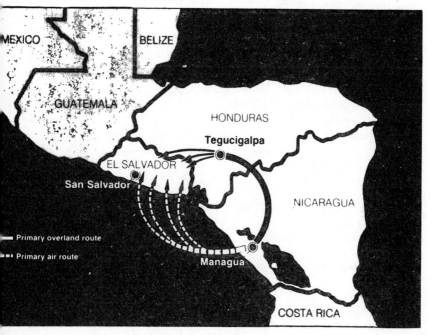

— Primary overland route

∎∎ı Primary air route

APPENDIX B

DISSENT PAPER ON EL SALVADOR AND CENTRAL AMERICA

DOS 11/6/80

To: Dissent Channel
From: ESCATF/D

Re.: DM-ESCA No. 80-3

TABLE OF CONTENTS

Statement of purpose

The Reagan Administration's first international crisis may well be in El Salvador. Candidate Reagan's foreign policy advisors have made deeply disturbing statements about their plans for Central America and the Caribbean basin.

However, should President Reagan choose to use military force in El Salvador, historians will be able to show that the setting for such actions had been prepared in the last year of the Carter Administration. There may still be time to change course during the transition period. If the effort fails we will continue to argue for a negotiated resolution of the conflict. We recall, perhaps with unwarranted optimism, that it was Mrs. Thatcher – and not her Labor predecessors – who brought the Rhodesian crisis to a peaceful end. We hope that moderation and reason will prevail among President Reagan's appointees.

We see current US activities in El Salvador as leading to increased military engagement with far reaching implications for our strategic interests in the Caribbean basin. Support for our policies is limited and unreliable. Our identification with the governing Junta in that country has placed us in a collision course with key regional actors with whom we need to maintain friendly and cooperative diplomatic and economic relations.

By contrast, the non-military, negotiated solution proposed in this paper may well enjoy broad international support and acceptance. This option is seen as most effective in achieving the two key objectives of US policy in this region: limiting Cuban and Soviet expansion and promoting the emergence of stable and pluralistic governments.

The views articulated in this paper are shared in private by current and former analysts and officials at NSC, DOS, DOD and CIA. Employees from other agencies active in El Salvador and Central America – but normally excluded from policy debates – also contributed to these notes. In this case, their close contact with the situation in the field provided us with valuable insights and uncommon objectivity.

Members of Congress and their staffs, concerned by developments in the region and disturbed by the implications of some aspects of current policy, also participated in this effort.

It is our intention that this dissenting paper circulate widely among makers and executors of policy, in the Carter and Reagan administrations. We trust it will promote open discussion of realistic alternatives to our potential escalated military involvement in Central America and the Caribbean.

Washington D.C., November 6, 1980

Summary and recommendations

The Carter administration has gradually increased US political, diplomatic, economic and military involvement in support of the civilian-military coalition government in El Salvador. This involvement is extensive and growing. The resources invested in this effort exceed those allocated to any other hemispheric crisis since 1965.

Resource allocation and official public statements have identified our strategic interests in Central America and the Caribbean with the fate of a relatively weak, unpopular and internationally isolated regime.

Various government agencies have taken preparatory steps to intervene militarily in El Salvador. Policy makers appear to have concluded that such a move could succeed in preventing the collapse of the current regime.

Current policy consistently underestimates the domestic legitimacy and international support enjoyed by the opposition FDR/DRU coalition. Furthermore, policy makers fail to recognize the scope of military capabilities of opposition guerrilla forces and ignore the logistical value and potential impact of their support in neighboring countries.

Contingency scenarios for US military deployment tend to underestimate troop requirements, estimates of casualty rates, and the time and geographic scope of required engagement. Politico-military analysts downplay the potential for regionalization of armed conflict in the isthmus. In particular they underestimate the implications of the Nicaraguan and Cuban commitment to provide military support to Salvadorean guerrilla forces in the event of continued escalation of US involvement. No serious consideration appears to have been given to global security implications of an escalated regional conflict involving US, Cuban, Nicaraguan, Venezuelan and other participants. Diplomatic analysts overestimate the extent of current Venezuelan and Costa Rican commitment to continue to support our current policy in El Salvador. They also tend to minimize the political costs of world reaction to follow any increased deployment of US military personnel or equipment in the area.

The articulation of US policy for public and congressional audiences has misrepresented the situation in El Salvador emphasizing the viability of the current regime, downplaying its responsibility for the excesses being committed by security and paramilitary forces, exaggerating the positive impact of current reforms and portraying opposition forces as terrorists unsuitable for and unwilling to engage in constructive dialogue. These misleading rationalizations of our policies have played upon domestic frustrations resulting from perceived setbacks in other theaters, and have legitimized grossly inadequate arguments in favor of military intervention.

Our actions and our words have narrowed down our policy options to a single path of gradual escalation of direct military involvement in a region vital to our national interests and within a political context that gives the use of force few chances to achieve a satisfactory outcome.

The search for a non-military option in El Salvador must be urgently reopened. The process must begin with a realistic redefinition of our objectives, it must be based on unbiased intelligence analysed within a framework that reflects the new power distribution in the Caribbean basin.

A key objective of US policy in Central America is to limit Cuban and Soviet bloc influence throughout the region. Communist potential for projecting their influence relies principally on the opportunistic willingness to provide military equipment and training to subversive groups. Their obvious weakness under conditions of political stability and relative peace gives way to ominous strength when armed conflict spreads.

To limit opportunities for Soviet-Cuban expansion, the US must avoid the regionalization of armed conflict in Central America by reversing the current trend towards escalation of our own military involvement.

A second strategic objective of US policy should be to promote the emergence of stable governments capable of effective management of sorely needed reform programs while encouraging responsible private sector activity and normal economic relations with foreign business communities.

Clearly the current government of El Salvador is not stable and the security forces are unable to win a military confrontation on their own. Local and foreign businesses have already been severely weakened. Continued warfare will further erode their influence and limit their role in the post war period. Polarization and the hatred built up through years of violence will continue to reduce tolerance and eliminate respect for individual rights.

The sooner the conflict is brought to a negotiated end, the easier it will be to moderate the policies of the new status quo.

The two principal objectives and arguments presented apply with equal weight to the Guatemalan situation. Our support for a negotiated solution in El Salvador will serve notice to the Guatemalan hardliners that their time has run out. The chances for a less radical and less traumatic transition in Guatemala will be greatly improved.

Recommendations

A new policy towards El Salvador will have to address the following issues:

1. *Recognition of the FDR/DRU*

There can be no improvement of our negotiating position and no resolution to the current conflict without the US officially signaling the world community that it acknowledges that the FDR/DRU coalition is a legitimate and representative political force in El Salvador.

This recognition will be a key indicator to intransigent sectors on the left and the right that a real change of attitude has taken place in Washington.

2. *Signal our willingness to abandon the confrontational track*

Salvadorean and international public opinion perceive the US as being committed to a military solution in Central America. We must signal our willingness to abandon this course of action under certain conditions if an appropriate environment for negotiations is to emerge. To do so we must consider:

1) Taking actions which will clearly separate us from those sectors inside and outside the armed forces responsible for gross excesses against the population. The individuals involved have been identified by the FDR/DRU and by our own intelligence services.

2) Taking actions to reduce the level of military support we are currently providing to the armed forces, for example, by reducing or interrupting our training program and military supply flows.

3) Condemning the intervention plans of Guatemalan military and paramilitary forces and indicating our opposition to Honduran encouragement of hostile actions against Nicaragua.

4) Expressing privately and publicly our concern regarding continued involvement of Southern Cone countries in El Salvador and urging all our allies, including Israel, to act with caution in the region.

3. *Maintain a low profile throughout the process of disengagement*

The US does not have at this time the political credibility to spearhead a mediation effort. We should encourage and support initiatives taken by other regional actors avoiding direct participation. Our direct involvement may limit our ability to influence the process and may become an obstacle to mutual concessions.

4. *Encourage pluralistic media coverage*

Conditions in El Salvador and our official posture have not encouraged adequate media coverage. Influential US journalists have been banned from the country by threats on their lives. Salvadorean government restrictions on visiting reporters have kept a tight lid on many critical events in the past six months. Informal signals to foreign desk editors during the electoral campaign discouraged their interest in the region.

Appropriate, objective and pluralistic media coverage will make a positive contribution to the search for a peaceful solution to the conflict in El Salvador and, indeed, throughout Central America.

A.   CURRENT US ROLE IN EL SALVADOR

Policy statements on Central America, whether for internal use or for congressional or public consumption are inadequate starting points for discussion of our current role in the region. Rather than focusing on the articulation of policy objectives and their rationale, we prefer to outline the actions of our government agencies which affect developments in El Salvador.

We have ascertained that the activities grouped and listed below are being implemented by no less than twelve agencies of the government and supported by numerous NGO's.

The following is a partial list of these activities:

1. *Improving political and economic conditions to increase viability of current governing coalition through:*

   − Accelerating disbursement of bilateral economic aid and providing administrative and technical assistance.

   − Supporting approval and expediting disbursements of IBRD, IDB and IMF new and pipeline programs and projects under consideration.

   − Setting up of US/Salvadorean technical and managerial team to assist in government planning and administration to prevent economic collapse.

   − Expanding resource flow and tightening administration of agrarian reform program to reduce its impact on traditional elite and to increase short term benefits to target population.

   − Expanding short-term resource flow to private sector to discourage current capital exodus and strengthen sectoral confidence.

   − Monitoring closely and moderating latent and open differences among members of governing Junta and the officers corps.

2.   *Improving and protecting the international legitimacy and prestige of the regime through:*
   - Encouraging Salvadorean recruitment of moderate, reformist personnel for diplomatic representation.
   - Providing logistical support and orientation through US embassies and missions.
   - Actively encouraging increased diplomatic support from sympathetic Latin American and other allied governments.
   - Discouraging resolutions and other diplomatic initiatives critical of current government or possibly contributing to the legitimation of opposition forces.
   - Activating mechanisms to disrupt opposition efforts to obtain international support and legitimacy and to limit the impact of such efforts.
   - Creating favorable conditions for other countries' involvement in support for US initiatives in the OAS and the UN in relation to the situation in Central America.
   - Closely monitoring and feeding US and world media coverage of the region and publicizing widely US confidence in and support for current process in El Salvador.

3.   *Strengthening counter-insurgency capabilities of armed forces through:*
   - Increased training for middle and low ranking officers.
   - Improving military infrastructures for more effective urban and rural combat communications and for rapid troop deployment.
   - Setting up adequate supply lines and stockpiling materiel in cooperation with regional and extra-hemispheric allies.
   - Providing strategic and tactical command advisory assistance.
   - Increasing cohesion and coordination among various command structures within Salvadorean armed forces.
   - Seeking to bring under unified command the paramilitary units operating in the country.
   - Establishing and/or improving communications and cooperation among armed forces and paramilitary organizations in Guatemala, El Salvador and Honduras.
   - Making available US surveillance data pertinent to military developments in El Salvador to the armed forces.

4.   *Updating detailed contingency plans for US alternative responses to deterioration of conditions in the region to include:*
   - Political and diplomatic initiatives to be taken in the event that military engagement of US forces is required to preserve the current regime.
   - Operational plans for multilateral and unilateral deployment of military forces in El Salvador and Guatemala.
   - Cost, casualty and time estimates under favorable and unfavorable conflict scenarios.
   - Evaluation of readiness status and recommendations on preparatory exercises to be undertaken.
   - Assessment of the need and preparation of contingency plans for actions intended to disrupt support and supply lines of Salvadorean guerrilla forces in Cuba and Nicaragua.

5.   *Assuring continued congressional and public opinion support for current policies through liaison and press relations efforts that emphasize:*
   - A moderate and reformist image of the current government.
   - US support for extensive but moderate reforms in the region as a means to contain extremist and communist expansion.
   - Linkages between opposition guerrilla groups in El Salvador and Guatemala with Cuba.
   - Discrediting centrist spokesmen of opposition as puppets of hardline guerrilla leaders.
   - Careful monitoring of US press coverage of developments in El Salvador to avoid Nicaraguan style publicity for opposition insurgents.
   - Arranging regular closed session briefings for congressional committees, subcommittees and key MC's concerned with the issue.
   This partial list of activities implies an allocation of bureaucratic and financial

resources exceeding those made to any other hemispheric crisis since 1965. No such allocation could have taken place without a major high level decision in the administration. This decision was made in part to prevent the crisis in El Salvador from climaxing prior to the elections. However, the choices made have strategic implications reaching beyond domestic political considerations.

The Carter administration came to the conclusion that the collapse of the current civilian-military coalition government in El Salvador and its replacement by a left wing regime would constitute a threat to our strategic interests in the Caribbean basin.

Policy makers also agreed that the US still has a chance of preventing such developments through the provision of overt and covert political, military, economic, technical, diplomatic and public relations assistance to the current regime. However, if this effort failed to stabilize the local situation, the US would let it be known that it is prepared to and will use military force in conjunction with others, or, if necessary, unilaterally.

We consider these activities and the policies they imply to be dangerously misguided. Current policy, as we interpret it, is based on inaccurate intelligence, and on the suppression within various bureaucracies of verified contradicting information.

The options and recommendations on which policy decisions were made have been based on irresponsibly self-serving evaluations and analyses of intelligence reports available within the agencies. Critiques and dissenting views were systematically ignored.

Underlying these apparent bureaucratic maladjustments one finds a fundamental lack of understanding of general conditions and trends in Central America and the Caribbean.

B.   AN ALTERNATE VIEW OF REGIONAL AND INTERNATIONAL FACTORS AFFECTING EL SALVADOR

In this section we outline a characterization of the situation in El Salvador and its international context which is drastically different from the one commonly accepted within the Department.

The outline is based on a condensation of statements, commentaries, reports and memoranda available throughout various agencies of the government. We are not aware of any request for this information to be assembled for evaluation or for discussion.

1.   *El Salvador's domestic situation*

- The governing Junta and the armed forces have failed to rally significant support for their reform and counter-insurgency programs.
- The land redistribution effort has failed to neutralize the peasant population and has not succeeded in isolating the guerrilla forces.
- The urban middle class is divided among those who have already chosen to side with the FDR opposition, those seeking to leave the country and those remaining neutral for the time being. Only a small fraction of this sector can be said to be committed to the survival of the current regime.
- Domestic and foreign businesses have nearly completed liquidating their assets and withdrawing their capital from the country. No significant private investment is taking place. Infusion of foreign assistance and loans is not having any significant impact on economic recovery.
- Conflict among members of the ruling coalition continues to spread. New defections from the Christian Democratic party and factional fighting among and within branches of the armed forces impede regime consolidation.
- The documented expansion of military capabilities of the opposition forces, including their ability to recruit and organize large contingents of displaced peasants, and to cause heavy casualties among government forces, makes it highly unlikely that a short term military defeat of the guerrilla forces might be achieved.
- Neither the government nor the armed forces have been able to demonstrate their will or ability to avoid indiscriminate repression of civilian personnel thus contributing to the rapid deterioration of their image among the population and internationally.

2.   *Regional factors*

It is misleading to examine developments in El Salvador outside the Central

American and Caribbean context. Although policy statements and analyses routinely include references to regional concerns, seldom is an attempt made at relating domestic developments in one country with those within its neighbors'.

GUATEMALA

The trends below are pertinent to short term developments in El Salvador:
- Political power in the country is firmly in the hands of the hardline faction of the military, paramilitary and civilian elites. Among them there is near unanimous rejection of any reformist or moderating changes in regime composition or program.
- In recent years, the Guatemalan military have been referring to an expanded definition of their country's national and territorial interests that contemplates the possibility of intervention in neighboring Belize and El Salvador.
- Opposition forces have unified in a broad coalition which includes moderate reformers, parts of the church, and the marxist and populist guerrilla groups.
- A paramilitary strike force made up of former members of the Nicaraguan National Guard, anti-Castro Cubans, Guatemalan military personnel and mercenaries has been formed in the past year. Spokesmen for this contingent have expressed their intention to intervene in El Salvador "when the situation requires it."
- There has been a significant improvement of the military capabilities of the guerrilla forces in Guatemala. Their prestige and following among Indian peasants as well as among the urban middle classes has been well documented.
- Repression of moderate political and trade union leaders continues to accentuate political polarization and has led to the practical liquidation of the political center. Reflecting this internal situation, the international image of the regime continues to deteriorate.
- In the past year Salvadorean and Guatemalan opposition forces have increased contacts, communication and cooperation on political and military matters.

It should be noted that US intelligence has kept informed of the plans and capabilities of the paramilitary strike force in Guatemala. US intelligence has been in contact with Nicaraguan exile groups in Guatemala and in Miami and it is aware of their relationship with Cuban exile terrorist groups operating in the US. Charges that CIA has been promoting and encouraging these organizations have not been substantiated. However no attempt has been made to restrict their mobility in and out of the US or to interfere with their activities. Their mobility and their links with the US — it seems reasonable to assume — could not be maintained without the tacit consent (or practical incompetence) of at least four agencies: INS, CIA, FBI and US Customs.

HONDURAS

During 1980 DOD has devoted considerable resources to expanding communications and improving relations with the Honduran armed forces. DOD's stated objective has been "to create a new balance in the region" after the fall of Somoza's National Guard. The discussions with Honduran officers have been characterized as "encouraging," "fruitful," and "successful" at different stages of the process. These discussions included the following topics:
- Agreement on role of the US as mediator in seeking a settlement of disputes between El Salvador and Honduras.
- The need for increased cooperation between Honduras and El Salvador armed forces to reassert government control over disputed border areas currently held by Salvadorean guerrillas.
- US and Honduran cooperation in resupply efforts to El Salvador's armed forces in the event of a large scale insurrectional offensive.
- US willingness to assist Honduras in case of outbreak of open hostilities with Nicaragua.

Although our efforts in Honduras have already proven very useful, their impact has been exaggerated by a failure to take account of domestic developments in that country:

– A hard line majority within the military establishment has been pressuring to contain and even reverse the democratization process. It is with representatives of this faction that the agreements above were discussed.

– This hardline faction favors counter-insurgency cooperation with El Salvador, tolerates and encourages National Guard exile groups hostile to Nicaragua to operate from Honduras, and believes it could win a military confrontation with Nicaragua.

– A minority moderate faction within the armed forces is seeking closer relations with the civilian democratic opposition. It favors friendly relations with the Nicaraguan government and with the FSLN. It wants no Honduran involvement in El Salvador. It considers that open conflict with Nicaragua could prove dangerously destabilizing for Honduras and is not convinced of the possibility of defeating the new Sandinista army and militias.

– There has been a notable increase in trade union, religious, professional and political activity in Honduras. The organizations involved share a sympathetic view of the Nicaraguan process and oppose Honduras support for El Salvador's armed forces.

– Rural and urban guerrilla groups have begun to operate in Honduras in the past year. Although their capabilities pose no threat to internal stability, their disruptive potential in the event of gradual regionalization of conflict should not be underestimated.

NICARAGUA

The following background items should be kept in mind in attempting to predict Nicaraguan behavior in the event of escalated US involvement in El Salvador:

– Cooperation between the FSLN and various branches of the Salvadorean guerrilla groups can be traced back to the mid 1970's. Salvadorean contingents participated and provided logistical support during the war in Nicaragua. Historically, cooperation between the two countries against US interventions is documented in the 1920's and during the 19th century.

– Prior to July 1979, the FSLN maintained support networks in Honduras, El Salvador and Guatemala. FSLN commanders and troops are familiar with the terrain and the population. Nicaraguans have extensive family ties in these countries.

– Widespread popular support for the opposition forces in El Salvador and Guatemala, the high level of military preparedness of the population, the recent combat and insurrectional experience, and the high levels of unemployment would make recruitment and training a relatively simple and rapid operation.

– Despite economic recovery and surprisingly effective planning, administration and management, the Nicaraguan economy remains weak and vulnerable to a war effort. An outbreak of hostilities would force the Nicaraguan authorities to adopt "war communism" methods. This would imply labor conscription, extending government control over private sector activities, and generally would radicalize the Nicaraguan political process.

– Nicaraguan military supplies are sufficient to cope with internal disorders and limited border skirmishes. Nicaraguan involvement in regional hostilities would require expanded supplies and would provide ample opportunities for increased Cuban and Soviet bloc leverage in that country.

– The FSLN has consolidated firm control over government, armed forces, and mass organizations. The size, discipline and morale of regular army and militia units are impressive. Their newly acquired transport and communications equipment would make them serious contenders in any regional conflict.

Other political and diplomatic factors also deserve our attention. The FSLN and, in general, the Nicaraguan process continue to enjoy broad international support. During their first year in government the Sandinista government has gained influence and legitimacy in international forums notably in the OAS, the UN and the non-aligned movement. The Nicaraguan government and the FSLN have opened diplomatic and party relations in most Soviet bloc countries.

The Nicaraguan leadership remains divided on how to respond in the event of a direct US military intervention in El Salvador or in Guatemala. A moderate wing favors emphasis on diplomatic actions, extending humanitarian support for refugees and opposition forces but avoiding a military engagement that would severely hurt the prospects for economic recovery. The hard liners on the other hand favor full support for the guerrilla forces and, if needed, direct participation of Nicaraguan forces in regional operations.

MEXICO

US policy makers have failed to give adequate consideration to the potential impact of Mexico's policy towards the conflict in El Salvador. Yet Mexico's continuing economic growth, its oil wealth and its internal political stability have sharply increased its prestige, capabilities and willingness to influence developments in the Caribbean basin and Central America. Analysts in Washington project a continuation of Mexico's rhetorical posturing and downplay recent changes. But current intelligence suggests that Mexico is unusually determined to promote the emergence of stable, progressive and representative governments in Central America capable of asserting their independence from the US and willing to develop friendly and cooperative relations with their powerful northern neighbor. There are two principal reasons for this affirmative policy:
1. Mexico sees with growing concern and displeasure Venezuelan and US involvement in security matters close to its own oil fields.
2. PRI analysts have concluded that the process in El Salvador is irreversible. In their view the best way to influence developments there is to establish early friendly relations with opposition forces and provide political and economic support for the new regime.

The PRI would like to limit the domestic impact of the Central American process and capitalize for itself Mexican sympathies for opposition forces in El Salvador and Guatemala. The PRI feels that the best way to insure non-interference in Mexico's internal politics by the new governments is to recognize and to support them.

This policy does not depart significantly from Mexico's diplomatic tradition. Their current position towards Central America can be seen as an updated version of the successful and mutually convenient arrangement maintained between Mexico and Cuba for the past two decades.

The following factors link Mexico with the current situation in El Salvador:
— The PRI maintains cordial relations with and recognizes the legitimacy of the FDR/DRU coalition.
— Relations between the Mexico Government and the Salvadorean Junta have deteriorated steadily in the past six months.
— A significant percentage of the arms flowing into Guatemala and El Salvador originate in Mexico. This flow could not take place without the tacit consent of the Presidency.
— Mexico has already indicated to the US that it opposes current and escalated US and Venezuelan involvement in El Salvador. It has shown its willingness to lead a diplomatic counteroffensive and may link withdrawal to other bilateral issues of concern to the US.
— Public opinion in Mexico enthusiastically supports the Guatemalan and Salvadorean opposition forces. Government and private print and electronic media give clearly biased and distorted coverage of Central American events reflecting almost exclusively the views of the opposition in the two countries.
— Mexico has recently signed a series of accords with Cuba. Some of these include clauses that pertain to the two countries' common security concerns in the Caribbean and in Central America.
— Mexico is providing generous economic and technical assistance to Nicaragua. The PRI maintains fraternal relations with the FSLN. Some reports indicate that Mexico may have agreed to increase its economic support to Nicaragua in case of regionalized conflict.

VENEZUELA

The government of President Herrera Campins has become an indispensable ally in our current policy in Central America. Venezuelan policy towards El Salvador – and indeed on most regional and global issues – largely coincides with our own. COPEI's Social Christians identify with and support in many valuable ways their Christian Democratic colleagues in the Salvadorean Junta. Venezuela's official economic and security assistance to El Salvador complements and provides needed legitimation to our own efforts.

It is especially pertinent to examine some factors that might alter their current position:

– Venezuela's domestic situation has continued to deteriorate during 1980. The economic picture is not encouraging. Trade, fiscal and inflationary problems have led to increased unemployment, lower wages and a restless social environment.

– Social Democratic and left wing opposition to the government's economic and social policies has been growing. The opposition's control over the trade union movement gives their tactical coordination significant disruptive power.

– Herrera Campins' foreign policy does not have broad popular support in Venezuela and does not attract international sympathy. In many circles the release of Cuban terrorists is seen as damaging the country's democratic international image and prestige.

– Accion Democratica recognizes and supports the FDR/DRU coalition. AD has shown its determination to use this issue to build up their pressure on Herrera Campins. Some COPEI congressmen do not share their party's position on El Salvador. There are indications that a single issue coalition could be formed in the Congress that could impose a policy change on the executive.

– Officials in Herrera Campins' entourage are increasingly concerned about the implications of developing tensions with Mexico as Venezuelan involvement in El Salvador escalates.

These factors will become more critical in the event of a joint US/Venezuelan military deployment. The possibility of de-stabilizing developments in Venezuela should not be ignored. As pressures on the COPEI administration mount, the US should expect policy differences between the two countries to emerge.

COSTA RICA

The domestic political and economic situation in Costa Rica in many ways parallels that prevailing in Venezuela. President Rodrigo Carazo supports Venezuelan and US policies in El Salvador and his party maintains cordial relations with the Duarte/ Ehrlich wing of the Salvadorean Christian Democratic Party.

But Costa Rican support is largely symbolic as the country lacks the economic, security and political resources to make a significant contribution to the joint effort. Furthermore, President Carazo and his party have become sensitive to domestic pressures seeking a change in Costa Rica's position towards El Salvador.

Finally, Costa Rica's energy-short and trade-dependent economy makes the government sensitive and vulnerable to Mexican and Nicaraguan pressures.

PANAMA

The US is making extensive use of its remaining military facilities in Panama in the expanded training program for Salvadorean personnel. This training program is the largest ever sponsored by the US for any Latin American country in a single year.

The Latin American press has carried accusations suggesting that DOD may be using our facilities in Panama for stockpiling military supplies intended to play a key role in an eventual logistical supply air-lift to Salvadorean armed forces. We have obtained some evidence supporting these allegations.

The critical importance of Panama for the US in the current scenario would be sharply increased should we become more heavily involved in the escalating conflict in El Salvador. Yet General Torrijos – who continues to exercise control over the armed forces and veto power over government policies – is described in our character profiles as "volatile, unpredictable (. . .) a populist demagogue (with) a visceral anti-American bias (. . .) and a penchant for the bottle," hardly the description of a reliable ally. Our precarious situation in Panama was recently evidenced by President Royo's public condemnation of our training program for the Salvadoreans.

Consider the following additional links between Panama and El Salvador:

- Although initially supportive of the 10/15/79 coup, General Torrijos – and the Panamanian government – have improved ties with the FDR/DRU coalition moderates.
- Panama's economic difficulties and its dependence on the US banking community make it potentially responsive to our pressures. However the same factors combined with our tendency to act heavy-handedly may encourage a resurgence of "anti-imperialist" sentiment.
- In the past six months Panama has been expressing its displeasure on a number of issues related to perceived grievances linked to the implementation of the treaties.
- General Torrijos is in a position to assert control over two key tactical resources in any direct US military operations in the region: the canal and the bases.

ECUADOR

Earlier this year there were widely circulated allegations in Ecuador to the effect that DOD and ARA envoys had visited the country seeking to enlist government and armed forces support for the set up of an Andean Pact "peace keeping force" that could move into El Salvador in coordination with Venezuelan, US and Costa Rican contingents. Subsequent official denials did not change the perception that domestic and international counter pressures had succeeded in blocking the US initiative.

Despite its limited military capabilities, Ecuador's democratic government and relatively healthy economy wield disproportionate political and diplomatic influence on its Andean Pact partners and on other Latin American countries.

Since May, President Roldos' position on El Salvador has shifted further in favor of recognition of the FDR. European Social Democratic sources believe that Roldos may support diplomatic initiatives in favor of a new government which would include their participation.

3.   *International context*

In the aftermath of the 10/15/79 coup, international public opinion was unanimous in its support for the new government and its proposed reform program.

That first coalition Junta had the participation and support of Social Democrats, Christian Democrats, Communists and even some sympathy from the "popular organizations." A fact seldom referred to by official spokesmen of our government is that the first, broadly representative coalition government collapsed in early January 1980. Junta members and their organizations felt the government was powerless to implement the reforms and control repression. From that moment on, international support for the successor coalitions dwindled rapidly. A year after the October coup the international context has changed drastically.

A brief review is pertinent to assess the support to be found for current US policies:

- The Christian Democratic movement and its member parties are divided. Its conservative wing favors continued support for the current government and for US policy. The youth sector of the movement – considered by many observers to represent majority factions in most parties – identifies with the FDR opposition.
- The Social Democrats have unanimously moved to provide active political and humanitarian support for and through the FDR leadership. SD commitment to the Salvadorean opposition is seen consolidating along the same lines it did with respect to the FSLN in late 1978. The German Social Democratic Party, a key actor in the movement, appears determined to continue its support for the FDR. This has already been a source of some tension between us and the German government.
- Communist parties around the world also abandoned their "wait and see" attitude when the CPES resigned from its positions in government ministries in

January 1980. Not surprisingly, the Cuban CP is advising their Salvadorean counterparts to moderate their program, to broaden their alliances and to continue to seek compromises with the "progressive sectors in the military." Above all, the Cubans (and the Soviets) are urging utmost caution to avoid a direct confrontation with us.

— The most solid bloc of support for the current government and its counter-insurgency efforts comes from the southern cone military regimes. Among these, Argentina, Chile and Uruguay provide training and advisors on intelligence, urban and rural counter-insurgency, and logistics. Argentina has become the second largest trainer of Salvadorean officers after the US.

— Protestant and Catholic religious hierarchies in the hemisphere had been divided along the same lines as the Christian Democratic parties. The assassination of Archbishop Romero had a profound effect both on the hierarchies and on the village level priests and pastors who held the armed forces and the government ultimately responsible for the killing. Since then, a consensus in favor of the FDR has emerged.

The above changes in organized public opinion have had an impact on the expected behavior of governments in the international organizations. UN voting patterns on resolutions on El Salvador would show, at this time, a two thirds majority against the government and opposing US involvement. High ranking UN diplomats familiar with the Central American situation affirm that reaction to US military engagement would be equivalent to that which confronted the Soviets after their invasion of Afghanistan. The important diplomatic gains we made since would be lost overnight.

At the OAS the situation is not more encouraging. An unpublished study among representatives to the OAS found that about half of the members would oppose any form of military intervention in Central America regardless of the circumstances, about one in five would support it and the rest would abstain, support or oppose "depending on the circumstances."

4.   *US public opinion*

Public awareness of the situation in Central America was increased through mass media coverage of the Canal treaty negotiation process and the war in Nicaragua.

A poll conducted in June 1979 found that 2 of every 3 Americans opposed the Somoza regime and about half of these were sympathetic to the Sandinista insurgents. More pertinent however, is a poll conducted in August 1980 which found that the public attitudes of June 1979 had not changed significantly despite critical media coverage of the first anniversary of the Sandinista government.

However, our efforts to emphasize the differences between the situation in El Salvador today and the one prevailing in Nicaragua before July 1979 have had an impact on public perceptions. Media coverage of El Salvador has been responsive to official government policies: greater emphasis on US interests in the region, continuous reference to Cuban involvement, understatement of the "human rights" dimension, effective use of the "extremists of the right and the left" formula. Therefore, the current domestic environment is generally supportive of current policy as articulated for public consumption.

We believe that this support would not survive the introduction of US troops in the region. For example, an October 1980 poll found that 60% of all males and 68% of females interviewed opposed the use of US military force in trouble spots in developing countries. The still to be analysed reaction to the draft registration drive and the drop in support for intervention in Iran after the rescue attempt, suggest that assertions to the effect that we have overcome the "Vietnam Syndrome" may be premature.

There are also some indications that church involvement in the current drive to attract attention to the situation in El Salvador in support for opposition forces and against US intervention may begin to influence public perceptions of our role in that country. Congressional staff familiar with the lobbying potential of this network foresee some changes in current attitudes and voting patterns in the event of escalated US involvement in Central America.

C.   IN SEARCH OF A NON-MILITARY OPTION

In this section we propose a redefinition of US objectives in Central America and argue that conditions exist for achieving them through a negotiated solution to the conflict in El Salvador.

1.   US objectives

A key objective of US policy in Central America is to limit Cuban and Soviet bloc influence in the region. We do not agree with those who belittle the threat of Cuban expansionism. But we try to distinguish between Cuban desires and intentions and their actual capacity to expand.

Cuban and Soviet bloc domestic political and economic difficulties and their overextension in Africa and Asia severely limit their ability and willingness to make new and potentially costly economic and political commitments. Neither Cuba nor its Soviet bloc backers are capable or interested in assuming the costs of displacing the US as the region's major aid donor and trade partner. We should be reminded that in Nicaragua – outside the highly publicized volunteer teachers and doctors from Cuba – Soviet bloc assistance has been minimal, a fact which has been a source of sobering frustration to the Sandinista leaders' expectations of a year ago.

But Cuban and Soviet bloc limitations in the economic field should not be mistaken with powerlessness. Their potential for projecting and expanding their influence relies fundamentally on their opportunistic willingness to provide military equipment and training. Their obvious weakness under conditions of political stability and relative peace gives way to ominous strength when armed conflict pervades.

Few developments would open more opportunities for Cuba in Central America and the Caribbean than the regionalization of armed conflict that would follow the escalation of US military involvement in El Salvador.

The Sandinistas, threatened by what they will perceive as the beginning of an offensive against them, would be under strong pressure to make a strategic alignment with the Soviet bloc through response mechanisms similar to those that pushed Cuba into their orbit in the 1960's.

Regionalization would justify the emergence of "internationalist brigades" that could roam the isthmus from Colombia to the Mexican border. And any government that might emerge during or after a military confrontation with the US in El Salvador would be forced to seek the protective umbrella of other regional powers. A likely candidate is, obviously, Cuba.

Therefore, to limit opportunities for Soviet-Cuban expansionism, the US should avoid regionalization of armed conflict by reversing the current trend towards escalating its own military involvement.

A second strategic objective of US policy should be to promote the emergence of stable governments capable of effective management of sorely needed reform programs while encouraging responsible private sector activity and normal economic relations with the foreign business communities.

Clearly the current government of El Salvador is not stable. It can not carry out the reforms it decreed and it can not provide a social and political environment conducive to economic normalization. Growing casualty rates and continued destruction of property make it apparent that the Salvadorean security forces can not gain a military victory on their own. The private business sector and foreign investors have already been severely weakened. Continued warfare will further erode their influence and limit their role in the reconstruction period.

Political analysts tend to overlook the radicalizing effect of prolonged "liberation wars" on the insurgent leadership and on the masses. Polarization, widespread destruction, and the hatred accumulated through years of bloodshed reduce tolerance and eliminate respect for individual rights. The longer the process, the more evident this trend will become. The sooner the conflict is brought to a negotiated end, the easier it will be to moderate the policies of the new status quo.

The two principal objectives and arguments made apply with equal weight to the Guatemalan situation. We have tried unsuccessfully for nearly four years to strengthen centrist moderate forces in the country and to press the government to limit repression and allow for political relaxation. Our support for a negotiated solution in El Salvador will serve notice to the Guatemalan hardliners that their time has run out. The chances for a less radical and less traumatic transition in Guatemala would be greatly improved.

2. *The context for dialogue*

Conditions for a negotiated resolution of the conflict in El Salvador will be present when the principal domestic contenders and their respective international allies conclude that complete military victory is no longer possible, or that the costs of achieving such victory are no longer justifiable.

In this section we argue that most key actors are now prepared to consider supporting and/or participating in a negotiated disengagement.

We have been saying privately and publicly that the Salvadorean opposition is unwilling to dialogue with the armed forces or with the Junta. We have been promoting the view that the guerrilla leadership is seeking a full fledged military confrontation to liquidate or dismantle all existing political and military institutions. These are gross misrepresentations that, through mere repetition, have acquired an aura of veracity that does not correspond to reality.

The FDR/DRU leadership feels confident about their continuing growth in and out of El Salvador but two major tactical currents remain clearly identifiable:
- One argues that they have sufficient power to impose their own terms on the armed forces and the Junta. In their view mediated negotiations are identified with the 78/79 US promoted, tripartite effort in Nicaragua. This form of dialogue they reject.
- The other tendency, reportedly gaining influence within the coalition, favors opening discussions along the lines of a Zimbabwe type transitional arrangement

Both tendencies are aware of the following factors:
- An insurrectional offensive may not be completely successful or sufficiently swift to avoid a stalemate in the internal war and a dual government situation that may sharply increase the social costs of their insurrection as well as the chances of US intervention.
- Even a successful insurrection might entail such high human and material costs that a military resolution might make reconstruction and regime consolidation dangerously difficult.
- Direct US intervention would impose a change of tactics away from localized insurrections to "prolonged people's war" on a regional dimension. This would postpone indefinitely the emergence of a representative popular government and would raise the social costs of the war effort beyond all previous projections.

Both tendencies reject any dialogue with representatives of groups or sectors identified with or directly responsible for "acts of indiscriminate repression and genocide." But they also agree on the need to reopen conversations with representative spokesmen for the private and foreign business sectors currently identified with the Junta. Close international allies of the FDR/DRU feel that a more conciliatory attitude is a necessary prerequisite for resolving the present stalemate. They also feel that such an attitude is steadily gaining ascendancy within the coalition.

A similar trend is also discernible on the government's side away from continued confrontation tactics towards a recognition that negotiations with the insurgent opposition might be unavoidable. There is a growing realization that a total military victory is no longer a realistic objective for the government and for the armed forces. Thus, the options facing the more lucid sectors identified with the governing coalition are:
- Defeat following insurrectional offensive
- Complete identification with and reliance on a US rescue operation
- Starting a mediated negotiation process towards a new coalition government

Clearly the situation in El Salvador is highly complex. Its complexity contrasts with the simplistic generalizations being made by senior US officials to the effect that the opposition is only interested in a military resolution of the current stalemate.

3. *The Zimbabwe option*

The Junta's proposal to hold elections in two years was officially predicted and denounced by the FDR as a political maneuver. Internally however the electoral offer is being discussed as one component of the "Zimbabwe option." The argument being made is based on the conviction that they would win those elections if they had the freedom to mobilize their supporters and access to mass media. However, even the strongest supporters of this option admit that the sector of the armed forces now in control of the political process – who know the extent of mass support enjoyed by the opposition – have no intention to allow a truly participatory electoral dynamic to develop.

There are obvious differences between the situation in Zimbabwe in 1978 and 1979 and the current situation in El Salvador. But there are also numerous structural parallels worth the attention of policy makers:
- The Patriotic Front was a coalition of centrist and marxist forces each with its own strong guerrilla army.
- Outside support from Cuba, the PRC and the Soviet Union, and a long and bitter guerrilla war had strengthened the liberation armies and weakened the Rhodesian forces. Terrorism on both sides became common in the last year of the war and brutal acts continued even as the Westminister talks proceeded.
- The threat of South African involvement, the Cuban commitment to intervene with troops and the implications of a regional war were important factors in favor of reaching a negotiated solution.
- The Muzorewa regime lost prestige and credibility through its identification with traditional white interests, its participation in the counter-insurgency efforts and its inability to implement structural reforms.
- The international climate around El Salvador is beginning to approximate the one prevailing in the last six months of the Muzorewa regime.

What is most clearly missing in the Salvadorean case is the will of the regional dominant power – the British in Rhodesia, the US in El Salvador – to concede that the time has come to grant its recognition to the new emerging status quo. It is interesting to recall in this context that a majority of US congressional and executive branch policy makers maintained the view that Mr. Mugabe was a marxist extremist with limited representation until his landslide electoral victory made him a prestigious and influential head of state.

4.   *Attitudes of regional actors*

In our review of regional trends running counter to current US policy we made reference to factors favoring a negotiated solution; these were:

MEXICO

Washington policy makers do not wish to recognize the extent and significance of the changing power relations between the US and Mexico. Yet this change must be reflected in the two countries' attitudes and actions in Central America and the Caribbean. Mexico has already indicated that it will support any initiative directed at containing the conflict in El Salvador as long as such an initiative enhances the chances of a truly representative popular government with FDR/DRU participation coming to be in that country.

NICARAGUA

Nicaragua's commitment to the FDR/DRU has been noted. The Nicaraguan Junta and the FSLN are keenly aware of the social costs of a prolonged war in El Salvador with regional repercussions. There are clear signals coming from Managua that they would support a solution that would lead to a transitional government with FDR/DRU participation.

VENEZUELA

We already noted President Herrera Campins concerns relating to the rising domestic and international political costs of his policy in El Salvador. But COPEI has invested its reputation within the Christian Democratic Movement on continued support for their Salvadorean colleagues. COPEI wants to avoid the appearance of betraying its friends, and abandoning Venezuela's senior partner. A bipartisan consensus wants to ease the growing tensions with Mexico. President Herrera Campins would probably welcome a face-saving formula that would allow for a needed policy adjustment without domestic or international humiliation.

PANAMA

Negotiations in El Salvador would serve conflicting currents in Panamanian domestic politics. General Torrijos' dual allegiance to the reformist wing of the armed forces and to the centrists in the FDR/DRU would allow Panama to play a key role in a mediation effort. The broad based anti-interventionist sentiment now focusing on the use of Panama's territory for support of counter-insurgency in El Salvador could be diffused through a negotiated disengagement. The threat of disruptions to the peaceful implementation of the Canal treaties would be largely neutralized.

CUBA

Cuban attitudes towards a negotiated settlement in El Salvador would largely depend on the nature of the process itself, on the response of the FDR/DRU and on their perceptions of the chances for adequate representation in a coalition transitional government.

It is pertinent to examine briefly aspects of the Cuban government's attitudes vis-a-vis the Zimbabwe negotiations. We stress that Cuba was prepared to intervene militarily in support of the Patriotic Front under the following conditions:

- A formal request from the two factions of the Patriotic Front, a formal request from the front line states, acquiescence from the OAU.
- Escalated South African intervention in Zimbabwe initiating the internationalization of the conflict.
- Formation of a Provisional Revolutionary Government.

From the Cuban point of view, the costs of involvement in Zimbabwe were much lower than those associated with their intervention in El Salvador. Their actions in Zimbabwe were surprisingly cautious even under such favorable circumstances. Mr. Castro surprised international observers when he gave full support to the negotiations in Westminister. We will emphasize again the strategic importance of reaching a solution in El Salvador that proves that Cuban military assistance is a dispensable factor in the democratization of Central America.

OTHER REGIONAL ACTORS

The list of likely supporters of a negotiated settlement that would guarantee FDR/DRU participation in a new coalition government is extensive. The arguments in each case may become repetitive. Costa Rica would follow with relief Venezuela's lead. President Roldos of Ecuador would see the opportunity to cancel out competing pressures on his administration. Caribbean countries would perceive US support for such a process as a step away from gun boat diplomacy and in favor of political pluralism. Religious organizations would support the moderating potential of negotiations and as a way to heal internal differences.

D.   OPENING MOVES FOR AN ALTERNATIVE POLICY

The results of the elections, new appointments in Washington, and, above all, events in El Salvador will confirm the need for a new US policy. There is a wide gap between the prevailing attitudes among policy makers in Washington in November 1980 and those that will be required for the US to be able to make a positive contribution to this process. When re-evaluation gets underway the following key issues will need to be addressed:

RECOGNITION OF THE FDR/DRU

There can be no improvement of our position and no resolution of the current conflict without the US officially signaling to the world community that it acknowledges that the FDR/DRU coalition is a legitimate and representative political force in Salvadorean politics.

This recognition will be a key indicator to intransigent sectors on the left and the right that a real change of attitude has taken place in Washington.

When and how this recognition is extended is a critical factor in the prospects for success, in discouraging or encouraging flexibility on the part of the contenders.

We must be willing to meet privately or publicly with a representative delegation of the opposition FDR/DRU coalition. We must avoid the temptation to try to choose or impose interlocutors. The instinctive tendency on our part to speak only with accommodating moderates named by us beforehand will have the effect of limiting these individuals' chances of playing a constructive role within the coalition. If a preference needs to be stated, the US should choose to meet with representatives of the toughest and least likely to compromise factions of the coalition. We must seek to overcome the view that recognition and negotiations are only tactics to divide, or just another form of intervention.

SIGNAL OUR WILLINGNESS TO ABANDON THE CONFRONTATIONAL TRACK

Salvadorean and international public opinion perceive the US as being committed to a military solution in Central America. We must signal our willingness to abandon this course of action under certain conditions, without necessarily closing that option. To do so we must consider:

1) Taking actions which will clearly separate us from those sectors in and out of the armed forces responsible for gross excesses against the population. The individuals involved have been identified by the FDR/DRU and by our own intelligence services.

2) Taking actions that indicate our willingness to reduce the level of military support we are providing to the armed forces, for example by reducing or interrupting óur training program and supply flows.

3) Condemning the intervention plans of Guatemalan military and paramilitary forces, indicate our opposition to Honduran support for hostile actions against Nicaragua.

4) Expressing privately and publicly our concern regarding Southern Cone countries' involvement in El Salvador, and urge all our allies, including Israel, to act with caution in the region.

MAINTAIN A LOW PROFILE THROUGHOUT THE PROCESS OF NEGOTIATIONS

Political analysts reflecting on the US role during the mediation efforts in Nicaragua point as its main weakness to the insistence of the Carter administration and the Congress to spearhead the effort. We should not initiate any mediating effort. Instead we should support such initiatives and encourage those with whom we maintain influence to join in. Our direct participation may actually limit our ability to influence the outcome and may become an obstacle to mutual concessions.

ENCOURAGE PLURALISTIC MEDIA COVERAGE

Conditions in El Salvador and our official posture have not encouraged adequate media coverage. Influential US journalists have been banned from the country by threats on their lives. Salvadorean government restrictions on visiting reporters have kept a tight lid on many critical events in the past six months. Informal signals to foreign desk editors during the electoral campaign discouraged serious investigative journalism.

Appropriate, objective and pluralistic media coverage will make a positive contribution to the search for a peaceful solution to the Salvadorean, and indeed, the Central American conflict.